THE PRICE OF
IMMORTALITY

ALSO BY PETER WARD

The Consequential Frontier:
Challenging the Privatization of Space

THE PRICE OF IMMORTALITY
THE RACE TO LIVE FOREVER

PETER WARD

MELVILLE HOUSE
BROOKLYN • LONDON

The Price of Immortality

First published in 2022 by Melville House Publishing
Copyright © Peter Ward, 2022
All rights reserved
First Melville House Printing: April 2022

Melville House Publishing
46 John Street
Brooklyn, NY 11201
and
Melville House UK
Suite 2000
16/18 Woodford Road
London E7 0HA

mhpbooks.com
@melvillehouse

ISBN: 978-1-61219-952-8

ISBN: 978-1-61219953-5
(eBook)

Library of Congress Control Number: 2021953017

Designed by Patrice Sheridan

Printed in the United States of America
1 3 5 7 9 10 8 6 4 2
A catalog record for this book is available from the Library of Congress

For Seren and Leeloo,
with whom forever would seem so short.

TABLE OF CONTENTS

Introduction   ix

1. The Immortalists of Hollywood, Florida   3

2. A Drastic Plan B   19

3. The Curious Case of the Missing
   Frozen Head   41

4. How to Pay for a Second Life   61

5. The Eternal Prize   79

6. The Valley Shadowing Death   97

7. Know Thyself   115

8. DIY Immortality   133

9. Regeneration   151

10. The Immortal Jellyfish   165

11. The Digital Resurrection   183

12. A Race to the Bottom   203

13. The Consequence of Immortality   219

Epilogue   233

Acknowledgements   239

Endnotes   241

Index   261

INTRODUCTION

In Ancient Greek mythology, Orpheus was one of the first men to challenge the concept of death. When his wife Eurydice died, he was overcome with grief. Refusing to accept her fate, the hero traveled to the underworld in an attempt to bring her back to life. There, he charmed the guardians of the River Styx, ferryman Charon and the many-headed dog Cerberus, with his musical talents. The depth of his suffering moved Hades, the king of the underworld, who allowed him to take Eurydice back to the land of the living on one condition: As they left the underworld, neither of them could look back. When Orpheus approached the surface, he panicked and wanted to make sure he wasn't leaving alone. Without thinking, he turned to check that his wife was there, and just like that, she was gone.

The tale of Orpheus was among the first to emphasize the dangers of rejecting death, and cautioned the reader about the perils of looking back instead of forward. But neither the legend of Orpheus nor the thousands of stories that followed managed to deter people from seeking a cure for mortality. For centuries, wide-eyed optimists from all over the globe have sought magical potions, traveled to obscure and mythical destinations, and made deals with devils and demons to try to ward off death. None of them succeeded, and yet the attempts keep coming.

The potions and elixirs may have new names, but they still appeal to one of humanity's strongest instincts: survival, no matter the cost. The race to immortality has various definitions. To some, eternal life is a spiritual pursuit, and for others it can refer to leaving a lasting impact through their acts or work. But this book is about the most literal take on immortality—to live forever physically in the world as we know it now. Those who chase such a lofty goal call themselves immortalists.

There are enough immortalists in the world to warrant annual events on different continents, and there are several groups, communities, and even religions that bring together people who believe a never-ending life is possible. I first encountered this way of thinking while working on my first book *The Consequential Frontier*, about the privatization of space. Space enthusiasts, particularly those looking forward to settling on other planets in the solar system and beyond, often see life extension and immortality as a key part of that process. Prolonging life by putting people in stasis would allow humans to travel much farther distances. Sending humans off to live on other planets is also frequently cited as a solution to the potential overpopulation that could arise from ending death.

The modern interpretation of immortalism emerged in the postatomic world of the United States, where science fiction merged into reality. (Isaac Asimov said, "The dropping of the atomic bomb in 1945 made science fiction respectable.") After World War II, the planet was gripped by apocalyptic anxiety, but was also inspired by the endless possibilities of science. Against this uncertain backdrop, enthusiasts launched new and technology-driven projects to cheat death. Despite attracting cult followings, these movements made little tangible progress. Most of their hope was poured into cryonics, the practice of freezing the dead so they could be reanimated in the future, a technique that remains unproven today.

But at the turn of the millennium, cause for optimism emerged. New thinkers in the field made startling declarations about the prospect of immortality. Hope was placed in the emerging field of biotechnology, where huge breakthroughs were being made. One of the major thinkers in this domain, Dr. Aubrey de Grey, captured the burgeoning enthusiasm with his theory of "escape velocity," which told immortalists they only had to stay alive for a few more decades and they would reach the point when biotech would keep them alive indefinitely. As the understanding and mastery of fields like gene therapy, stem cells, and gene editing increased, the immortalists were faced with a scenario most thought would never happen: They might be proved correct.

Immortalists believe escape velocity is in sight, but they remain in the minority. In the vacuum between scientific theory, discovery, and real-world solutions, a familiar crowd of con artists and fraudsters have emerged to take advantage of those seeking never-ending life. Against this weird set of circumstances, I plunged into the world of immortalists, hoping to unravel what was real and what was false, and to discover the real price of the modern pursuit of immortality.

Like Orpheus, this book straddles two worlds, one considerably darker than the other. My first trip to Florida to seek out a community of immortalists took place months before the COVID-19 pandemic ravaged the world as we knew it. The rest of the reporting occurred after.

When the virus struck, the path to immortality became even more difficult, as did my own task of getting to know the people who believed they would never die. A pandemic is one of the worst nightmares of an aging immortalist. Many of them went underground, a necessary measure to increase their chances of living forever. Meetups were canceled, in-person conferences moved online, and even some laboratory space used to investigate death was repurposed for the more immediate battle facing humanity.

COVID-19 forced the rest of us to confront death in a way each generation believes it never will. Almost overnight, desperate yet pragmatic decisions were forced on the world, from doctors choosing who to treat and who to let die, to politicians and talking heads justifying rising death rates by pointing to underlying conditions and the ages of those who were lost. As the immediate fear of our own death increased, our sensitivity to others dying fell. Every report on coronavirus statistics came with the caveat that a significant percentage of deaths were made up of either the elderly or people with pre-existing conditions, as if this somehow excused their passing. This qualification soothed the subconscious of the general population, reassuring them that death was something that happened to other people. As Ernest Becker says, paraphrasing Aristotle in his book *The Denial of Death*, "luck is when the guy next to you gets hit by the arrow."[1] It's extraordinary how far we'll go to believe we are lucky. One of the interviewees for this book, George Church, described this phenomenon as the "flip-side of the lottery delusion."[2]

Even the most relentless optimist would struggle to find anything positive in a pandemic, but there is one consequence that offers humanity hope—illumination. Like a UV light on a grubby motel bed, COVID-19 has highlighted the seedy, dysfunctional foundations on which our society is constructed. America's health care system, built for the profiting few rather than the needy masses, predictably failed to respond to such huge pressure, as over 750,000 people in the US have lost their lives as of early November 2021.[3] Populist leaders around the world were exposed as fraudulent opportunists, unable to cope with a truly dangerous scenario not fabricated by their own spin doctors. And all the while inequality rattled on, underpinning the depth of this crisis and feeding the basis for the next one.

"'Tis a fearful thing, to love what death can touch," wrote the Hebrew poet Judah Halevi. I would add it's quite fearful to write about what death can touch, particularly during a pandemic. Studying the concept of immortality and those who seek it inevitably always leads back to death. At times, the characters in this book seem like lighthearted eccentrics, but it all circles back to the fear of mortality, usually brought on by a tragic loss. In the aftermath of COVID-19, no doubt there will be plenty of others drawn to the quest for immortality—spiritual or physical—unable and unwilling to confront and accept the limited time we have before we die. Their paths will be littered with fraudsters, con men, and falsehoods, but the past few decades of technological progress have offered immortalists hope that their ultimate goal may yet be achievable. In this book, I wanted to establish if this was another false dawn in humanity's pursuit of everlasting life—or if we really need to prepare for a world where some people can choose not to die.

THE PRICE OF IMMORTALITY

1

THE IMMORTALISTS OF
HOLLYWOOD, FLORIDA

On a humid morning in the summer of 2019, I stepped out of my Airbnb rental apartment in Hollywood, Florida, with a great sense of purpose. But as I reached the curb, I found a dead possum staring back at me, legs in the air, eyes wide and tongue protruding, a look of shock on its tiny face. Flies buzzed around the corpse as the rising temperature hastened its decomposition. It must have been there for a few days now. Usually I'd have walked by, attempting to avoid the smell and sight of the poor creature, but that day I paused and contemplated the finality and inevitably of death. I'd always believed that, like the possum, we were all on a preordained trip to the metaphorical gutter. But on that weekend I was about to meet a group of people who thought the exact opposite, the immortalist congregation of the Church of Perpetual Life.

The church itself towers over the untidy rows of bungalows lining the streets of its quiet residential block in an otherwise nondescript neighborhood. Each month, the giant, bulky building hosts this crowd of unconventional worshippers, who don't gather to celebrate a god but instead an idea—that everyone should live forever. Followers of the church believe they can achieve immortality by surviving to a point in the future when technology and medicine are advanced enough to save them from death indefinitely. They meet to discuss the best ways to reach that golden age, taking inspiration from scientific breakthroughs, wellness practices, and plans to reanimate themselves should death catch up with them.

The community, unsurprisingly to outsiders at least, attracts a large number of eccentrics, both in the congregation and the leadership. All of them are regularly wheeled out for TV and print interviews, in which a fair amount of mockery seeps through the page or screen. It's easy to see why: their declaration of impending immortality goes against everything we know about biology and science in general. But it's worth remembering that they are far from the only group seeking to live forever. Every Sunday in the United States, tens of millions of devoted followers gather to worship some form of deity in the hope they will achieve a kind of everlasting life. Yet they largely escape the kind of mockery the immortalists endure, despite the Church of Perpetual Life's version of eternal bliss sounding far more appealing than the judgement-heavy utopias offered as bait for a lifetime of religious service.

But when you're chasing eternity in this life, rather than the next, it's easy for detractors to accuse you of being deluded or, even worse, fraudulent. Selling immortality is an old trick. Ancient Egyptian pharaohs, Roman emperors, medieval knights, and many others since have all pursued some form of the elixir of life, a potion or medicine which can grant the drinker an unnaturally long existence. And many have fallen victim to con men and scam artists, eager to exploit humanity's weakness for a superpower of dubious worth. In many ways, the immortalists of Florida are just another of those groups pursuing an unlikely and elusive dream. But this is the age of the computer, and science is now advancing at a pace previously thought impossible. Medicine has extended the average life expectancy significantly in the past century, and scientists now turn their expertise to more extreme measures to stop people from dying. For the first time ever, immortalists may actually have hope.

Each immortalist has their own personal tool kit for defeating death. Over time, as new technologies have been developed, that kit has expanded. Initially, their best hope was cryonics, the practice of freezing people after they die with the hope of bringing them back to life at a later date. Cryonics has a brilliantly bizarre history and remains a fringe science, denounced as nonsense by some but promoted as an effective Plan B by others. More recently, immortalists have looked to breakthroughs in the understanding of the human body for inspiration. They follow rigid diets, take a long list of supplements, and sometimes dip their toes in experimental treatments with little chance of success. Most follow science like a religion, desperately searching through published research for any sign of any means of extending their lives. This takes them into some cutting-edge areas of medical technology, including gene therapies and editing, nanotechnology, stem cell therapy, and more speculative areas like brain interfacing and mind uploading. In each of these fields, researchers and scientists come under pressure from the immortalists, who want to see their work fully operational and used in humans as soon as possible. I set out to find if there was a Holy Grail buried among this research, or if the immortalists, including those in Florida, had just fallen for one of the oldest scams in human history.

Philosophers, prophets, scientists, and salespeople have proclaimed immortality to be within our grasp since the dawn of time, but now there's a chance they could be right. If a cure to death is found, groups like the Church of Perpetual Life will be the first to volunteer to take the elixir in whatever form it is offered, and no matter how costly it proves to be. I couldn't wait to meet them.

• • •

I arranged to meet Neal VanDeRee, the pastor of the Church of Perpetual Life, the day before the start of their monthly meet-up. The weather that week in Hollywood was hot and sticky, and every few hours a storm would roll in, bringing a hefty downpour. In the past, the sturdy church building was used as a place of shelter for the locals when these storms became hazardous. The church's role as a safe haven from nature's wrath fit well with the message it was preaching: that its members could outlast disease, old age, and any other ailments inhibiting immortality.

When I arrived at the church in the late afternoon, VanDeRee's assistant Josh greeted me at the door. He was in his mid-twenties and looked sweaty and stressed. He explained he was setting up the church for the events of the next few days but could take time to show me around while we waited for his boss. When we first entered the building, I was a little disappointed. The first room looked like a community center, furnished with long tables and plastic chairs. The real place of worship was upstairs, and when Josh took me up there, I was happy to see it was closer to what I expected.

Like a regular church, there were pews, an altar, and a stand from which to give sermons. The decor looked remarkably like a Christian establishment, with crosses everywhere. I then spotted a sign informing the congregation that no women were allowed to sit in the front row and immediately worried about what kind of eternal future these people were planning. Josh, perhaps noticing my confusion, told me the church was rented by a nondenominational Christian group most of the time, and the Perpetual Life crowd only used it once a month. It was his job to transform it from Christianity to immortalism.

On this particular weekend, the church was hosting a special event, beyond the scope of its usual monthly meetings. The First Annual Cryonics Symposium was taking place, during which the practice of freezing corpses to be reanimated at a later date would be discussed at great length. The three-day conference was sure to draw a bigger crowd than the average service, and people had traveled from all over the world to be there.

The church was founded in 2013 by Bill Faloon, a well-known and outspoken immortalist among the transhumanist movement; Saul Kent, a key figure in the world of cryonics; and VanDeRee himself. They chose Hollywood because it was central to South Florida, close to both Miami and Boca Raton, and an easy drive from Palm Beach. There are also two international airports nearby, which makes it easier for global followers to jet in for a service.

Hollywood itself was founded in the 1920s by a man named Joseph Young,[1] who envisioned his "dream city" in Florida. He built hotels and a casino in an effort to make it the Atlantic City of the South, and the city became a popular destination for northern industrialists and celebrities. But Hollywood's location meant it was battered by hurricanes and other major weather events fairly frequently over the years. Over time, the city lost its luxurious appeal, but did manage to lure in the church, one of transhumanism's most curious attractions.

Transhumanism is the larger umbrella belief group within which immortalism sits. The philosophical movement argues for the enhancement of the human condition. This can be achieved through subtle acts like wearing glasses or working out but sometimes gets quite extreme. More outlandish wings of transhumanism include advocating dangerous experiments to make the human body physically more capable and merging with computers to improve the human mind. And then there is immortalism, the branch that prophesizes humans who are so advanced they can choose when they die, and perhaps takes transhumanism further than any other area.

Most immortalists subscribe to the theory of biological immortality. This means they can live for as long as they choose in their current bodies, providing a grand piano doesn't fall on their head, for example. But for others, this doesn't go far enough. Americans have a one in six chance of dying from heart disease, one in seven chance of succumbing to cancer, and one in twenty-seven chance of chronic lower respiratory disease ushering in their downfall, according to National Safety Council statistics from 2019.[2] Biological immunity would remove those threats, but others would remain. For example, there is a one in 107 chance of dying in a motor vehicle crash, while your chances of dying from a gun assault in the United States are just one in 289. The particularly positive immortalists believe they can ensure they live on, despite such calamities, through various means such as augmenting their bodies or backing up their minds.

Transhumanism and immortality have largely been in the news because billionaires, presumably bored of ways to flaunt their wealth, are relentlessly pursuing the goal of everlasting life. The usual suspects in this quest are Silicon Valley tech magnates. Peter Thiel is perhaps one of the most well-known and notorious. Faloon might not be a Silicon Valley billionaire, but he raised the money to buy the building in Hollywood and tasked VanDeRee to officiate the church. Together with a host of volunteers, the pair run the community. The website lists two other leaders, both of whom are dead.[3] The first is the science fiction author Arthur C. Clarke, who died in 2008. Clarke was best known for cowriting the screenplay of the movie *2001: A Space Odyssey*, one of the most influential science fiction films ever. He was a prolific author of nonfiction and novels, often on the topic of space travel and exploration. The Church of Perpetual Life lists him as one of their prophets and describes him as a futurist of "uncanny ability." The other prophet listed on the church's leadership team is the Russian philosopher Nikolai Fedorov. (Federov will make a spectacular appearance in a later chapter.)

These older inspirations underline the fact that the immortalists of Florida are hardly the first to chase eternal life. There are plenty of stories from fiction and real-life history that detail humanity's desperate struggle against death. Immortality features heavily in one of the earliest forms of literature, *The Epic of Gilgamesh*, a story of a mortal demigod King of Uruk thought to have been written between 2150 and 1400 BCE. In the grandiose tale, Gilgamesh's friend Enkidu dies unexpectedly, and the titular hero begins to fear his own mortality. He embarks on a long and perilous journey to find Utnapishtim, the only known immortal in the world, to find his secret to living forever. When he finally hunts down the immortal, whose backstory is remarkably similar to Noah's in the Old Testament, Utnapishtim tells him that "there is no permanence" and attempts to dissuade him from the idea:

> Do we build a house to stand forever, do we seal a contract to hold for all time? . . . When the Anunnaki, the judges, come together, and Mammetun the mother of destinies, together they decree the fates of men. Life and death they allot but the day of death they do not disclose.[4]

Gilgamesh refuses to let the idea drop, so Utnapishtim challenges him: if he can stay awake for six days and seven nights, he will tell him the secret to immortality. Gilgamesh fails the test, but Utnapishtim's wife persuades her husband not to let him leave empty-handed. He tells Gilgamesh of a plant in the sea that can restore youth. The hero wastes no time obtaining the plant and plans to test it on an elderly person when he returns to Uruk. But when he is bathing, a serpent steals the plant and escapes by shedding its skin.

Gilgamesh goes home to Uruk with nothing to show for his journey, but he does appear to have learned his lesson. Throughout the story Gilgamesh is told how he should react to his friend's death: to live his normal, mortal life.

There are other similar tales from ancient history, including that of Qin Shi Huang, the founder of the Qin dynasty and the first emperor of a united China. By 221 BCE, Qin had conquered all the Chinese states, organized the building of the Great Wall of China, and commissioned the life-size Terracotta Army to guard the city-sized mausoleum he built. But toward the end of his life, despite such a long list of achievements, he began to crave a few more years and became fascinated by the concept of immortality.[5] As one of the most powerful men in the world, he presented a lucrative opportunity to tricksters, who were keen to sell him phony cures to death, and Qin is said to have fallen prey to many schemes. He sent Xu Fu, the court sorcerer, to find a supposed thousand-year-old magician who lived atop the mythological Penglai Mountain. Xu Fu took hundreds of young men and women with him and never returned. Some believed they were too scared to face Qin without the secret to immortality, but other legends suggest Xu Fu took them to the island now known as Japan and colonized it. Qin, meanwhile, decided ingesting mercury would grant him immortality. He died of mercury poisoning.

Immortalists candidly acknowledge these cautionary tales and agree the concept is prone to attracting fraudsters. But they are not put off. At the church on that stifling Thursday afternoon of my visit, dead Chinese emperors appeared to be the last thing on Josh's mind as he raced around trying to get the space ready for the activities to come. Furniture needed to be moved, leaflets laid out, and the entire building made ready for the incoming crowds. Josh seemed relieved when his boss arrived and he was able to pass me off.

VanDeRee, tall, slim, and in his late fifties, offered me a firm handshake and within two minutes of talking declared his intent to live until he's at least three hundred years old. He followed this by giving me a testing glare, as if daring me to mock him, query his sanity, or shout all sorts of questions directly into his face. I suggested that we instead we go for dinner at a salad bar restaurant five minutes away. When we arrived, VanDeRee piled mountainous amounts of salad onto his plate, including an extraordinary number of peas. So many peas, in fact, I began to wonder if there was a link between them and immortality. When I asked VanDeRee, it turned out he was practicing intermittent fasting, a diet where people forego eating for large amounts of time in an effort to become healthier. He also liked peas a lot. Fasting is widely used in the immortalist community

and has been linked with life extension. In 2018, a group of researchers from the National Institute of Aging (NIA), the University of
Wisconsin-Madison, and the Pennington Biomedical Research Center
in Louisiana found that increased time between meals lengthened the
lives of male mice compared to mice who ate more frequently.[6] The
study showed that this benefit was seen regardless of what the mice ate
or what calories they consumed.

This type of study is typical of those which inspire the immortalists. It's all part of a plan to survive until that crucial time when
technology will enable them to live forever. Not long into my conversation with VanDeRee, he told me immortalists have a phrase for
that watershed moment. "There are things that you can do right now
to ensure that you live to be 150, and if you can live to be 150 then
you can catch the age-reversal escape velocity, the escape velocity for
longevity," explained VanDeRee. "In a hundred and some years from
now, when you're 150, medical technology will be up there, and then
you're going to shoot for three hundred and then five hundred and
then one thousand. Then it goes on exponentially, until we have hit essentially an immortalist phase for humanity where we can then decide
if we want to die or not." For immortalists, escape velocity has become
similar to judgement day in religions; it is the moment when all their
long-held beliefs are proven accurate and they reach the point when
they no longer have to die.

VanDeRee is a soft-spoken man who displays genuine care toward
whoever he is talking to. When he's not hosting events at the Church
of Perpetual Life, he works in real estate as a broker and an auctioneer,
a job he had long before he founded the church. He lives in Venice on
Florida's Gulf Coast, frequently traveling across to the opposite side of
the state to Hollywood. During the two hours we spoke that evening,
the topic meandered from immortalism to my own personal history,
to his hopes for the future and back again. At no point did I feel he
was trying to recruit me to the immortalist way of viewing the world,

but his warmth, positivity, and optimism drew me in regardless. One of the themes that came up often was his worry and pity for those who will die in the future, a fate he sees as avoidable.

"Right now, we're forced, we have to die," he said. "There's no way to escape it for everybody in this room except me. I know I'm going to live for five hundred, one thousand, ten thousand years. I don't see an end to my life, but there are so many people that don't seem to care about age reversal. They don't seem to care about the fact that we have a real chance at reversing aging and living forever. And it boggles my mind. I can do a speech to three hundred people. Maybe one of them gets it, maybe one of them has a glimmer of thought in their eye: 'Maybe that could be me.'"

VanDeRee is genuinely baffled as to why more people don't seek eternal life. He believes that skepticism of the idea comes from pretenders in the past and naysayers in the present.

"Peer pressure and humanity seems to tamp it down and say, 'Oh no, you can't do that. That's not good. That's not right,' for whatever reason," he said. "I think some of it has to do with people thinking that a hundred years ago we had snake oil salesmen say if you take this elixir, it'll give you vibrance and youth, and they sell them the snake oil and then they don't live. You'd probably die from it. There's always the worry that they're going to do something that all of society is going to laugh at them about, the peer pressure. They're going to laugh at them for taking the tonic that can make them potentially live forever. And yet here's peer pressure, saying, 'Well, you shouldn't think about living forever. You should do this, that, or the other thing instead. It's more important than you personally living for a thousand years,' and yet if good people can live for five hundred, one thousand, ten thousand years, those good people can turn this planet around, can make this planet a cleaner, better place. And that's really what this is about. Creating heaven on earth and not leaving it."

VanDeRee's frustration toward people who do not choose the path of immortality is also born out of not being able to save more people close to him. He got into the immortalist world in his early thirties when he was diagnosed with a disease that he was told was going to kill him. He preferred not to name or talk about the disease itself, but at that time he began exploring cryonics, the process of freezing and preserving a body so it can be reanimated in the future. He wasn't just researching for himself, but also for his father, who was born in 1917 and "saw more horses than cars." After becoming convinced of the idea, he tried to persuade his father to accept cryonics. But VanDeRee said as the fifth child of seven kids, the "jury was rigged," and neither his father nor mother signed up to have their bodies preserved.

This was the first time I saw the sadness, not just the optimism, which motivated VanDeRee to seek out immortality. He told me if he had a time machine he would go back and try and convince his parents again, and this time save them from death.

This is an important motivating factor for all immortalists. In my conversations and in public profiles of the more well-known eternal life seekers, their desire to live forever comes from having to confront their own mortality at some stage, either because they have experienced sickness or have been in danger of dying themselves, or because they have had to deal with the death of someone close to them. To immortalists like VanDeRee, death is a tragic and unnecessary waste, and even if he couldn't save his parents, he remained determined to save himself. "I looked at cryonics and I said, okay, well this is an option, but right now I need to study these other things to get rid of the disease and be healthy and do what I can. And I stayed in with things. And then Aubrey de Grey gave a talk at the Orlando Science Center. So I went to the talk, and I brought a couple of people with me," recalled VanDeRee of the event held in the spring of 2008.

If the Church of Perpetual Life were to elect a living prophet today, there's a strong possibility Aubrey de Grey would be top of the list. He's a British scientist who is renowned in the field of age reversal, and perhaps the most influential of the current crop of demigod-like figures leading the immortalist movement. After VanDeRee listened to de Grey's talk, he stayed in contact with him. Later on, the British scientist introduced him to Bill Faloon, and together they built the church which VanDeRee leads today.

VanDeRee's personal history made him the perfect clergyman for the church, an establishment which follows much of the same structure as any other religious institution. For any church or religion establishing itself in 2012, there's a tried-and-tested playbook to follow, and the Church of Perpetual Life doesn't stray too far from it. There have been articles written in the past speculating the church was formed simply for tax purposes, and even some attendees I spoke to over the weekend suggested that to be true. There are significant tax incentives to declaring your organization a church in the United States, and there's no doubt that this had an impact on the decision. But I suspected that by creating a quasi-religion, the organizers were infusing scientific speculation with a thick layer of mysticism, a tactic that has succeeded in spreading a message that is still gathering congregations around the world today.

By tapping into the politics, mythology, and spiritualism of organized religion, this branch of immortalism succeeded in drawing much attention to its cause and has raised significant amounts of money. Donations are first applied to running the church itself, but VanDeRee said when members of the church learn of longevity projects, research that focuses on extending life, they give money or help in other ways, either by volunteering or as test subjects.

VanDeRee believes their time has finally come. "There are some amazing things happening right now. We have for the first time in human history a real chance for age reversal and life extension," he said. "For the first time we have a scientific real chance at immortality. And so that's what we're working on. It's going to revolutionize humanity."

As officiator of the church, VanDeRee hosts the monthly gatherings and also keeps his congregation informed of any scientific breakthroughs that can give them hope. Despite being kept busy selling real estate, he still finds time to send emails to the group when a particular piece of news, or scientific paper, is worthy of passing on. For example, in December 2019, VanDeRee sent an email inviting people to the latest gathering of immortalists but also sharing news of George Church's work at Harvard University using the gene editing tool CRISPR to try and make humans immune to viruses, disease, and aging.[7] This is just one scientific area that legitimizes the claims of the church.

In the same month, the congregation was sent an article from *Medical News Today* that heralded the anti-aging properties of a drug called rapamycin on human skin.[8] The drug was discovered in the soil of Easter Island half a century ago and gets its name from the native term for the island—Rapa Nui. It is said to be able to repress the human immune system and prevent cell replication. VanDeRee brought up many similar studies when we met, and it was somewhat jarring to hear so many scientific papers quoted in the style of an American preacher.

At the end of our meal, I told VanDeRee I looked forward to the weekend's events, and we went our separate ways: he returned to the church to continue the preparations, and I went back to my Airbnb to deal with the smell of a rotting possum.

I next saw the Church's officiator at the drinks reception held at a nearby Holiday Inn the next evening, where event attendees had the chance to network and meet old friends prior to the start of the event. Here I was introduced to a community stranger than I could ever imagine.

Meeting VanDeRee was one thing—he was the welcoming face of the movement—but these were hardened believers. As I sipped a drink and lingered uncomfortably by the buffet, I noticed almost all of them had something in common—they were old. One or two younger faces were dotted among the crowd, but I guessed the average age of an attendee was way over fifty. These were the people striving to reach the escape velocity age VanDeRee talked about, and they knew it was touch and go whether they'd survive long enough to make it.

I tried to speak to some of the younger people in the crowd. One utterly confused me when he told me he was making a documentary and threatened to film me, leering over me with his smartphone. Another, a man in his thirties named Diego, was a lot easier to talk to. He was a health enthusiast who had left the Jehovah's Witnesses, losing friends and family in the process. His old religion had preached about a form of everlasting life on Earth, and Diego was there to see what the Church of Perpetual Life had to offer. He wasn't convinced by some of the arguments he had been hearing but wanted to see if he could pick up any tips on staying healthier for longer.

Much of the elderly crowd were wearing the same bands around their wrists that I noticed VanDeRee sported at dinner the previous day. This was not a particularly fashionable piece of jewelry, but a calling card for those who are signed up to be cryogenically preserved after death. The band lists the details of the facility where the body must be taken, and the account details for when they get there. Small details like this make the whole group seem a lot more cultish, and it's easy to feel out of place in their presence. The immortalists are a deeply optimistic group of people, but I couldn't shake the overwhelming feeling that their optimism was misplaced. Advances in medical technologies bring great hope of better, healthier lives, but with a broken health care system and a world of accelerating inequality, would many of the attendees truly be able to reap the benefits? The topics of conversation varied from new diets to supplement doses. But the main topic of discussion on the weekend I visited the Church of Perpetual Life was cryonics. Companies traveled from as far away as Russia to discuss the latest advances in this experimental and controversial field and gave polished and professional talks, showing slides packed with medical advice, technical details, and scientific procedures.

Prior to the event, my thoughts on cryonics probably fell in line with the majority of the population—it all sounded a little weird. The idea of having my body stored in a frozen cylinder after I died was not the problem; after all, we all end up in either a box in the ground or burned to ashes anyway. But the thought of waking up at some point in a strange and mysterious future was disconcerting. It was with these hesitations that I delved into the history of cryonics. The industry is a lot older than most people may think. Its origin story spans decades and, as you'd expect with such a strange topic, features plenty of eccentric and fascinating characters.

2

A DRASTIC PLAN B

The founding years of the cryonics movement are dominated by three key characters: Robert Ettinger, Evan Cooper, and Bob Nelson. This unlikely trio thrust cryonics into global consciousness, transforming the practice from a science-fiction fantasy to a hotly debated topic of the future. But none of them were able to unite the fractured cryonics community, as backstabbing, jealousy, and outright fraud ran rampant in the early years.

Cryonicists today describe Ettinger as the grandfather of the industry, and his work from the 1960s continues to inspire and motivate those practicing the art of freezing the dead. He was born in Atlantic City, New Jersey, in 1918 and was, unsurprisingly, something of a nerd. He developed a love of *The Jameson Satellite*, a science fiction series which ran in the magazine *Amazing Stories* in 1931.[1] The stories were written by Neil Ronald Jones and followed a Professor Jameson, who managed to have his preserved corpse launched into space. He orbited the Earth for forty million years before passing aliens called Zoromes, who had achieved immortality by transferring their brains into machines, picked him up. These half-alien, half-machine hybrids resurrected Jameson and made him one of their own, and the stories followed his adventures as an immortal traveling around the universe and generally having a great time. It's easy to see why a thirteen-year-old would find the tale appealing, but Ettinger took the possibilities to be much more practical than fiction. "It was instantly obvious to me that the author had missed the main point of his own idea!" he later wrote. "If immortality is achievable through the ministrations of advanced aliens through repairing a human corpse, then why should not everyone be frozen to await later rescue by our own people?"

Ettinger's fascination with the concept of freezing the dead became the central theme of his life. He obtained a master's degree in physics and mathematics before serving in the United States Army during World War II.[2] He reached the rank of second lieutenant but was wounded in combat. During his long recovery, he read up on some of the science emerging around the concept which had captured his imagination as a young boy. His research led him to French biologist Jean Rostand, who explored the possibility of using low temperatures to affect the properties of living things in the 1940s. What he read inspired him to write science fiction of his own. In 1948 he penned a sci-fi story called "The Penultimate Trump," which thankfully was not a prophetic warning of what the world would endure decades later. The pulp science fiction magazine *Startling Stories* published the tale in its March issue, and it was notable for containing many of the concepts of cryonics which emerged later on. Still, cryogenic preservation remained a topic of fiction, while Ettinger grew frustrated at his own inability to lead the revolution he so desperately wanted to see. He became a physics teacher at Highland Park Community College, just outside Detroit, and waited for the spark that would ignite this next great medical age, but nobody stepped up. By the 1960s, he'd waited long enough. "As the years passed and no one better came forward, I finally had to write . . ." he later proclaimed.

The United States at this time was fertile ground for ideas that blurred the lines between science fiction and fact. The development of the atomic bomb during World War II, which was predicted by the major science fiction magazine of the day, *Astounding*, altered the

way science fiction was viewed. The United States became the leading economic, industrial, and scientific power in the world, and rapid
technological advancement created a feeling that anything was possible. This was particularly evident during the 1960s, as the Space
Race between the United States and the USSR brought regular and
astonishing feats, culminating in Neil Armstrong and Buzz Aldrin's
trip to the moon in 1969. In the same decade, science fiction classics
like Frank Herbert's *Dune* and Philip K. Dick's *Do Androids Dream
of Electric Sheep?* were published. In cinemas, Stanley Kubrick's *2001:
A Space Odyssey* elevated the genre to a new level, prompting people
around the world to ask major questions about the future of humanity. Against this backdrop, Ettinger attempted to launch cryonics into
the world.

His early efforts to drum up support for the idea were a little odd.
He wrote an article outlining the basic concept and explaining why it
was so important for the future of the human race, and mailed it to a
couple of hundred people he found on a Who's Who in America list.
One can only imagine their reaction at receiving such a document out
of the blue and, unsurprisingly, Ettinger did not get much response.
He realized he needed to present his ideas more comprehensively, so
he published what would end up being a preliminary version of his
book *The Prospect of Immortality* in 1962.[3] To Ettinger's delight, like-
minded people across the country responded to the self-published
book with great excitement.[4] One of them was Evan Cooper. While
Ettinger was a reluctant pioneer in the field, Cooper has since been
credited as the first person to take practical steps toward making the
idea a reality. There was undoubted enthusiasm around *The Prospect of
Immortality*, but before Cooper, followers of cryonics were yet to form
any kind of community.

Cooper published his own book about the future the same year as
Ettinger. *Immortality, Physically, Scientifically, Now* perhaps suffered
for its wordy title, as it never reached the heights of Ettinger's work.
But Cooper was ready to take action. On December 23, 1962, he

held an informal meeting in Washington D.C. for those interested in the concept of cryonics.[5] Around twenty people attended to discuss both books, and Cooper and others agreed to form the Immortality Communication Exchange (ICE), a special interest group promoting the "freeze and wait" idea that would be at the heart of all future cryonics. But ICE did not last long as a name. The group morphed into the Life Extension Society (LES) at its first formal event in Washington D.C. And in early 1964, LES launched a newsletter to better communicate progress to the fledgling community.

Ettinger's book, meanwhile, really took off. Doubleday Publishers released a hardcover version, buoyed by encouraging public interest. The publishers sent a copy of the book to the renowned science fiction writer Isaac Asimov, who apparently approved of the science.[6] *The Prospect of Immortality* became the cryonics equivalent to the Bible. The book has since appeared in nine languages and has had four editions. It's an interesting read. The tome contains a lot of wishful thinking and minimal science to back anything up. Ettinger wrote about a golden age, when overwhelming positivity would reign, but didn't go into any detail how a freezing process would be carried out, let alone the much trickier reanimation. At times Ettinger strayed into dark and dubious territory. For example, he suggested fetuses could be frozen and childbirth made a thing of the past but claimed those with cerebral palsy could just remain on ice without being reanimated. In a section called "Mercy Killings," he wrote:

> According to Jane Gould, "In all, roughly three newborn infants out of a hundred are seriously abnormal." Most of these, of course, will not be considered for early freezing; they will either die early natural deaths, or will be cured, or can be helped to lead lives not too pitifully far from the norm. But consider, for example, the worst cases of cerebral palsy. According to Jessie S. West, in the United States in 1954 there were around a half million victims of this disease. Many had normal intelligence, although the affliction produced symptoms

such as facial grimacing, drooling, and unintelligible speech which might make them seem subnormal to an uninformed observer. But many had serious mental deficiencies, and in fact 13 percent were considered uneducable. At present, we properly do not countenance euthanasia for this 23 percent, even though they may be suffering and even though there is a heavy emotional and financial burden on the other members of the family. But will not the situation be different when freezers are available?[7]

In a book about freezing people, it's genuinely chilling to see how quickly the utopian fantasy takes a wild swing into eugenics and dystopian nightmare. Ettinger wrote of an extremely positive future for the species, providing he saw people fit enough to be born in the first place.

The future will reveal a wonderful world indeed, a vista to excite the mind and thrill the heart. It will be bigger and better than the present—but not only that. It will not be just the present, king-sized and chocolate-covered; it will be different. The key difference will be in people; we will remold, nearer to the heart's desire not just the world, but ourselves as well. And "ourselves" refers to people, not just posterity. You and I, the frozen, the resucitees, will be not merely revived and cured, but enlarged and improved, made fit to work, play, and perhaps fight, on a grand scale and in a grand style. Specific reasons for such expectations will be presented.[8]

By the end of 1964, perhaps feeding off each other, both Ettinger's book and Cooper's LES gathered momentum. Ettinger became something of a celebrity: he was featured in magazine and newspaper articles and appeared on radio and television, including the Long John Nebel show, an all-night radio talk program.[9] Cryonics entered the national discourse, despite the fractures that had already begun to emerge in the community of enthusiasts. The LES newsletter, elaborately titled *Freeze, Wait, Reanimate*, became the conduit for the various squabbles that were roiling the immortalist communities. In the September 1964 issue, Leonard Gilley tore into Cooper for his perceived inaction. They saw a lot of talk and not enough practical steps being taken. "You are, to be very blunt, doing more waiting than freezing . . . have you personally planned specifically for freezing? What is that plan? . . . if you have not planned, then you are a hypocrite . . . intentions and speculations, hell! Let's see action!" he wrote in an impressively impatient and stinging letter.

And here begins the soap opera years of cryonics.

In the same September 1964 issue, two groups announced they were breaking away from LES, again over a perceived lack of action. "Tom Tierney's group, feeling the urgency of getting something done in the way of organization and freezing, considers that they will get there faster on an independent track. Tom informs us that his group voted to withdraw from LES," Cooper wrote of the first group, which formed its own organization in Southern California.[10] (Tierney's group rejoined the LES in 1965.)

Cooper further noted: "Bob Ettinger also feels that the physical freezing program has been too slow, and to remedy this he is considering beginning a commercial operation for the freezing and storage of bodies. He is more than willing to go full steam ahead, with any engine that can carry the freight, profit or nonprofit. Bob is becoming increasingly doubtful, however, that a nonprofit organization [like LES] can get the program in motion."

The next year, even Cooper lamented the lack of action. "Are we shouting in the abyss?" he wrote. "How could 110 million go to their deaths without one, at least trying for a life in the future via freezing? Where is the individualism, scientific curiosity, and even eccentricity we hear so much about?"[11]

Thankfully, before things could get too stale, the eccentrics emerged. Pioneers, bold, brave, and mostly misguided, made the first attempts at cryopreservation. New cryonics societies had emerged across the country as more and more enthusiasts turned away from the LES. In August 1965, Saul Kent and Curtis Henderson, who would both make important contributions to the community, started their own organization in New York called the Cryonics Society of New York (CSNY). The duo also coined the phrase cryonics in the process. Around the same time, more LES breakaways formed, including Cryo-Care Corporation in Phoenix, Arizona, which advertised its services as cosmetic rather than preparation for eventual reanimation.[12] Kent and Henderson made a trip across the United States in 1966 and helped organize more cryonics societies in Michigan and California as further societies continued to emerge. They were quick to make progress where the LES had failed.

Wilma Jean McLaughlin of Springfield, Ohio, died of heart and circulatory problems on May 20, 1965. A plucky group of cryonicists attempted to freeze her, but the procedure failed. Cooper recounted what went wrong in the next issue of *Freeze, Wait, Reanimate.*[13] He recounted an alarmingly long list of explanations gathered from newspapers, newscasts, and long distance calls from people present, most of which blamed meddling third parties. Although McLaughlin's husband favored freezing his dead wife, some of her relatives and her minister were deeply opposed to the idea. The minister, validly, noted that there were no laws or regulations in place to govern the procedure or keep the parties involved in check. Her physician agreed and refused to aid the freezing process, while hospital staffers where she passed away wanted no part in the experiment. Mistakes were made, apparently, by the cryonics practitioners themselves. Juno Inc., the company supposedly supplying the capsule to store the body, said the device was still being tested and only a prototype existed. Little is known of Juno, aside from it being one of the first commercial companies to attempt to profit from cryonics by building the equipment dreamed up by the enthusiasts. Cryonics capsules became a cottage industry over the years and, particularly in the early decades, almost always broke down at some point. Perhaps the McLaughlin attempt was always doomed to fail. The final reason Cooper listed for its foundering was the most damning: "The subject for freezing was unconscious and did not know anything about the plan according to most reports," he wrote in the newsletter.[14]

The LES refused to be deterred by one magnificent failure. The next year Cooper's organization offered to freeze someone for free. "The Life Extension Society now has primitive facilities for emergency short term freezing and storing our friend the large homeotherm (man). LES offers to freeze free of charge the first person desirous and in need of cryogenic suspension." Cryonics, at the level it was being attempted in the 1960s, required surprisingly little in the way of equipment. The facilities thrown up by the various organizations were usually warehouses or spaces where they could store the capsules or containers used to preserve the bodies. Over time, it would become more and more difficult to set up these spaces, as insurance concerns, health regulations, and the increased complexity of the operations limited their setup.

Nobody took up Cooper's generous offer, but the attempts kept coming elsewhere. Danbridge M. Cole, who wrote the book *Beyond Tomorrow: The Next Fifty Years in Space*, which, among its many lavish illustrations of moon colonies and rockets, included a section on suspended animation, died in October 1965 from a heart attack. Cole, an aerospace engineer, reportedly expressed a wish to be frozen after death to friends and colleagues, including Robert Prehoda, a curious individual with a large part to play in early cryonics. Prehoda was interested in cryobiology and later wrote a book called *Suspended Animation*, but he opposed cryonics because he felt the freezing process damaged the brain, making it unfeasible to reanimate anyone in the future. He convinced Cole to be buried, recalling in his book: "Rational counsel prevailed, and Dan was given a dignified burial."

On April 22, 1966, Cooper finally had reason to celebrate. "Someone has been frozen at last!" he wrote in the newsletter.[15] Cryo-Care, the Arizona-based company established in 1965, announced it had cryopreserved an unidentified elderly woman, but the results were far from promising. "There is little or no thought that this first frozen pioneer will rise again in the 21st or 22nd century as considerable time elapsed between death and freezing. If the cooling and perfusion of the person with cryoprotective agents isn't begun immediately at death the memory which is believed a matter of fine molecular placement would soon disintegrate. As this first person was frozen long after death there is no known hope for re-establishing the original memory and thus the personality. Yet this imperfect beginning may be a step forward toward bringing an extended life to others via cryogenics," Cooper wrote.

Within a few months, Cryo-Care thawed the woman for unknown reasons, removing her from suspension. Despite this setback, momentum continued to build. Each partial success brought new eccentrics to the cause. One of those newcomers became a (temporary) hero in the cryonics world: Bob Nelson, a TV repairman.

Nelson endured a tough upbringing in Boston, Massachusetts. His mother was an alcoholic, and his father left before he was born. His stepfather, a mobster named John "Fats" Buccelli, was jailed for his part in Brink's Robbery, dubbed "the largest heist in US history,"[16] in which nearly $3 million was stolen from a Boston office in 1950. Months after being released from prison, Buccelli was shot in the back of the head and killed, ending his complex relationship with his stepson. Nelson said his stepfather's death left him "devastated but not surprised," but he felt "strangely freed from his path" and knew his own journey was finally about to begin.[17] Nelson later moved to Los Angeles, where he read Ettinger's book and became obsessed with cryonics. While sitting in traffic, he heard a radio advertisement for a group of enthusiasts in the city. Delighted to meet like-minded people, he attended his first official LES meeting in May 1966.

Nelson documented his experience in 2014 in his book *Freezing People Is (Not) Easy: My Adventures In Cryonics*. He expected to walk into a room full of scientists and medical professionals, but instead found elderly people with no more idea of how to freeze someone than himself. Nelson had no medical training, no scientific knowledge, no degree or even high school diploma, yet in the second meeting the group voted to leave the LES umbrella due to a perceived lack of action and elected him president of a newly formed group, The Cryonics Society of California (CSC). The appointment didn't please everyone.

Dr. Renault Able—who Nelson said resembled Batman's nemesis, the Joker—attended Nelson's first meeting very briefly, claiming he wanted to be the group's appointed medical professional.[18] Able showed up at subsequent meetings sparingly, but when he learned a TV repairman had been made president he was outraged, claiming they would never be taken seriously. Nelson responded by offering Able the position of president, but the doctor, presumably worried about the potential damage to his reputation, turned him down.

As president, Nelson was tasked with raising awareness of cryonics, and he took up his duties with relish, making appearances on radio and television shows in California. Nelson also got in touch with his hero, Ettinger, with whom he struck up a correspondence. At one point he arranged a five-day visit to the CSC for Ettinger and gushed over his appearance, claiming it changed his life. He also described the pioneer as a father figure.

Nelson didn't want to just talk about the prospect of freezing people, he wanted to go ahead and try it himself. He began to learn more about cryobiology, the sister science of studying things at extremely low temperatures, and was introduced to Prehoda, an expert in the field and the same man who had opposed freezing one of the earlier candidates. When Nelson called Ettinger and told him he was meeting Prehoda, Ettinger bristled, saying he approved of the expert's knowledge of cryonics but didn't like his character, presumably because he had persuaded his friend to opt out of cryopreservation in favor of burial.[19] Nelson welcomed Prehoda into the CSC regardless, and they slowly patched together a team of experts and enthusiasts who would try to take cryonics to the next level. Nelson and Prehoda also assembled a scientific advisory council to conduct research into human suspended animation. The council was made up of respected scientists of the time, long since scrubbed from the history of the society, who agreed to join on one condition: if the CSC did eventually freeze someone, they would immediately end their affiliation with the group. The scientific council saw the field as an interesting subject worthy of further examination but feared any attempt to actually freeze a dead body would do irreversible damage to their own careers. They believed progress should be made through lab work and experimentation on animals.

It wasn't long until that agreement was tested.

In early 1967, Nelson received a call from a frantic funeral director at a mortuary in Glendale. He was trying to calm an irate gentleman demanding he arrange for his father, who was very close to death, to be frozen. The funeral director had no idea how to facilitate such a request, so he called the local cryonics society. Nelson took the number of the mortuary, promised to call back, then hung up. Here was just the opportunity Nelson and the nascent cryonics industry had been waiting for. He persuaded Prehoda to help, even if it meant losing the scientific advisory board, and the pair arranged a meeting with the interested party.

The irate customer was Norman Bedford. His father was dying of cancer, and he wanted to carry out his final wish—to be frozen.[20] James Bedford, who taught psychology at Glendale College, had put aside a sizable sum of money to fund cryonics research when he died. As he approached death, he decided he wanted to go a step further and volunteer for the procedure himself. Prehoda was concerned no freezing protocol had been perfected, and still held doubts that freezing humans was beneficial at all. Nelson cast these worries aside and sought Ettinger's advice. The founding father of cryonics, who hadn't frozen anyone himself, said it was an exciting opportunity for the CSC and shipped a cardiac compression machine from Detroit to help the freezing process. Prehoda then got over his concerns, and a hastily assembled team got to work with the preparations.

The group's main goal was to preserve James Bedford's brain. At a normal temperature when someone dies, their brain is damaged within five minutes of their breathing stopping. When the body temperature is lowered, the brain is less dependent on oxygen. Therefore, the group theorized, the body must be cooled as quickly as possible. You can't just plunge a human body into freezing temperatures without causing major damage, however. The human body is made up of more than 75 percent water, which expands when frozen. To prevent cells in the body from bursting, the team proposed injecting special chemicals into the bloodstream which would absorb the vast majority of water. This would ensure freezing took place outside the cells and not inside.

Nelson, a biophysicist named Dr. Dante Brunol, and Prehoda carried out the procedure. The trio began gathering the necessary tools and implements as Bedford's health deteriorated. His regular physician was replaced by the Joker-like Dr. Able. Nelson visited Bedford on his deathbed, and, to his surprise, the man about to be frozen was awake. According to Nelson, he said in a whisper: "I have little hope of ever being reanimated, Mr. Nelson, but I believe in the future of cryonics. I hope my children or grandchildren will benefit from the inevitable medicine of the future."[21] Nelson would much later be found to be economical with the truth in his recollections of the past, so it's hard to imagine Bedford offered up such a tantalizing soundbite as he lay dying, but perhaps it reflected his general sentiment.

On January 12, 1967, Nelson had just collected the last of the chemicals when Dr. Able called to say Bedford was dead, way ahead of schedule. Able managed to keep Bedford's body cold with whatever ice he could get his hands on, while Nelson rushed to reach the nursing home where Bedford had died. When he got there, he was joined by Prehoda and Dr. Brunol, and they set about packing the body with more ice before injecting the chemicals (essentially, biological antifreeze). They used the heart compressor device sent by Ettinger to pump the solution around Bedford's body, and after two hours of work, the primitive procedure was completed. The team moved the body into a container packed with dry ice and stored it at Prehoda's house.

The cryonics community rejoiced. Cooper responded in the hastily written and distributed January issue of *Freeze-Wait-Reanimate* with enthusiasm and a positive report on the procedure.[22] He believed there was hope of reanimating Bedford in the future and suggested nursing homes would be the best place to carry out subsequent preservations. Cooper also expressed surprise that cryonics skeptic Prehoda had participated in what they saw as a landmark case. Ettinger opined:

> Readers of the LES newsletter will probably be surprised to know that Mr. Prehoda provided such important help, in view of his expressed pessimism. He remains more pessimistic than most of us, and in fact says that at this date he still would not choose freezing for his own family, but it is greatly to his credit that he recognizes the possible validity of other viewpoints and is willing to help the optimists in practice. His chief concern remains to stimulate greater support for research, and we all agree on the importance of this.

However, it seems the extent of Prehoda's involvement surprised nobody more than his own wife. The CSC team stored Bedford's frozen corpse in Prehoda's garage. Next morning, his wife Claudette learned there was a dead body being stored on her property. She freaked out, telling him he had six hours to remove the body or she would call the police.

Nelson somehow managed to convince his "first-class hippie" secretary and her husband to keep the body in their home in Topanga Canyon. He hauled the container holding the body into his pickup truck and sped over to the new temporary lodgings. Bedford's corpse stayed there for a week before his son transferred the body to the Cryo-Care Equipment company in Phoenix, Arizona, where he could be placed in a cryogenic capsule. The maker of the capsule was Ed Hope, described by UPI as a "former night club owner and oilman" who was currently working as a wigmaker. Bedford's family paid him $4,000 for his services.

As if the previous week's events hadn't been entertaining enough, they were amplified by leading figures in the cryonics world descending on Los Angeles in pilgrimage. Ettinger himself flew into California from Detroit and appeared on *The Johnny Carson Show* (Zsa Zsa Gabor was apparently the other guest), as well as other celebrity talk shows. Meanwhile, the scientific advisory council of the CSC dissolved immediately and told Prehoda not to mention any of their names, as they didn't want to be associated with any part of the whole operation.

That same year, easily the most monumental in the industry's history up to that point, the cryonics community again went to war with one another. In 1967, Nelson froze another person through his California-based organization, a woman named Marie Phelps-Sweet who had been a prominent member of the early cryonics community. Three weeks after the publication of *The Prospect of Immortality*, she wrote to Ettinger expressing her support for the concept of cryonics. "Zestful living has been a long-time hobby of mine, so zestful departure from this vale, via freezeration, is a welcome release from the degrading and wasteful concepts of the past . . . What bothers me now is how any thoughtful people can fail to realize the scope of the program . . . [is] more immediate and necessary," the letter read. She threw herself into the cryonics cause and joined LES. Cooper said in his December 1964 newsletter: "We are fortunate in having the marvelous support and inestimable services of Marie Phelps-Sweet, our Western Coordinator in Santa Barbara. She is the spark-plug of LES." [23]

Two years later she became involved with Nelson's CSC, and both she and her husband Russ Van Norden agreed to be frozen when they died. Van Norden's time appeared to have arrived first when he had a heart attack in April 1967. Nelson and his team coordinated with the hospital in anticipation of freezing the body, but he recovered. Just four months later, Sweet was found dead in a Santa Monica hotel room. The events that followed caused another severe rupture in the cryonics community.

Sweet was taken to a mortuary, and the undertaker, having found a card she kept on her stating she was to be frozen, rang Cooper on a collect call to ask for advice on what to do with the body. Cooper refused to pay for the charges, believing it was a crank call, and hung up on the undertaker. "All I can say," a mortuary employee told the *Glendale News-Press* at the time, "is that it must be a pretty secret society. I called all up and down the West Coast trying to locate a representative."[24]

As a result, Sweet's body spent three days in a mortuary freezer before anyone could cryopreserve her.

Eventually, Nelson and his team froze Sweet's body, but Dr. Able was quoted in the *Glendale News-Press* saying the procedure was nothing more than a publicity stunt given the amount of time between Sweet's death and when she was frozen. To add to the drama, there were no mortuary facilities available, so the team had to take the body to the CSC offices, where it was technically illegal to work on it. Sweet was an incredibly popular member of the cryonics community, and yet she was let down. Accusations quickly began to fly. Another CSC member, Russ Stanley, attempted to find out where Sweet was being stored, and when he couldn't reach Nelson, he wrote to Cooper expressing his frustration. "I'm not picking at him, but if this is a downright hoax, then I'd rather have no one [at all] than [someone like] Nelson. He has alienated himself from those who wanted to help, but demanded to know where the money was going."

When Ettinger got wind of the situation, he sprung to the defense of his protégé Nelson. "I must comment on what I consider the shameful attitude you and Russ Stanley are displaying toward Bob Nelson," he wrote in a letter to Cooper which was also sent to other cryonics organizations. "There is nothing to justify your suspecting him of a 'hoax' in Marie's freezing; quite the contrary." He then chewed Cooper out over the refused collect call, describing it as "one of the most stupid and irresponsible things I've ever heard of."

The October issue of *Freeze-Wait-Reanimate* made it clear how much Ettinger's letter had hurt Cooper. Two weeks after the newsletter was distributed, the LES was to host its fifth conference for the cryonics community. Cooper canceled it, blaming the fallout from Sweet's death. "First, an unexpected increase of mail came, much of which remains unanswered and a corresponding backlog of office work has accumulated. Second, a very nasty letter was received from a usually respected authority in the freezing movement accusing the President of LES of poor judgment, bad motives, stupidity, irresponsibility, etc., etc. a letter that a paranoid would consider a veiled threat," Cooper wrote.[25]

Although the event did go ahead the following year, the LES effectively ceased to function by 1970. Cooper became marginalized in cryonics. He attempted to build his own cryobiology laboratory, which would also serve as a storage center for cryopreserved people. He was not wealthy but in 1968 managed to borrow enough money to purchase land in Maryland, where he built a small facility. However, his hopes were ruined when the basement flooded and he couldn't fix the damage.[26]

Cooper, who had done so much to organize the movement, walked away from cryonics. His former wife Mildred attributed his abrupt exit to "overload, burn-out, and a general sense that it was not going to be a viable option in his lifetime." He focused his attention on his other passion, sailing. In 1982, he left Martha's Vineyard in his boat *The Pelican*, heading for his home in Beaufort, South Carolina, but never reached his destination. Cooper's body was never found, and he was lost at sea forever.[27] He never returned to cryonics, despite having his hunch over Nelson's conduct proved accurate. After Bedford's freezing, the story of the most successful man in cryonics quickly turned both gruesome and tragic.

In the aftermath of the Bedford preservation, Nelson was slightly underwhelmed. The media attention was impressive, but somehow it didn't translate into genuine inquiries from people who wanted to be frozen. He also battled new competition. Organizations around the country, buoyed by his success, started accepting patients. One such company was Cryo-Care, where Bedford's relatives had taken him to be fitted for a capsule. The Arizona firm was run by the wigmaker Ed Hope, whose interest in cryonics was purely financial.[28] He built his own capsules, which were easily transported around as they had wheels. Hope advertised his services as purely cosmetic rather than a means to be reanimated in the future, but it didn't deter the cryonics enthusiasts knocking on his door. He froze a man named Louis Nisco in September 1967 following a sizable delay after the time of death. Eva Schilman followed the next year, along with a third patient, a man who had committed suicide. All three were stored at the company. But after just two years Hope realized he wasn't going to make a profit from freezing the dead and told relatives they must find alternative means of storage for their frozen loved ones. Schilman was driven around in a truck packed with dry ice for a period by her son before being handed over to a mortuary and buried. The man who committed suicide was also buried by his son a year later. Nisco ended up at CSC with Nelson.

In the eighteen months after he froze Bedford, Nelson attempted three more cryopreservations.

The first was Sweet, the case that provoked skepticism from Cooper. Nelson realized neither she nor her husband had enough money to cover the upkeep of her body. Cryo capsules, like those built by Hope, could keep bodies preserved effectively but needed topping up with liquid nitrogen every now and then and were expensive to procure. The only other option was to keep the body stored in a container and pack it with dry ice, a much more labor-intensive process. Nelson attempted to raise the thousands of dollars needed to buy a capsule for Sweet but fell short, so he resorted to Plan B, paying $90 a week for the dry ice. He stored the body at the mortuary of Joseph Klockgether, a new CSC recruit whose skills as a mortician were very much welcomed.

Helen Kline, another CSC member, whose house was used for Nelson's first-ever LES meeting, was frozen next. Again, she lacked the riches required to pay for her body's long-term upkeep, but Nelson went ahead and placed her in the same dry ice container as Sweet. Stanley, another paid-up member who accused Nelson of being a fraud after Sweet's preservation, soon joined them. Nelson was certain Stanley had settled his affairs to ensure his suspension was fully funded but was again left disappointed: he'd left just $10,000 in his will to CSC. The funding provided some relief to the society's stretched finances, but Nelson still found himself in an awkward and draining situation with three bodies stored in one container. And the bodies couldn't stay at the mortuary for long. A state rule forbade holding corpses at mortuaries for more than six months, and Klockgether began putting pressure on Nelson to move the container.

Nelson came up with an unorthodox but surprisingly impressive plan. He found a plot with an underground crypt at the Oakwood Memorial Park Cemetery in Chatsworth, a suburb of L.A.[29] The team would need to make changes to the crypt, but legally the bodies would be interred in a cemetery with no limit to how long they could be kept there. But until he could afford a capsule, even a crypt couldn't save him from financial difficulties. Luckily, Hope's exit from the cryonics game meant a capsule landed in Nelson's lap. The only problem was it was occupied.

In late 1968, Marie Brown called the CSC and explained her predicament: Hope was shutting shop, and her father Louis Nisco needed a new home.[30] Nelson smelled an opportunity. He agreed to take Nisco's body—capsule and all—and store it in the cemetery for $150 a month. He even paid the remaining balance she owed for the capsule. Nelson hatched another plan, this time a little less ingenious.[31]

The way Nelson saw it, Nisco's capsule was a little roomy. He planned to open it up and give him some company—the three bodies he was storing in the cemetery. He didn't tell Brown her father was about to get three new roommates, let alone any relatives of the other

three deceased. The plan worked perfectly: Nelson now had four frozen people in a single-person capsule, but nowhere to store them. The
crypt worked well for the low-maintenance container packed with
dry ice, but a capsule would need electricity, ventilation, and access to
refill it with liquid nitrogen. He stored the capsule in a nearby heavy
equipment yard while he searched for a solution, but new problems
continued to arise. The capsule was leaking and needed a vacuum
pump to make sure there was a sufficient seal between the inner wall
and the outer chamber. The leak meant the liquid nitrogen needed to
be replaced every week instead of every month, while the vault itself
was filling with water and needed to be pumped out regularly.

The pressure was getting to Nelson. Money was running out. In
the run-up to a 1970 cryonics conference held in L.A., he managed
to get the crypt in decent enough shape to accept visitors and showed
some enthusiasts around. He hoped that display would encourage
donations, the bigger the better. But the event came and went, and the
CSC left empty-handed.[32] The money ran out, and Nelson could no
longer afford the liquid nitrogen. Now he faced the unthinkable. With
no liquid nitrogen and a leaky capsule, the temperature of the preserved bodies would quickly climb. The people stored in the cylinder
were not just pioneers of cryonics, they were also Nelson's friends. At
some point in 1970, Nelson drove out into the desert, emotional and
disconsolate, and said a ceremonial goodbye to his frozen comrades.[33]
Then he let them decompose.

For many, that horrendous experience would have turned them off
cryonics for life. Nelson had given a large part of his third decade
to the endeavor, to receive only scant acknowledgement. But a few
months after he abandoned the capsule, he received a call from two
brothers in Iowa and jumped right back in, hoping for a fresh start.
Dennis and Terry Harrington offered a $10,000 donation for Nelson
to freeze their mother Mildred's body, ship it to California, and keep
it in temporary storage.[34] They would pay $150 a month to keep it in

a container with dry ice until CSC finished building a thirty-person cylinder, a long-term plan that never reached fruition.

Nelson was back in the body-freezing game, and in July 1971 was contacted by the father of a seven-year-old girl who was terminally ill. Genevieve de la Poterie had a Wilms tumor, which was fatal at that time. Her father, Guy de la Poterie, wanted her body to be preserved but seemed to lack the resources for the eternal upkeep.[35] Again, Nelson couldn't find it in himself to turn the desperate family down. Genevieve was transferred from her native Montreal to a hospital in California, and Nelson grew close with the family and the girl, even taking her to Disneyland before she died.[36] After she passed, Nelson oversaw the freezing procedure and placed her in temporary suspension with Mildred Harrington.

Later, he welcomed another guest at the Chatsworth cemetery plot, Steven Mandell, whose mother was having issues keeping him stored in a similar facility on the East Coast. He also helped a man named Nick de Blasio set up a chamber in a New Jersey cemetery for his frozen wife and agreed to store Pedro Ledesma in a paid-for capsule.[37] Now Nelson had four bodies to care for. Mandell and Ledesma were in a cryonics capsule, meaning they just needed the liquid nitrogen topped up monthly, but the other two, Harrington and young Genevieve, were being stored in a temporary container and needed their dry ice replaced each week. Facing a similar workload to before, he revived an old plan. He cut off the top of Mandell's capsule and placed the bodies of Genevieve and Harrington inside with him.

Nelson enlisted the help of a welder to work on the job, which took a full day. The welder later said that as he was fixing the top back on, he could smell burning hair, such was the proximity of the three crammed bodies to his equipment.[38] Another person who worked on the procedure said the bodies initially wouldn't fit into the capsule because they were too rigid and frozen. Nelson reportedly took a hairdryer and began thawing out parts of their bodies so they could all be slid into the container.[39] The resurrected plan ran into familiar problems—the capsule was not well made. And when Nelson was away on vacation in Boston in 1974, the pump failed. He returned to the cemetery and found that far from being freezing cold, the capsule was incredibly hot.[40] He instantly knew all three bodies were already irretrievably decomposed.

Nelson claimed he contacted the relatives of Genevieve and Harrington to tell them the capsule had failed and their loved ones had been without cooling for several days. The way Nelson tells it, they replied nonchalantly, simply telling him to start it back up again despite knowing any hope of resurrection was almost certainly gone. Both Genevieve's father and Harrington's son later told a journalist from *This American Life* that Nelson never spoke to them.[41] Either way, he had the pump fixed, replaced the liquid nitrogen, and continued to maintain a capsule full of dead bodies which had absolutely no chance of being resurrected. He even continued to add people to the vault at Chatsworth.

In October 1974, Nelson agreed to place six-year-old Sam Porter in storage in the cemetery.[42] Porter's father paid for a cryonics capsule and for the upkeep. But Nelson's other charges were not paying for themselves. According to the beleaguered CSC president, he received no money from Mandell's mother, or the sons of Harrington. Guy de la Poterie sent the occasional $50 or $100, but that was all the money coming in, and the liquid nitrogen expenses were crippling Nelson financially.[43]

Three years after the second capsule failed, Nelson admitted defeat. His wife had divorced him, and he was neglecting his children. He told the families of the dead he was financially and emotionally exhausted and would no longer be taking care of the vault. Around March 1979, Nelson cut open the capsules and took out the bodies.[44] Genevieve and Sam Porter were taken to a mortuary and buried conventionally in Orange County. Harrington, Mandell, and Ledesma were placed in metal boxes, while the original frozen members, Nisco, Sweet, Stanley, and Kline, were left sealed in the capsule. It was a sorry end to Nelson's great experiment, but his life in cryonics still had one painful and expensive twist.

Unhappy relatives of those left to rot in the Chatsworth vault sued Nelson. In the court case, he was portrayed as a cult leader trying to scam mourning people at their most vulnerable. In 1981, Nelson and the mortician Klockgether were both told to pay $400,000 in damages to relatives.[45] Klockgether paid the fee using his malpractice insurance. Nelson had no such insurance and was left financially decimated. The affair was labeled the Chatsworth disaster, a low point for the young cryonics industry.

Thus, the three pioneers of cryonics met vastly different fates. Cooper died first and died permanently, his body never found. Opinion on Nelson varied within the community. Some felt he did the best he could with the resources he had, while others labeled him a con artist and a fraudster. He wrote two books about his experience in cryonics and died in 2018. He was cryopreserved and stored at the Cryonics Institute, where he was reunited with his old mentor and inspiration Ettinger. His former collaborator and codefendant Klockgether oversaw the procedure.[46] Ettinger, the grandfather of cryonics, enjoyed the happiest ending. He was well respected in the cryonics community throughout his life. Stanley Kubrick, in the wake of the release of *2001: A Space Odyssey*, spoke admiringly of Ettinger and his work, saying, "I believe that freezing of the dead will be a major industry in the United States and throughout the world; I would recommend it as a field of investment for imaginative speculators."[47]

Ettinger died in 2012. He was also cryopreserved at the organization he formed in 1976.

After the Chatsworth disaster, cryonics needed new faces to advance the practice and restore its reputation. Happily, there was already a new generation of eccentrics ready to take up the challenge.

3

THE CURIOUS CASE OF THE
MISSING FROZEN HEAD

Mike Darwin was something of a prodigy in the cryonics industry. He witnessed its most crucial formative events over a decades-long career, and even crossed paths with Bob Nelson before the pioneer was outed as a fraud. Darwin brought a new approach to freezing dead people—a scientific process that encouraged caution and gradual discovery—but eventually found himself in jail and accused of murder, with the whole concept of cryonics on trial.

Darwin was born in Indiana in 1955 and given the name Mike Federowicz (he adopted the name Darwin for his work in cryonics). He described his childhood as happy and stable with a loving family, but his early life was punctured by a traumatic confrontation with death. When he was around seven years old, Darwin visited his maternal cousin Rae Rohrman, who lived a few doors down the street from his home. What he found inside shaped his entire life. Rohrman had died suddenly from complications of diabetes, and young Darwin walked in and found her about a week after she'd passed away in an advanced state of decomposition. This sudden and dramatic introduction to death, without the softening context of a hospital or mortuary setting, impacted the young boy profoundly. He soon set out on a life mission to "halt decomposition" and "prevent death."[1]

Darwin's ambitions were bolstered when he found a box of Ace D series science fiction novels in the attic of an abandoned house in 1965. The books had a profound effect on him, none more so than *The Mechanical Monarch*, by E.C. Tubb, in which a marooned astronaut floats around space for two hundred years, frozen, before being restored in a medical facility on Mars.[2]

He began experimenting with ways to interrupt and restart life through cooling and freezing, and by 1967, when he was around twelve years old, he began trying to freeze plants and animals. The next year he won first place at a local science fair with a project titled "Suspended Animation in Plants and Animals" and advanced to the regional finals. Darwin was one of the youngest competitors, and a registration error meant he was unable to win a prize, but the competition still had a massive impact on his life. One of the judges asked if he'd seen the news from California—a man who had died from cancer had been frozen, to be reanimated at a later date. The judge was referring to Nelson's freezing of James Bedford.[3] At first he was incredulous: from his studies he knew it was impossible to freeze even a mouse or a human organ, let alone a whole person. The next day the judge brought a clipping from a newspaper to the science fair, detailing the attempt at preservation.

Darwin read everything he could get his hands on about Nelson's feat and developed an obsession with the cryonics industry. He contacted every cryonics organization he found and joined the nearest one, the Cryonics Society of New York (CSNY), which was run by Curtis Henderson and Saul Kent. He became an associate member when he was thirteen and signed up to be cryopreserved two years later. As a teenager he mowed lawns and cleared yards so he could buy cryonics equipment, and kept in constant contact with the biggest names in the nascent field, bothering the likes of Kent, Henderson, and Nelson with letters.

When he was fifteen, Darwin spent a summer at CSNY getting hands-on experience with dead people, the freezing process, and the challenges of the practice. The management team of CSNY showed him everything he wanted to see and were completely open when they didn't know the answer to his endless questions.[4] Their honesty was a revelation to Darwin, but it soon dawned on him that the entire operation was far from professional. He was disappointed to find unrefined methods, poor practices, and an organization constantly on the brink of financial ruin.

Let down by his own cryonics society, Darwin looked west for inspiration. He was in contact with Greg Fahy, a California-based cryonics enthusiast and Nelson's protégé, and two other members of the California Cryonics Society, Linda and Fred Chamberlain. Nelson had largely ignored Darwin's letters, but by badgering the cryonics superstar through intermediaries, the youngster finally managed to persuade him to meet. In 1972, seventeen-year-old Darwin took the train from Chicago to Los Angeles, keen to hear more about the CSC and its mercurial leader.

At the time of his trip, Darwin already harbored deep suspicions about Nelson's conduct. He called around the short list of liquid nitrogen providers in Los Angeles and asked about the president of the CSC. One told him Nelson owed him money. Darwin also tracked down the welder who helped fit three people into a single cryonics cylinder, who described the ordeal as the worst experience of his life. Finally, Darwin and Fahy met Nelson at a coffee shop in L.A.[5]

These days, Mike Darwin is a tough man to track down. He has since dropped out of the cryonics scene, and I was only able to find him via a Reddit post in which he tore strips out of the major cryonics providers of today. He was initially hesitant to talk to me, but after some persuading, I spoke to him for several hours. He was an intense and accurate speaker, pausing regularly to check names and dates, and incredibly honest and forthright. And when he met Nelson back in the '70s, he was just as straightforward with his approach. He immediately grilled him about the various processes used in the CSC's underground facility.

Darwin recalled, "He developed this really bad facial tick, and his hand would shake holding the coffee cup, and he said, 'Oh, we have experts of our own with PhDs and stuff, but I can't let you meet them because they're afraid of their professional reputation.'" Nelson refused to allow either Darwin or Fahy to see the facility that housed the supposedly frozen bodies, despite the fact that Fahy was his golden boy. This secretive attitude was a far cry from CSNY, which laid bare its weaknesses for all to see, and all but confirmed Darwin's suspicions.

When the full truth of Nelson's operation came out, Darwin was unsurprised. He later became baffled and irritated by the cryonics community's reaction to the man who performed the first ever cryopreservation. The general feeling decades later is that Nelson tried his best with limited resources and suffered on behalf of his patients, who he ultimately couldn't help but fail. It's a view that Nelson himself attempted to cultivate unsubtly in the last book he wrote before his death. But Darwin has nothing but scorn for his actions. He told me Nelson was a sociopath and claimed he was involved with the Boston mafia and had no remorse for those he hurt.

He later sent me a letter Nelson wrote to his assistant Marcelon Johnson telling her that everything was fine with the facility, despite the fact he knew beyond doubt at the time that the bodies had decomposed. Johnson was made acting president of the CSC before the lawsuits arrived, leaving her to face an avalanche of criticism and controversy. "This woman basically lost [everything], they had to mortgage their home again, they had it all paid off, they had to take a mortgage for the full value of her home. She didn't pay that off until shortly before she died. That's the kind of harm Nelson did, and he did it casually," Darwin said.

In a 1991 issue of an industry magazine, *Cryonics*, Darwin wrote an open letter to the body of James Bedford in which he criticized Nelson. "It may shock you, but it is something of an understatement to describe Nelson as a pathological liar and an outright fraud. It is a testimony to the good judgment and determination of your wife and son that you were removed from his clutches only six days after your suspension and shipped to Cryo-Care Equipment Corporation in Phoenix, Arizona," the letter read.[6]

Nelson faded into obscurity following the lawsuits, but Darwin's star was on the rise. He had met with the Chamberlains in Los Angeles and was impressed with their vision for the future of cryonics. When Fred Chamberlain's father died in 1976, the couple asked Darwin to build the necessary equipment for the cryopreservation—the first of their new organization, Alcor Life Extension Foundation.[7] Darwin didn't join Alcor initially, and instead set up his own cryonics team in Indianapolis, called the Institute for Advanced Biological Studies (IABS). The organization amassed an impressive array of equipment and a strong reputation among the cryonics community. In 1979, another cryonics provider, TransTime, asked Darwin and IABS to secure a dying patient and transfer the body to be cryopreserved. Darwin accepted the request on the condition he was allowed to conduct the hand-off himself and was able to meet the expert who was responsible for the preservation. That person was Jerry Leaf, a researcher at UCLA. While the pair were working on the original body, another TransTime member died nearby in California. Leaf and Darwin did two "back-to-backs"—seventy-two hours of nonstop action freezing dead people. Exhilarated by his work with Leaf, Darwin moved IABS to California to work more closely with the man he felt had expertise to advance the art of cryonics substantially.[8]

In California, Darwin pursued a worrisome matter for the cryonics crowd. After Nelson's disastrous caretakership, it became clear that every body frozen before 1973 had been thawed with the possible exception of one, James Bedford. There was a major problem, however—Bedford's body was missing. Here was the last great hope for the first generation of frozen patients, and yet the community had lost track of Bedford's movements, an impressive feat considering he was dead. It turned out the former Pasadena psychology professor had been taken on an odyssey through the cryonics world, stopping off at several organizations, each of which either shut down or turfed the body out when an insurance company complained about storing humans on their premises. Darwin had a suspicion that at some point Bedford's family had taken over guardianship of his corpse. He tracked down Bedford's son and found he was caring for his father's body at great expense and difficulty. Darwin made his pitch and, with the help of Leaf, transported the first man ever cryopreserved to Alcor, the organization founded by the Chamberlains.

At that time, Alcor was in a sorry state. The company held only four patients in suspension and the founders had moved to Lake Tahoe, entrusting a president who Darwin described as "incompetent . . . in literally every way" to run operations. In 1982, Alcor reached a nadir, and Darwin was approached to help. An IABS conference for cryonics enthusiasts collapsed into farce when Alcor members, demanding to know what the then president had done with funds collected for an investment club, approached Darwin in the restroom and begged him to become their next president. Despite having misgivings initially, he relented and accepted the position, and IABS merged with Alcor.[9] Soon after, Leaf joined Alcor as well, forming, on paper at least, something of a dream team at a company that was soon to become the largest and most established cryonics provider in the world. And the duo did lead cryonics into a golden age. Yet disaster was just around the corner.

In the early years of Darwin's tenure as president of Alcor, the industry moved forward quickly. New processes were put in place to ensure the freezing process was as efficient as possible, and a different type of cryopreservation was introduced. The likes of Bedford had their entire bodies preserved, and most of the problems associated with their upkeep came from the need to keep a human-sized cylinder cold. Hypothetically, Bedford would wake up in a world where his cancer could be cured, but his body would still be old. For many, it made sense to downsize the whole operation, to leave the broken body behind and just take what matters into the future—the head. Neurosuspension had been around since the late 1970s but was growing in popularity. It was cheaper—you can fit more heads in a cryonics capsule than full bodies—and there was the hope of being attached to a mechanical body in the far-flung future when you were reanimated. It was one of these procedures that nearly brought Alcor's operations to an abrupt end.

In 1986, the landlords of Alcor's headquarters in Fullerton, California, told their tenants they had a year to leave the premises. The organization raised enough cash from its members and supporters and identified a new headquarters to buy outright. Darwin, in his role as president, did the due diligence on the area of Riverside, California. He visited the local coroner's office to broach the subject of having a cryonics facility in the county. The coroner was a crucial official to get on their side, as they would be handling dead bodies regularly. Darwin met the chief deputy coroner Carl Smith, who was receptive to the idea and thought having a quirky company like a cryonics provider would be a unique point of interest for the area.[10]

Darwin was satisfied; Alcor completed the deal and moved into its new property. But the president then failed to follow what was going on in the coroner's office. Smith was exposed as a convicted felon and was unable to take up the position of coroner for Riverside county, despite receiving strong support in the 1986 election. His nearest competitor got the job—a man named Ray Carrillo, a highly controversial figure who would do his best to take down Alcor.

On the morning of Wednesday, December 9, 1987, Saul Kent, the former president of CSNY and Darwin's mentor, received a call from the nursing home where his mother, eighty-three-year-old Dora Kent, was being cared for. Her doctors told him she was critically ill and likely to die soon. Osteoporosis and senility had consigned Kent to a bed for four years, and her son decided there was no reason to prolong her life by attempting to treat the pneumonia which had brought her so close to death. [11]

He ordered an ambulance to pick her up and take her to the Riverside facility of Alcor, where she was a paid-up member and would undergo neuropreservation. By bringing her into the building prior to her death, the Alcor team hoped the outcome of the preservation could be improved by carrying out the procedure just seconds after she died, rather than waiting for her to pass away elsewhere.[12]

Throughout the calamitous events of the weeks that followed, Mike Perry, a long-term caretaker of patients and the unofficial Alcor historian, kept notes in his diary. When Kent entered the facility on December 9, her condition initially appeared stable, although she was very weak, according to Perry. Darwin put the suspension team on high alert. The next day, her condition worsened. "There is a strong feeling that she will go down, as we hope, and she is no longer being fed through tubes as she was at the nursing home," Perry wrote. At 10 p.m. that night, the Alcor team wheeled Kent into the operating room, where they shaved her head and removed her oxygen supply. Kent's breathing stopped completely around 11:30 p.m., but her heart was still beating. Darwin then jumped in and performed mouth-to-mouth resuscitation, and her breathing returned, although it was shallow.[13] (It was later speculated that he did this because the team was not completely ready for the preservation to begin. Darwin said no such procedure was carried out until she was medically and legally dead.) Under an hour later, Kent stopped breathing again, but this time her heart slowed and then stopped. Darwin and Leaf confirmed the heart had stopped and prepared for the preservation. But in the adrenaline-filled moment, the team had overlooked the importance of one factor—there was no physician present to declare Kent dead. Darwin later told me the law did not require the physician to be present at the time of a patient passing but did have to confirm the death within twenty-four hours. He called the doctor at 8 p.m. that evening to inform him Kent was expected to die soon, but the doctor angrily replied he would not be driving two hours to the facility that evening.[14]

Despite having no physician, the suspension team jumped into action. They cut Kent's chest open and massaged her heart to maintain oxygenation of the tissues, then went ahead with the vitrification process they hoped would preserve Kent for future reanimation. Due to the short time between death and suspension, the team achieved their best results to date. Perry carried out smaller chores like refilling an ice chest while the senior members worked. Eventually he clocked off and got some sleep.[15]

At 7 a.m. on December 11, while Perry was asleep, Darwin and his team decapitated Kent.

After the marathon procedure, the Alcor suspension team rested. All seemed well. Perry hurt his middle finger ensuring enough dry ice was packed into the container holding Kent's head and then joined three fellow Alcor employees for dinner that evening at a Pizza Hut. When he told his colleagues he had written about Kent in his diary, they jokingly suggested it should be shredded.[16]

On December 14, the first signs of trouble hit Alcor.

The mortician contracted by Saul Kent to dispose of his mother's body attempted to file a death certificate with the Public Health Service to obtain a cremation permit.[17] However, the eagle eyes of a registrar spotted that the place of death was in an industrial zone, not a residential or commercial zip code, which was most common. She flagged this up to the attention of the Riverside County Coroner, who then contacted the physician who had belatedly signed the death certificate.[18] The coroner's office brought up the matter of the physician's attendance at the time of death and decided an autopsy was necessary.

Still, Darwin remained unworried. He knew an autopsy was not ideal in a cryonics case, as the body would be destroyed and all prospects of reanimation removed. But they'd already preserved Kent's head, and the coroner's office was welcome to the body.

The next day, Saul Kent visited the facility and asked Perry why the physician was not present when his mother died. Perry, unaware of the conversation Darwin had with the doctor, believed it was his own fault, as he hadn't called himself.[19] On December 16, employees from the coroner's office removed Kent's body and reportedly told Alcor they "might" do an autopsy, although it was "by no means a certainty."[20] Five days after Kent's body was taken away, the coroner's office called Alcor and told them an autopsy confirmed the cause of death was pneumonia.[21] Darwin and Leaf went to pick up a copy of the death certificate and met with the two coroner's deputies handling the case, Rick Bogan and Alan Kunzman. Darwin also encountered the man running the office.

Ray Carrillo was already smelling publicity. "I got chills down my spine when I went to pick up the death certificate, because on his desk he had a little grand piano with a candelabra on it," Darwin said. The candelabra was a sick memorial to Carrillo's previous brush with fame, earlier that year. When Liberace, the famous pianist, singer, and actor, died in 1987 from pneumonia as a result of AIDS, his personal doctor attributed the death to anemia (brought on by a diet of watermelon), emphysema, and heart disease. Liberace had been diagnosed as HIV positive eighteen months before but kept the news completely secret. Carrillo wasn't happy with the cause of death on the certificate, but instead of asking the doctor to change it, he dug up Liberace's body and had an autopsy carried out before announcing to the world he had died from an AIDS-related illness.

"He did it because he wanted the press. When I saw that I thought, 'I'm dealing with a sociopath here, I'm dealing with a guy who will do anything to further his political career.' Nothing could be more attractive [to him] than a big scandal over cutting a little old lady's head off while she was still alive, so I had a very bad feeling," Darwin told me.

The two deputies were initially more helpful. They handed over the copy of the death certificate and explained that the matter was closed.[22] Darwin, who had told colleagues he thought the incident could be the end of Alcor, began to see things more positively before another issue cropped up. After Kent's cryopreservation, her hands had been cut off as part of a perfusion study. Perry fretted in his diary that the hands were not given over to be the coroner's office with the rest of her body, prompting frantic phone calls to the mortician. Perry wrote possibly one of the greatest diary entries of all time. "We don't know what we'll do with the hands. I saw Mike sitting morosely on a stool, head in (his own) hands, all cheer evaporated, situation normal again."[23]

Darwin later refuted that claim, saying the hands and the body were always together. "I don't have any moral or ethical concerns, but public relations–wise, it was very difficult to explain to the general public," he said.

The next day, Christmas Eve, the coroner's office went on the attack. That evening a local news station aired some particularly grisly stories. A chainsaw murderer was convicted, a baker fell into a vat of batter and nearly died, and a cryonics group reportedly chopped an old lady's head off while she was still alive. A crew from the local TV station had attended a press conference earlier that day in which Bogan and Kunzman suggested there was a possibility Kent was not brain-dead when she was decapitated and announced the coroner's office would investigate Alcor.[24]

The news spread fast. Soon after, Darwin sat in his office listening to NPR, worrying about the future of the company. To his dismay, Alcor's story was about to be featured on *As It Happens*, a popular Canadian show focusing on news from around the world that was picked up by many NPR stations. Bogan was the guest and told listeners that if there was even a spark of life in Kent when she was decapitated, they would prosecute Alcor to the full extent of the law. Darwin knew what was coming next. His father had been a cop for thirty years, and he fully expected the police to be knocking on the door within days.

Alcor faced a monumental choice. If the police arrived with a search warrant, they would most likely demand the only part of Kent they didn't already have: her severed and cryopreserved head. If the coroner's office performed an autopsy on the head, she would be lost forever. Darwin gathered the executive team and board members and told them they had to decide—either they hand over the head willingly or move it from the premises.

"Everybody agreed that we were not going to surrender this patient, we had not done anything wrong, we certainly hadn't killed her. What would be next? Would they accuse us of doing this to other patients, would other patients be brought out of storage?" Darwin recalled.

The group initially considered moving all the frozen corpses of Alcor's customers but didn't have the manpower to get it done. The facility stored full bodies like Bedford's as well as just heads, and they lacked the space or logistical ability to move them all to new locations. They decided to move just Kent's head.

Even years later, Darwin refused to tell me where the head was hidden but did say people from outside the world of cryonics—who didn't even believe in the practice—were a great help. While all this was happening, Perry carried out a bizarre list of chores, presumably handed to him by management so he wasn't incriminated by helping to move the head. He mailed out copies of the company's magazine and spent a large part of one day licking and sticking stamps. On his way out of the building, he was given strict instructions to knock on the door and say he was selling Girl Scout Cookies when he returned.

Between Christmas and New Year, very little happened. Some of the Alcor team began to build hope that nothing more would come of the matter despite the continuing media frenzy. But the peace came to an emphatic end on January 7, when deputy coroners and police arrived at the Alcor facility with a search warrant.[25] They were there for the head. While the cops searched the building, Darwin called Leaf and told him the facility was being raided. Leaf urged Darwin to stay calm and said he'd be there as soon as he could. He never showed.[26]

During the search, police were happy to converse with the Alcor team, left them unrestrained, and even allowed them to go to lunch. When Darwin, Perry, and their colleagues returned, the atmosphere had soured. Angry they couldn't find the head, the cops placed the whole team in handcuffs and carted them off to the station to be interrogated. The police, Darwin told me, were "very unhappy. Very, very, very unhappy" when they realized the head was no longer at the facility.

Officers booked in the six Alcor employees, one by one. While Perry had his fingerprints taken, an official asked him if he believed he'd have new fingerprints when he was reanimated in the future. He replied that he imagined he would, much to the amusement of the police. Perry was questioned "rather sternly" by the two deputies, particularly about the location of the head.[27] But Darwin received the harshest treatment. His interrogators threatened him with the downfall of Alcor and warned him he would be dragging the reputation of Leaf "through the mud" if he didn't comply.

"If you just give us the head of Dora Kent," he was told, "you'll still have a salvageable business here."[28]

After several hours, the police released all six employees. They returned to the Alcor facility to survey the damage, fearing the worst for the other patients stored there. To their immense relief, they found the various bodies and heads untouched and still frozen. With Kent's head stored safely in a secret location, they felt things could have been a lot worse. But the day's events took a heavy toll on Darwin.

"After we were released from being arrested, I was psychologically incapacitated," he said. "I was a total basket case. I couldn't eat, I couldn't sleep, I was paralyzed with terror and fear. I thought the odds of us surviving this were low. Not zero, but very low. And I couldn't lead. You can't lead when you're literally sobbing half the time and are curled up into a ball, immobilized with anxiety—you can't function."

Alcor made the decision to replace Darwin as president; this was a great relief to him. Leaf appeared to be the most logical replacement, but he was still on the run after refusing to present himself to police on the day of the raid. Perhaps Leaf's colleagues questioned his commitment or solidarity when he failed to show at the facility that day, but in reality, his actions, after receiving the call from Darwin, gave Alcor a fighting chance against the coroner's office. The organization had $30,000 raised from patients in gold Krugerrands, which they stored securely away from the Riverside facility. After he heard about the raid, Leaf immediately retrieved the Krugerrands and consulted Linda Abrams, an Alcor member and a lawyer. She recommended her friend Chris Ashworth, a noted constitutional lawyer who Darwin said had previously handled high-profile cases for the Church of Scientology. Leaf drove to Ashworth's office in Century City Towers and retained him with the $30,000 worth of Krugerrands.[29]

On January 12, Carrillo sent police back to the Alcor facility, only this time they took a SWAT team with them.[30] The Alcor employees watched on in horror as tens of thousands of dollars' worth of equipment was hauled out of the premises in the hunt for more incriminating evidence. Officials took computers, medical equipment, chemicals, prescription drugs, floppy discs, videos, and even personal effects, including Perry's diary, which revealed sensitive information about some of the employees.

Carrillo's timing of the raid was no coincidence; the next day Ashworth had secured a hearing in court requesting a temporary restraining order against the coroner's office. Ashworth was joined on the case by Saul Kent's lawyers, Garfield, Tepper, Ashworth, and Epstein, but despite the robustness of the legal team, few on the inside or outside of the case gave them much chance. The lawyers put forward their argument on behalf of Alcor—that the cause of death had already been ascertained, so there was no need for the coroner's office to have the head, and everything was conducted above board.

They filed for a restraining order against Carrillo, and Superior Court Judge Victor Miceli granted it, turning the tide of Alcor's battle. "You could have knocked me over with a feather when it was granted," said Darwin. "I'm not an optimistic guy in general, and I was very stunned and pleased. That was the turning point, clearly."

The order stated the coroner's office was not allowed to autopsy any Alcor members, including Kent, and lasted until February 1, at which point another hearing was scheduled.[31] Carrillo, meanwhile, called a press conference to get his side of the story across. Before the event, Carrillo's office started feeding the media false information, according to Alcor, including that a cache of weapons, explosives, and satanic reading material had been found at the facility. During the conference, Carrillo couldn't help making several inflammatory statements. When asked what the cause of death could be, he replied: "The toxicology will possibly prove that agents were used for the acceleration of her death. This would possibly later come out. But this is purely conjecture at this point."

Of the restraining order, he told reporters that Alcor wanted to stop the investigation. "They claimed we were going to take all the heads and melt them. I was very upset when I read the papers this morning. We were going to chop up the head . . . we don't chop up heads, we do autopsies. This shows the deviousness. It shows they're working on the people's minds to show that we're doing something illegal, which we are definitely not."[32]

On February 1, Alcor and the coroner's office returned to court. Supreme Court Judge Miceli again ruled over the case, which would decide if the temporary restraining order could be made permanent. Ashworth immediately went on the offensive: "Dora Kent didn't go through all this crap to have her brain end up in a blender," he argued, claiming it was Kent's constitutional right to have her remains treated in whatever manner she thought fit, providing it did not go against any health regulations.[33] Ashworth and the rest of the legal team also presented statements from medical experts who said cryonic suspension might work in the future, and by going ahead with an autopsy on Kent's head, they would be removing this possibility.

"It is her life in the balance against almost a technical curiosity of whether a homicide had been committed," Ashworth argued.

Joyce Manulis Reikes, the deputy county counsel representing the interests of the coroner's court, claimed that ruling in favor of Alcor would inhibit the coroner from conducting future investigations and would set a dangerous precedent. After all the arguments were put forth, Miceli again ruled in favor of Alcor. The judge concluded that under state law Kent had the right to determine how her remains were disposed of, and that the potential damages to Kent outweighed the arguments of the coroner's office, which had failed to show how an autopsy on the head would have yielded any information on the cause of death. Outside the court, Alcor and the wider cryonics community rejoiced.

"This is the first time that most people have taken cryonics seriously, although it may have taken my mother's death to call attention to it," Saul Kent told reporters.[34]

Alcor had won a huge battle, but the war rumbled on. Carrillo refused to drop the matter and masterminded three legal challenges against the cryonicists. His office issued a revised death certificate that proclaimed Kent's death a homicide, alleging barbiturates were used to help her die prior to her suspension. They argued the drugs must have been administered prior to death because the body had metabolized them, something not possible after death. Alcor refuted the claim completely. The homicide case lingered for years but never got anywhere because of a lack of evidence. Ultimately, no charges were even filed.[35]

The California Medical Board raised the next legal issue with Alcor, claiming personnel who carried out the Kent suspension were guilty of "felony practice of medicine without a license." Both sides argued over whether Kent was dead or alive when they began practicing any kind of medicine on her, something the authorities believed would be resolved with a murder investigation. This case also dragged on, causing genuine friction between Alcor and the medical board, to the point where an Alcor employee ejected an official from the state out of the facility at gunpoint. (The staff member was fired, but the case was bogged down by the murder claim and never went anywhere.)[36]

The final legal battle from the Kent case was, perhaps, the most desperate of all attempts by authorities to take down Alcor. The state accused the organization of grand theft of medical supplies from UCLA after many items stamped with the university's name were discovered when the initial searches took place. All the items turned out to be purchased from the surplus sales department of UCLA; Alcor was even able to provide receipts for most of the equipment.[37]

The Kent case, besides being another episode of fiendishly dark comedy in the history of cryonics, gave the industry hope that legal battles could be faced down and won. Media perception changed over the course of the saga. Initially, the press characterized Alcor as bloodthirsty cult killers chopping up old ladies and putting them on ice, but over time that view softened, and they were presented as the plucky underdogs. According to Perry, much of that shift occurred when the world got to know the band of misfits and eccentrics running the organization. Overall, Alcor saw the incident as a major victory. Membership reportedly increased as a result of the publicity, providing a welcome boost to the entire cryonics business after earlier catastrophes like the Chatsworth disaster. Alcor also won a financial windfall, as it sued the county for false arrest and illegal seizure of property and won both suits.

Darwin told me he believes the case was only won because the prosecution was vastly overconfident. "They felt they were dealing with crazy people. They felt there would be no support from the community or from the judiciary, and they had good reasons for feeling those things, I probably would have made the same mistake if I was a bureaucrat. You had this kooky bunch of people, easily less than one hundred of them in the world, and they're up against the might of the state, and the state says these people are not scientists, they're not doctors, nobody in the scientific medical community will back them or step forward. No expert is going to step up and say, 'Hey, I think this has a chance of working if we keep proceeding in a rational and responsible way toward finding out if it can work.' There was none of that. I think they felt it was going to be a slam dunk."

Over the next decade, Alcor became the biggest name in cryonics. By 1990, the organization had grown to three hundred members and was fast outgrowing its Riverside headquarters. In 1993, partially due to worries about California's vulnerability to earthquakes, Alcor bought a building in Scottsdale, Arizona, and moved its frozen patients there the following year.

Still, more controversies followed, including the most famous example—the Ted Williams fiasco. Williams, a well-known and popular baseball legend, died in 2002 and was placed in cryonic suspension. A brutal legal battle then erupted between his living relatives. His son John Henry and daughter Claudia both claimed Williams had expressed a desire to be preserved at Alcor, but their half-sister insisted he had wanted to be cremated. The next year Larry Johnson, the former COO of Alcor, told *Sports Illustrated* the company had botched the preservation of Williams, drilling holes in his head and accidentally cracking it.[38] Johnson also said some of William's DNA went missing, apparently because his son John Henry wanted to sell it. John Henry's attorney denied the claim, while Alcor also denied that any DNA was not accounted for.[39] The story once again catapulted Alcor and cryonics into national attention. Here was a beloved sports personality: the thought of his head being drilled and mishandled enraged many and further damaged the reputation of the industry.

Lawsuits and controversy played a huge role in the formative years of cryonics. Aside from the most famous examples, many other unhappy parties have sued cryonics organizations, usually over a loved one's decision to be cryonically preserved. Perhaps surprisingly, the cryonics companies have largely avoided any major losses. It helps that they don't promise all that much. Those being preserved are never told they will definitely be reanimated, only that they will be kept on ice until a means of reanimation is discovered. The only promise really made is the storage, which is what got Nelson in so much trouble all those years ago.

Few modern-day cryonics practitioners brought up the industry's worrisome past when I spoke to them. To its credit, Alcor retains detailed accounts of some of the most controversial incidents on its website, meticulously documented by Perry. But unsurprisingly they aren't shouting about their fraudulent forefathers and brushes with the law at immortalist events. The cryonics industry of today continues from its wildly eccentric beginnings but presents a more polished front to the world. I wanted to find out if this was merely a façade, or if cryonics really matured into a genuine scientific endeavor. For that, I needed to talk to the man in the middle of everything, who was on stage the day I visited the Church of Perpetual Life—Rudi Hoffman.

4

HOW TO PAY FOR A SECOND LIFE

Hoffman, white-haired, wide-grinned, and sporting a terrifically loud bright lime blazer, hosted the First Annual Cryonics Symposium in Florida. He organized the event to bring together the great and the good of the industry, and to make money selling life insurance to the gathered immortalists.

On that stiflingly hot weekend in Florida, Hoffman pushed cryonics hard. He greeted almost every attendee like a friend and pointed those he was meeting for the first time to his large brass nameplate. His mannerisms reminded me of a suburban car salesman, while the toothy smile screamed daytime gameshow host. In many ways, Hoffman is a very typical cryonicist. He rejected religion in favor of humanism, a past event forced him to confront his own mortality, and he is fiercely loyal to the community. Hoffman used to describe himself as a libertarian, but during the COVID-19 pandemic, the anti-mask and anti-vaccination views of those with libertarian leanings shocked him, and he now says he's a "recovering libertarian."[1]

His symposium was packed with speakers from the world of cryonics, including some familiar names from its history. Mike Perry gave a talk on the origins of the art, and Linda Chamberlain, one of the founders of Alcor, talked about the company. Some of the

topics were clearly widely speculative, and others were straight advertisements for cryopreservation companies. In between these talks,
Hoffman gave plugs for his business and his book, and, when it came
to his own twenty-minute slot, explained in detail how anyone can
afford cryonics.

Ettinger and Cooper, the two forefathers of the industry, disagreed on how cryonics should be made available to the masses.
Cooper believed it fell to the United Nations to ensure preservation
after death was a human right for everyone on the planet,[2] while
Ettinger believed corporations and capitalism held the key. Ettinger
correctly predicted in his book that life insurance would make cryopreservation affordable for everyone,[3] something Hoffman has now
made reality.

Over the course of the weekend, Hoffman was clearly very busy.
When he wasn't presenting on stage he buzzed around making sure
the event ran smoothly, while attempting to meet as many people as
possible. It was clear this was a man right at the center of the cryonics
industry. He held the financial keys to immortality and was happy
to hand them over in exchange for a commission. When I grabbed
rushed moments with Hoffman, he was in full salesman mode and
spoke in soundbites rather than offering the in-depth answers I had
hoped for. But even in these brief chats I saw why he's considered the
top cryonics life insurance seller in the world.

Life insurance salespeople shock and spook potential clients every
day. They remind them of the fragility of life, try to force them to
confront that reality, and then insist on preparing for the inevitable.
In that sense the job is quite morose. But Hoffman offers his clients something else aside from fear and alarm: hope. He still reminds
clients that one day their hearts will stop beating and they will be
declared dead, but the plan he's selling isn't quite so bleak. A policy
from Hoffman works in much the same way as a regular life insurance
policy, but the cash payout when you die goes to a cryopreservation
company instead of family, friends, or your favorite charity. It pays

a company like Alcor for the preservation itself and the immortal upkeep. Although the money goes to a company, the policyholders themselves will theoretically enjoy the rewards, unlike most life insurance deals.[4] With modest monthly payments (at least initially), immortalists can book their ticket to the future. Hoffman enjoys close to a monopoly in this weird niche of the insurance market.

Hoffman signed up to cryonics himself many years ago and proudly displays his Alcor wristband to anyone who asks. He also practices various life extension techniques, although not to the same alarming extremes some immortalists implement. When the Cryonics Symposium reached an end and the Church of Perpetual Life was restored to its regular Christian appearance, I reached out to Hoffman to talk over a video call, away from the chaotic buzz of hosting an industry event. To my surprise, he was a completely different person to the one schmoozing the crowd of immortalists. He was thoughtful, introspective, and thoroughly likeable.

Hoffman was raised in a Christian home in Indiana. His grandfather was president of the local church-focused Anderson College, and he described his family as "pretty open-minded Christians." He developed doubts over Christianity early on yet still attended Anderson himself before later moving to Florida to teach fifth grade at a private Christian school. Inwardly, he didn't see himself as a Christian in a theological sense but did see the benefit of the community aspect of people gathering regularly with the goal of spiritual enrichment.

"While I was never really a Christian cultist, I did get plugged into that whole church thing when I was teaching at the Christian Academy and singing in the choir," Hoffman recalled on our Zoom call. "But I would find myself singing in the choir and then I'd listen to this sermon, and I kept wanting to literally jump up in the middle of the service and yell, 'Come on folks, can we not see this as really, truly, bullshit?' Even though I never actually jumped up and said that, I realized my participating in that infrastructure was inherently kind of hypocritical."

Hoffman didn't leave religion altogether, however. He moved to the more open-minded Unity Church, where he met his wife Dawn, to whom he is still happily married. But his drift away from religion was already well underway. He took up a career in insurance, and in 1994, when he was thirty-seven years old, he read an article in *Omni* magazine about cryonics, a concept he believed to be science fiction. When he learned there had been several organizations quietly cryopreserving people for decades, he quickly became seriously interested. The magazine suggested the expensive procedures could be made affordable through life insurance, and Hoffman realized he could simply sell himself an extra policy and potentially live forever.

Wary of jumping in, he took five or six months to seek out more information on the process, then made the commitment. After becoming a fully fledged member of the cryonics community, companies like Alcor directed potential customers to him because they knew he was both an independent insurance broker and ideologically on board with cryonics. Cryonics members became 90 percent of his business over time, and he estimates around 67 percent of people who have signed up to be preserved by cryonics have gone through him.

Hoffman's customers first fill out a form on his website which asks for the personal details needed to begin the process. Hoffman then arranges a call, during which he presents three life insurance quotes from cryonics-friendly carriers. His organization fills out the application to the life insurance carrier for the customer. After it's signed, the customer gets a call from a local nurse within a week or two who carries out a physical examination. Once their health status has been established, the insurance carrier sends a solid offer. Hoffman reminds interested parties that it pays to take out the policy earlier, as they can be rejected on health grounds just as easily as financial.[5]

His battle to the top of the cryonics insurance provider league table has been far from easy. Initially the insurance carriers reacted with scorn, and some still refuse his business today. "I really expected the life insurance companies would embrace this market that I was bringing to the table because these are self-selected, highly educated people who basically are taking every possible step they could to not die," said Hoffman. "Instead, I found this absolute brick wall of lack of understanding and bias and prejudice that was in many cases, I believe, a religious bias or prejudice. Turns out you become an insurance executive not by huge amounts of outside the box thinking."

Hoffman regularly encountered two major objections from insurance companies. Firstly, they worried about the "insurable interest question," where they want to establish if the beneficiary of the insurance claim has a vested interest in a person staying alive. In the case of cryonics, it could be argued the company doing the cryopreserving would prefer them to die so they could cash their policy and begin storing them. Hoffman argues the insurable interest is the policyholder's clear desire to live as long as possible, given their immortalist leanings. It's unclear how the insurance industry would react if the cryonics providers worked out how to revive someone. Would they still accept the same policies, or would they no longer consider cryonics practitioners technically dead? It's not hard to imagine an insurance company taking the moral low-road to avoid paying out.

The second objection was reputational risk. Insurance providers saw cryonics as a lawsuit waiting to happen and wanted to avoid getting dragged into the negative stories which peppered the industry's early years. Hoffman was unperturbed and slowly built a rapport with a selection of life insurance carriers who were happy to take his lucrative—if unorthodox—business. Kansas City Life became his preferred carrier. He described the company as "tremendously committed and supportive of what I do," and the company even featured him in its corporate magazine in an interview explaining the cryonics niche he'd made his own. "They can't endorse cryonics, but at least they understand this is something that is not going to cause them reputation risk problems, and that I actually bring a really good demographic to the table," Hoffman said.

He's one of the company's most successful salespeople. During our call, he proudly displayed an award he received for the last quarter of 2020, when he topped the leaderboard for sales in the whole United States, beating competition from 2,800 other brokers. But Kansas City Life is only licensed in certain states, so Hoffman must find a different insurance carrier for people in places like New York. This brings back all the problems he faced when he first started out, and a host of questions about insurable interest and reputational risk.

Again, Hoffman told me a lot of these negative attitudes toward cryonics can be traced back to religion. "There seems to be a disproportionate amount of resistance to the idea of cryonics. And I think it is because we are stepping on some toes," Hoffman said. He sees a "religious undercurrent" in society that undermines the concept, as it goes against some of the building blocks on which a lot of faith is built. "Cryonics is the archetypal, leading bleeding edge of modernity, where we're basically saying the biggie, the big condition, the human condition, is the fact that we age and die, and we want to fix that. And it may be possible for science to fix that. You don't fix that through belief in superstitions and religions and everything your mama and your pastor told you, they lied to you because they didn't know any better."

Hoffman describes himself as a humanist and says he is anti-religion. Instead of having faith in a deity, he puts all his hopes into cryonics and science to eliminate death.

In 2016, that faith was put to the ultimate test. He woke up one morning and felt a lump on his thigh. Doctors told him he had stage two lymphoma, and that the cancer had spread throughout his body through the lymph system. The cancer hit his spleen the worst. When he saw his scan, there were two glowing red balls visible that even he as a layperson could tell were bad news. "All of a sudden your life changes in a day," Hoffman recalled. "It was really weird, really pretty surreal. And I of course handled the news with great spiritual discipline, saying 'fuck, fuck, fuck, fuck, fuck.'"

Doctors gave him six rounds of strong chemotherapy, and five years later Hoffman was declared cured.

"Going through the Valley of Death, where you almost die, should make you wiser and smarter and more tolerant of things and all that stuff. And it turns out it doesn't, which is kind of a rip-off," he said. "But the fact that I was signed up for cryonics really did give me a much greater sense of peace that I had done everything I could do as a fallback. It also made me super glad that I was smart enough to jump on a bunch of life insurance early, even before I could afford it." (Hoffman had sold himself additional life insurance to fund cryonics in 1994.) He happily acknowledged his answer sounded like a story any good insurance salesman would know how to tell, but he was completely earnest when describing the sense of relief he felt knowing his body would be preserved and his wife and dogs taken care of. If one of the central purposes of religion is to make you feel better about dying, then cryonics (and the insurance industry) filled any gaps created when Hoffman walked away from Christianity decades before.

Since the inception of cryonics, the ignorance of the rest of the world has exasperated the cryonics community. Hoffman is no different. He admits the chances of reanimation are slim, but he's still baffled by the majority's decision not to pursue the possibility. "I'm frustrated and angry that I've not been able to promote this mindset more effectively because it is such a reasonable, smart, rational thing to do, and should be adopted by literally tens of millions of people," said Hoffman. "If there's not a lot of downside and there's a whole bunch of potential upside, it's just a no-brainer for people to do something. But most of them don't, and I've learned to live with that."

Hoffman will fight for the cause of cryonics until the day he's put in a cylinder himself and, should he be proven correct, afterward as well. But while he's enjoyed great success personally, the secret to selling cryonics to the majority of world's population remains elusive. In response, the industry has switched up its marketing techniques to try and attract more believers. Cryonics was always sold as the key to immortality, but more recently, the major players have shied away from the word entirely.

When I mentioned the title of this book to Michael Geisen, a board member of Alcor, he bristled at the word immortality. On a video call, Geisen spoke with the typical cryonicist self-assurance, as if he'd uncovered a secret others had missed. He told me he doesn't believe he'll ever use his Alcor membership, and that by living his life a certain way he can survive for hundreds of years. "I think of Alcor as an insurance policy that I hope I'll never have to use," he said.

Geisen first contemplated the idea of extended life when he read Doris Lessing's cycle of science fiction novels Canopus in Argos. Years later he read *The First Immortal*, a novel by James L. Halperin, considered educational material by both Alcor and the Cryonics Institute. "Halfway through the book, I thought, 'Oh, that's the missing piece, because in my plan to live a long life, to eliminate aging, if I got hit by a bus or cancer or something like that, game over. But with cryopreservation as my backup, which I've had for over twenty years now, I don't have to worry about it.'"

Despite his involvement in cryonics and life extension, Geisen does not consider himself an immortalist. "In my mind I can imagine going on for hundreds of years, maybe thousands of years, but to imagine going for hundreds of thousands of years? That's even beyond my ability to imagine," he told me. Immortality, he says, is millions and billions of years, and that is "not what cryonics is about." I couldn't quite understand Geisen's viewpoint. If he truly believes he can live for thousands of years, way beyond his natural lifespan, why are millions or billions of years considered so unattainable? It was an argument I never truly grasped.

Geisen's opinion on immortality puts him at odds with the Church of Perpetual Life, and he was not afraid to speak his mind on its followers. He said some people have a genetic predisposition toward the spiritual. "I think it's just kind of a bridge for some people who don't want to, or can't, let go of religion in their lives. The Church of Perpetual Life fulfills that need," he said.

Geisen was the first person I'd met from within cryonics to outwardly criticize immortalism and the Church of Perpetual Life, so I was eager to explore Alcor's rebranding away from eternal life further. Over the years Alcor has entrusted the leadership of its organization to various different characters in addition to Mike Darwin. At the time of the Cryonics Symposium, the British philosopher and futurist Max More led Alcor. When I spoke to More at the event, he worded his answers carefully, as if he was wary of throwing cryonics into a pile of crackpot ideas. He is a huge name in the transhumanist movement and is even said to have originally coined the term transhumanism in his writings. His academic bent brought an intellectual rigor to the company, but a quick search revealed he also spent a good amount of time debating nonbelievers and Alcor naysayers on the internet.

By the time the pandemic shut the world down, More had been set aside for a new leader with a vastly different background. Former Chief Operating Officer Patrick Harris, who spent years in the pharmaceutical industry, took the reins. Harris endured an unconventional and difficult upbringing. He was born on an army base in the state of Washington, then lived in Germany for around five years where, he said, he had a good early life, with exposure to culture, science, and athletics. When he was seven or eight years old, he wrote a letter to NASA trying to convince them he should become the first child in space. The space agency replied with a polite no, but at that young age he was already looking far into the future. That was, until he was eleven, when his mother was diagnosed with breast cancer. A happy childhood filled with dreams of becoming an astronaut was transformed into a desperate search for ways to cure his mother. He became interested in health sciences and researched telomeres as a teenager. Before he'd finished high school, he attended a genetics conference, looking for hope for his sick mother. By the mid-1990s, Harris, still in high school, was researching bleeding edge technologies and came across the concept of cryonics in his local newspaper. He spoke to his mother and she was receptive to the idea, but they couldn't afford the cost. After seven and a half years of searching for new therapies, drugs, and technologies, Harris' mother passed away at age forty-one. Devastated, Harris was thrown off course by the loss. About a year later he found himself homeless and a high school dropout. He described the experience as "pretty traumatic." [6]

At the time Harris worked at a small local pharmacy, and his boss soon found out he was sleeping rough. Taking pity on his employee, the manager helped set him up in an apartment of his own. Harris immediately saw the pharmaceuticals business as "respectable and stable" and pledged to pursue a career in the industry. He obtained his GED and worked his way up the corporate ladder, studying for an MBA along the way. In 2018, Harris saw a job advertised at Alcor, where he'd become a member that same year. "I had planned to be a member the day that my mother died, which was January 1997. I always knew I was going to be a member. People are familiar with the word procrastinate, and it's funny how industries take a word and make it their own, so in cryonics when you delay signing up for your membership we call it 'cryocrastinate.' I was one of those 'cryocrastinators,'" Harris said.

He initially joined as chief operating officer, taking a hefty pay cut from his Big Pharma salary. "I thought, 'Man, I've been thinking about this since the '90s, since my mother passed away. I'm an Alcor member and with my experience I could probably help out the organization and its mission, which is the most aspirational goal in human history,'" Harris recalled in a phone interview. In the end, it was Harris' wife who convinced him, telling him they would find a way to live within a more modest budget if he really wanted to pursue the idea. "It was an interesting move from a career perspective," he said. The Alcor board made him interim CEO in May 2020, and he became the permanent leader in November that year. His background in pharmaceuticals and business make him a wise choice for an organization attempting to be taken more seriously. The old utter-ances of immortality are long gone, and Harris aims to steer Alcor away from science fiction and toward a health care–based approach.

"My view before I joined Alcor was this was bleeding edge re-search. I see it as a universal application of an emerging medicine," he said. "You hear people talking about how we need to perfect this if we're ever going to do interstellar travel, but what I saw coming from the health care industry is decades focusing on single diseases, whether it's diabetes or hypotension, which are very prevalent in the US, or on solving one issue, like Hepatitis B. If you can perfect the medicinal application of cryonics, it doesn't matter what disease state you suffer from. It could be a virus, bacteria, chemical, radiation, physical dam-age, you could stop and effectively freeze biological time to allow for new treatments to become available to save somebody's life.

"Medicine is so advanced, but it's still so early in its evolution. And what cryonics may potentially do, if we can make it work in the future, is just that, give medicine time to catch up with whatever ails us. And I think to myself, my mother who passed away at forty-one from breast cancer, if she were alive today, she would survive."

The shift toward a more health care–oriented approach suits loyal members like Geisen who take an extremely practical view of death. One of their biggest fears is being too far away from a cryonics facility when they die. Alcor has a set of protocols in place for when one of their members dies,[7] but it seems fraught with potential issues. All of its members wear a bracelet with a 1-800 number listed on it. When the patient dies, physicians are supposed to call that number and re-ceive instructions from Alcor to aid the cryopreservation process. The company immediately sends out an employee to wherever the person has died and eventually transports them to the facility. If a member is given a terminal diagnosis, they are encouraged to move closer to the company's headquarters in Scottsdale, Arizona. Geisen said if he was nearing death, he would immediately move, and he also has a plan for any disease of the brain. "If I somehow got Alzheimer's where my brain was being destroyed, I would not wait for natural death. I would end my life before my brain was destroyed," he said, matter-of-factly.

Just like in Mike Darwin's day, it's still vitally important that bodies are cryopreserved very soon after death. This urgency has spawned strange cottage industries. One of the presentations at Hoffman's Cryonics Symposium was by Suspended Animation, a company offering emergency remote preservation services. The two employees giving the talk, dressed in scrubs, traveled to the event in an ambulance decked out for one purpose—to prepare a corpse for cryopreservation. The vehicle parks outside a house, hospital, or nursing home where a paying customer is about to pass on. When the inevitable happens, they spring into action. In a hospital, they push past presumably bemused doctors and begin their work. If the deceased is at home they bring the body back to the ambulance. After draining fluids, icing the corpse, and preparing it for travel, they ensure it reaches the designated cryo facility in good time, even if that means chartering a private jet to move it across states.

All of this makes the modern cryonics business sound polished and professional, and that's exactly how it's trying to portray itself. But some of the old issues continue to surface. Competitors to Alcor have emerged around the globe frequently and sometimes bring bad practices with them. KrioRus, the Russian equivalent of Alcor, was in Florida that weekend to report on recent progress and apparently has cryopreserved seventy-eight people and forty-five pets since it was founded in 2003. The presentation failed to mention the crippling war between two founders tearing the company apart that has left one party with control of the company website and the other holding onto the suspended members.[8]

And at the symposium in Hollywood, Osiris Cryonics, a local for-profit company, was ordered by Hoffman not to attend. But they came anyway. Osiris founder Dvir Derhy was arrested in 2015 by the FBI when he attempted to bribe Miami fire inspectors with $10,000 cash stuffed in an envelope.[9] He went to prison for a month. Hoffman, understandably, felt his presence could harm the "fragile edifice the legitimate cryonics community has been trying to build," but when Derhy arrived Hoffman assigned people to watch him and keep him away from any press at the event.[10]

Murky characters like Derhy threaten an industry with an already compromised public image. For Harris, the challenge of selling cryonics to the masses rests on one aspect—education. "If you look back over history, a lot of people with any new innovation, they quickly jump to an assumption. They want to be an expert, they want to have an answer right away. And no matter what the advancement of technology is, medicine or otherwise, they are quick to judge. And they judge based on very limited information," he said. "The rise of the internet has educated people in so many different ways, where before that you would be educated based on the orbits and the spheres of people which you were associated with. I think a lot of it falls back to education. Cryonics is a multidisciplinary field. Unless you're one of the leading experts in the world it's very difficult to understand."

But criticism of cryonics also comes from within. One of the most important figures in the history of cryonics has since become a naysayer who walked away from the field completely. Mike Darwin, who performed the cryopreservation of Dora Kent all those years ago, has become a thorn in the side of Alcor, pointing out the organization's many flaws and demanding they do better. He believes wholeheartedly in the potential of cryonics and the mission itself, but claims the company has failed completely and utterly.

It can be difficult to find an informed critic of cryonics. Most scientists dismiss the concept out of hand, claiming it's not worth discussing as future reanimation would be impossible. Unfortunately, that means few look into the field in any great depth. But Darwin has a unique perspective. He was there for its formative years and helped shape many of the methods practiced today. In a long, late-night call, Darwin passionately explained the many failures of cryonics, breaking them down to three major arguments: the moral, the economic, and the philosophical.

Darwin's involvement in cryonics did not end with the Dora Kent scandal. He stepped down as CEO of Alcor but played a significant role in the company and performed the cryopreservation of Jerry Leaf when his former partner died suddenly from a heart attack.[11] Without Leaf to back him up, Darwin was soon forced out of Alcor. But while his operational role was minimal, he maintained his seat on the board and repeatedly took the organization to task. In the 1990s he disagreed with a new policy proposal to incentivize morticians to bring in business for Alcor by paying them a finder's fee for every body referred for preservation.[12] For Darwin, this was a terrible example of one of his chief criticisms of cryonics—that it's sold in an immoral manner. "I believe that it's the cryonics organizations' duty to ensure that the patients they accept know what is actually involved. They're stripped naked of the ability to rely on the normal mechanisms that are present to educate people about major life decisions," he said.

Because cryonics is unregulated, there is no way of going to a government agency and checking whether the company freezing your body has a history of malpractice, fraudulent activity, or even malicious intent. And because the customers are all dead when they finally receive the service they've paid for, there isn't even a Yelp review you can read to gauge how competent a cryonics provider may be. Darwin felt pushing sales in a mortuary was coercing business from mourning relatives lacking the emotional capability to make an informed decision. A friend or relative standing at the side of a loved one's body would likely do anything to bring them back, which makes hitting them up for business at that time predatory.

"My criteria and Jerry's criteria, and Alcor's criteria at that time, for dealing with somebody who came to us who was terminally ill was extensive counseling and evaluation by an independent psychiatrist who we had nothing to do with selecting," explained Darwin. "The person knew and understood what they were getting into, they were not under pressure or bereaved, and they were making this decision as rationally and informed as they could [be] about any other procedure, medical or otherwise, where there's a lot of unknown information."

Darwin also told me cryonics can be unfair to relatives of those who choose to be cryopreserved. "When someone starts dying, you fall back on what you've learned over a large time as to how to cope with that," he said. "Ministers, funerals, flowers, graveside ceremonies, wreath placing. Instead, you have these people who turn up that you don't know, who occupy the home or are by the hospital bed, and none of the normal mechanisms that are present for people to cope come into play. You can't sit there for an hour afterward in quiet solitude holding the person's hand or crying over them after they've experienced cardiac arrest. These people swoop in and do all these really invasive and, to someone who isn't used to it, shocking things."

On the practical side, there's a fair argument to make that cryonics is economically doomed. Financial problems have plagued the industry since the days of Bedford's freezing. In most businesses, bankruptcy is not the end of the world. But in cryonics, it can lead to customers decomposing, their dreams of a second life snatched away. Alcor appears from the outside to be in a better state than ever before, but there are still doubts around the economic principles underpinning its business plan. If an eighty-year-old goes to Alcor and pays $200,000 to have their head preserved, then dies a few years later, there's no problem. But if a healthy thirty-year-old buys a life insurance policy from Hoffman and signs up, there's an issue. The thirty-year-old is unlikely to die for at least another forty years or so but is committed to paying $200,000, just like the eighty-year-old. That sum will look pretty measly in forty years' time, given the rate of inflation. For comparison, something that cost $200,000 in 1950 would cost $2.1 million in 2021. Cryonics organizations don't seem to have accounted for that massive change in the value of money. Unless the likes of Alcor are continuously supported by very wealthy backers, they may not have enough money to keep the lights on and the bodies preserved.

Darwin's final point of contention with cryonics is philosophical. The practice was born out of science fiction and quickly moved into a fringe area of science, but has always flirted with the mystical. Cryonics, by its own admission, relies on future technology to solve the most pressing problem: how to reanimate a person.

This task will fall to the scientists of the future, but it's easy to get carried away with what they'll be able to achieve. "Once you have that problem, these god-like, all-powerful creatures on the other end, and you're relying on them, the tendency is to rely on them completely. And this reduces the front end of the procedure to ritual," said Darwin.

That means the cryonics companies of today can ignore science and best practice as they take increasingly large leaps of faith that the future will fix any mistakes. For example, if a corpse has been dead a week and has decomposed normally, by most cryonicists' logic they are unsavable. But if you were to put an increasing amount of trust in the science of the future, you might conclude that they could salvage something from even a completely decomposed corpse. "There's merit to that, I'm not denigrating it completely, but the consequence of it is it has an absolutely corrosive effect on progress, on trying to improve the state of the art. It prohibits you from establishing any standards. It locks you into some ritual that will only evolve when there's pressure from the outside," Darwin told me.

And worrying cases continue to emerge. According to Darwin, this erosion of principles and best practices is already evident. On September 6, 2019, Alcor member A-1100, a lifelong Alcor supporter, died with no suspension team nearby. He was shipped from Florida to Arizona by air freight, with no ice and no refrigeration. When he arrived at Alcor, his body was reportedly 68 degrees Fahrenheit, just under room temperature, with hope of reanimation all but lost.

"He wasn't a lovable guy, but he was honest, he sincerely believed in cryonics, and he put a lot of money into it and never did anything to hurt anybody," said Darwin. "And if you treat your own people that way, what have you become?" (The case is noted on Alcor's website but without detail. Harris said a more thorough case report will be published at some point in the future after a third-party review. He also said the company was unable to make a statement on a specific case. It should be noted that Hurricane Dorian was affecting travel at the time of the Alcor member's death.)

The types of characters attracted to the practice of cryonics continually threatens to undermine any credibility it has. A series of celebrities are rumored to have been cryogenically frozen, including most famously Walt Disney, but there still hasn't been confirmation of any well-respected people of note to add to the cryonics testimonies. In 2019, a report by *The New York Times* revealed that the accused sex trafficker Jeffrey Epstein had been obsessed with several controversial fringe sciences.[13] One of those was cryonics. Epstein was reportedly determined to have both his head and penis frozen, a terrifying thought—and another extremely damaging PR disaster for the industry.

Cryonics is one of the biggest parts of any immortalist's game plan. But it's hard to see how the practice in its current form can possibly achieve its goals. Nearly every cryonicist I spoke to expressed their shock that more people had not signed up to have their bodies or brains preserved. But given the chaotic history of the industry, it's no surprise the take-up hasn't been higher. For now, cryonics is destined to remain a fringe undertaking, at least until some kind of breakthrough is made on the reanimation side. There are no signs of progress any time soon, and that means cryonics practitioners need an awful lot of faith to sign up and maintain their memberships until they die. There are a lot of reasons to believe cryonics will ultimately fail, and even those within the industry acknowledge it is a long shot. The move away from science and medicine and toward some kind of religion could lead the community away from standards, regulations, best practices, and scientific rigor, and toward shoddy amateurism which will make their revered future scientists look back and wince.

The concept of faith in cryonics made me remember another, much older, game in town offering immortality and resurrection. Florida's immortalists gather every month in a church—but just how close to a religion are they really?

5

THE ETERNAL PRIZE

The final talk on the weekend of the First Annual Cryonics Symposium was given by Bill Faloon, one of the founders of the church. VanDeRee gave Faloon a big buildup when he introduced him to the crowd, and it was clear from their reaction that he was a well-respected figure among immortalists. And Faloon knew how to work an audience. His speech began with a list of updates from scientific studies showing any kind of promise that eternal life could be possible. As he gathered momentum, his talk turned into a sermon, and by the end he was rallying the crowd against death. He ran through a list of rich millionaires who had died, almost mocking them for not spending their money on immortalist solutions and finding a way to live longer. Faloon's heated finale featured legal wins for the immortalist movements and hit out at those who accepted death as part of life. For the first time, I felt I was at a church rather than a particularly strange hobby club. The talk made me realize just how closely immortalism resembles a religion.

It's easy to look at the Church of Perpetual Life and see a collection of misfits desperately chasing an unattainable goal. They make a soft target for mockery, sneering, and condemnation. But their fear of death is not unusual. And their belief in some sort of resurrection even less so. In the business of selling immortality, this small church in Florida is only the new entrant in an ancient marketplace. In order to understand what motivates the immortalists, I wanted to explore humanity's constant battle with the fact that we all die and religion's attempt to provide an answer.

There are two broad categories of immortality. One is the ever-lasting body, the other the soul. We usually associate the concept of an immortal soul with Western religions like Christianity, but it goes back much further than the Bible. Plato famously debated the immortality of the soul in *Phaedo*, one of his best-known works. In the ancient Greek dialogue, Plato details the final hours of Socrates as his fellow philosopher argues for the existence of the soul, life before birth, and life after death. In *Phaedo*, the state has sentenced Socrates to death for corrupting the youth of Athens and failing to profess his belief in the accepted gods of the time. When his friends appear and offer to bribe the guards so he can escape his execution, Socrates refuses, despite the highly questionable nature of his charges, and accepts his fate.

"Socrates represents something almost superhuman, because of course what Plato is recognizing is that fear of death is this very powerful part of what it is to be human," Professor Douglas Hedley, a professor of the philosophy of religion at the University of Cambridge, told me on a video call. Plato and Socrates saw philosophy as training for death, Hedley said, which made the actions of Socrates the ultimate mastery of his discipline and a way of conquering his mortality. Plato's musings on the presence of the soul greatly influenced the teachings of today's "mainstream" religions.

More modern philosophical takes on the subject come to similar conclusions. Ernest Becker's wonderfully argued book *The Denial of Death* suggests our mortality is the prime motivator of all our fears and anxieties. Becker, drawing on countless other works, contends that every human struggles with the paradox of their own existence— that our minds are overdeveloped thought machines, capable of taking us anywhere in time and space, but are housed in a frail, fragile, broken body which from the moment we are born begins to decay.[1] This makes death, or anything that reminds us of our mortality—including many basic bodily functions—a taboo topic. According to Becker, this way of thinking is not doing us any favors, and by confronting and accepting our own mortality we can live healthier and more fulfilled lives.

Becker also argued that each of us is compelled to think of ourselves as the hero of our own story, most likely as a means to make our short lives more relevant and meaningful. This obsession to see ourselves as the single most important thing in the universe led us to construct a society which offers ample opportunity to make ourselves heroic. Individuals are able to make themselves appear as heroes in the drabbest circumstances—somebody staying late at work to complete a menial task can convince themselves this makes them somewhat elevated from their peers, even if the effect on their job, company, life, or the universe as a whole will be inconsequential.

If Becker is correct, and purpose and distraction help us avoid the thought of our own impending doom, then Western religion ticks both boxes. Followers of religion can easily spin a hero story from their own existence because they believe they are doing the work of a greater power—the creator of the universe. Immortality, in this case, is usually considered a sure thing. Because of this, religion is one of the most effective suppressants of our fear of death.

Christianity has a strange relationship with death. The Old Testament laid out the story of humanity's soul quite clearly. Humans were first created immortal. Adam and Eve would have lived forever without ever knowing suffering but for the devious behavior of Eve, a part of the story which led to the demonization of women for centuries. To punish humanity, God took away their immortality, introducing pain, illness, and death. He then hatched a slightly convoluted plan to give them a second chance at living forever. That story involved Jesus and a crucifixion, and has been fairly well documented.

God's sacrifice opened the door to an eternal and blissful existence in heaven for anyone who lived the right sort of life here on Earth. There was a flip side to this, of course. Those who failed to meet the standards of the creator were handed an eternity of damnation in return. In theory, that stick-and-carrot system should bring Christians to a peaceful conclusion about death, but somehow it doesn't work out that way. For one thing, the rules of engagement are quite unclear, which must make it hard for even the most devout member of the church to be completely confident of their place in heaven rather than hell. To a lot of people, the idea of a physical heaven, another world where people presumably spend all day in devotion, either seems completely implausible or fairly torturous. Like most religions, Christianity swerves around the question of mortality by providing a strange and elusive answer which cannot stand up to the slightest bit of scrutiny.

Buddhism and Hinduism—the so-called "Eastern" religions—offer a different explanation. Instead of insisting the goal should be to live, in this world or another, they teach their followers to aim to achieve balance in death. Both religions claim we cycle through lives, constantly reincarnated and following a pattern of death and rebirth, until we reach a state where we overcome ignorance and desire. In Hinduism, a follower can skip ahead to that point if they die in Benares, the home of Shiva, the Hindu Lord of Destruction. Dying in this holy city is said to take the pollution out of death, breaking the cycle of life. Buddhists have no such shortcuts.

"Generally, Buddhists believe that there is no beginning to birth, and that once we achieve liberation from the cycle of existence by overcoming our karma and destructive emotions, we will not be reborn under the sway of these conditions. Therefore, Buddhists believe that there is an end to being reborn as a result of karma and destructive emotions, but most Buddhist philosophical schools do not accept that the mind-stream comes to an end," the Dalai Lama wrote in 2011.[2]

"I think the Eastern religions deal with the same worry differently," Dr. Tim Mawson of the faculty of theology and religion at the University of Oxford told me on a video call. "They don't say, 'That thing you want, it's only our religion that gives it to you.' They say, 'That thing you want, it's all right—we can stop you wanting it.' And that's the way to remove the itch rather than scratch the itch."

Some immortalists are also religious. VanDeRee told me many of the congregation of the Church of Perpetual Life go to other churches as well and find the idea of living forever works well with the teachings of their religion. It's clear the idea of physical immortality here on Earth fits better with some doctrines than others. For Diego, the man I met on the first evening of the cryonics event, the idea of living forever was not a new one but didn't conjure the most comfortable memories. Diego and his family were Jehovah's Witnesses, a religion born out of Christianity with strictly observed rules and regulations. The views of Jehovah's Witnesses are vaguely similar to modern day immortalists in that they believe one day every human on Earth will live forever. They see God's Kingdom, an oft-referenced part of Christianity, as a literal government, headed up by Jesus Christ and 144,000 Christians who are drawn from Earth. This kingdom, which was set up in 1914, according to the religion, is said to be the means used by God to accomplish his original plan for Earth, to transform it into a paradise where nobody gets sick and nobody dies. But while it's possible to fit the immortalist way of life into that part of the religion, other aspects just don't mix. Jehovah's Witnesses don't believe in some modern medicine and reject blood transfusions, even if it means they will die. Diego, a health nut, decided to leave the church his family had been part of for all his life and got his mother out as well. The result was complete ostracization from the community he'd grown up in.

Mormonism is another religion which perhaps surprisingly fits well with the immortalist view of the world. Every month, a group of Mormons meets to discuss how the various concepts of transhumanism interact with their religion. The Mormon Transhumanist Association takes a more liberal look at Joseph Smith's teachings and reached the conclusion that their beliefs are very compatible with some of the ideas thrown up by transhumanists. During a sermon in 1844 at the funeral of King Follett, Smith said, "God himself was once as we are now, and is an exalted man, and sits enthroned in yonder heavens! That is the great secret." He continued: "You have got to learn how to be gods yourselves . . ."[3]

Lincoln Cannon is one of the directors of the group. In a video call, he told me his upbringing in a Mormon household taught him that eventually humanity would overcome death. According to Cannon, heaven in Mormon teaching is a version of Earth transformed for the better, and immortality, far from being a spiritual or metaphorical goal, was a physical reality. "I was taught to hope for such things— that eventually the Earth would become our heaven, then our bodies would become immortal," Cannon recalled.

Cannon's father was a software engineer and computer scientist, while his mother converted from Catholicism to Mormonism before Cannon was born. His mother loved the epistle of James in the Bible, particularly the part about faith without works being dead. The combination of a technology-savvy father and a mother with a more hands-on attitude toward religion taught Cannon to look at Mormonism from the same practical angle. As a young adult, he moved away from the church and became an atheist for many years. It was during this period that he discovered transhumanism. "I recognized that it's something that I had always been, and just didn't know that there was a secular name for it," he said. When Cannon returned to Mormonism, he brought his transhumanist beliefs with him and found others with similar convictions. In 2006, along with thirteen others, he founded the Mormon Transhumanist Association, and for the first ten years served as president of the group. During this time, the fourteen members grew to between six hundred and seven hundred, and is now around one thousand strong.

Most Mormons have never heard of transhumanism, according to Cannon. But he says more people have become aware over time, particularly since the association began in 2006. When he explains transhumanism to Mormons, in a way "that's not intended to shock," he said most express a cautious interest. Others jump on board straightaway, seeing the parallels between the teachings of Mormonism and transhumanism.

The current CEO of the Mormon Transhumanist Association hails from a slightly different background. Michaelann Gardner was brought up in the 1980s in the South by a Mormon family but went to a school where most of the children were Southern Baptists. In 1982, two evangelical documentary makers released the film *The God Makers*, a stinging critique of Mormonism that drew a lot of unwanted attention to Gardner. She recalled her friends would tease her for being part of a religion that claimed its followers would become God, one of the tamer and more accurate statements made in the film. In response, Gardner played down that aspect of her religion, telling friends it was overblown. Now, as an adult transhumanist, she sees that belief as a key part of the doctrine. "One of the synchronicities between transhumanism and Mormonism is the idea of becoming God," she told me. For most Mormons, theosis, the belief that humans can become God, is an important part of their religion, but they can be strict about how that transformation can take place. "For them it's very, very important that it only comes about through the grace of God, through the atonement of Jesus Christ, through priesthood power." That causes some friction with the transhumanists, who believe that science could be one of the methods used by God to make humans deities.

The Mormon Transhumanist Association is far from the only religious transhumanist group, but it's a great example of how concepts like immortalism can fit into a wider religious belief. One of the most common ways immortalists synchronize their beliefs with their faith is to argue that humanity was made in God's image and God is immortal, so we are destined to follow suit. Others say it's our mission to build the most remarkable kingdom here on Earth, and ending the suffering of death would be one of the best ways to achieve that goal.

But there are some transhumanists and immortalists who see religion as a hurdle blocking their progress. For many of them, the pursuit of immortality has become something of a religion itself. To explore exactly how similar immortalism is to a faith-based system, I took a closer look at one of the Church of Perpetual Life's prophets, Nikolai Fedorov.

· · ·

It started, as many great tales have in the past, with a flaming ball of light in the sky. Biela's Comet, first correctly identified in 1826 by Wilhelm von Biela, a German military officer and amateur astronomer serving in the Austrian army, caused an uproar. Some scientists predicted the comet's trajectory would bring it crashing into Earth at some point in the 1830s, bringing about the end of the world. The news inspired three types of response. The first was mass global panic, the second a scientific retort stating the comet would in fact miss the Earth, and the third a massive increase in apocalypse-themed novels.

Prince Vladimir Odoevsky was one of the many authors inspired by the comet, and the Russian writer and philosopher got to work on *The Year 4338*. In his novel, a comet races toward Earth in the future and the world scrambles to avert disaster. Odoevsky's protagonist travels from Beijing to St. Petersburg on a high-speed electric train to meet fellow scientists. The Russia he travels through is eerily similar, in some ways, to our world today. Each household is connected via telegraphs, and the people read newspapers made from liquid crystal screens, eat synthetic foods, and wear electronic clothes, while the economy is completely moneyless. The story is told through a series of letters in a world in which humans can control the weather and look to conquer the threat hurtling toward them through space.[4]

Prince Odoevsky never finished his book, but fragments were published starting in 1835 that are thought to have directly influenced Fedorov, who began to develop an unusual branch of philosophy in the 1860s.[5] He was a devout follower of the Russian Orthodox Church. Despite writing prolifically, he didn't publish any work while he was living, partly because he felt his ideas would get him excommunicated.[6] Fedorov's father was a prince and his mother a noblewoman, but because he was an illegitimate child he was thrown out of the family home when his father died. Fedorov, four at the time, left with his mother and siblings, still living in relative wealth. In 1868 he became a librarian at the Rumyantsev Museum in Moscow, where he worked for twenty-five years and hosted an informal intellectual salon, earning himself the nickname "the Socrates of Moscow." After Fedorov died, his work was gathered and published in Almaty, Kazakhstan, under the title *The Philosophy of the Common Task*. Fewer than five hundred copies were printed, and they were not sold commercially.

Fedorov wrote about achieving immortality through technological means. He believed there was only one evil of consequence in the world: death. "Death is merely the result or manifestation of our infantilism," he wrote. "People are still minors, half-beings, whereas the fullness of personal existence, personal perfection is possible."

He tried to convince others that death was not a natural part of the human condition, but rather something to be conquered with technology. And he didn't stop there. As well as preventing death, Fedorov wanted to resurrect everyone who had ever lived, making a version of heaven here on Earth. If humanity were to achieve such a feat, the whole world would need to come together and treat the project as "the moral equivalent of war," according to Fedorov. He said that by attacking this one common foe, all the struggles of humanity, such as war, poverty, and disease, would be defeated, creating a perfect world. He also wanted to turn the entire universe into one united organism, all of which would be immortal, thus creating a god by scientific means.

Fedorov influenced other meaningful thinkers of the period. At the beginning of his time at the Rumyantsev Museum library in 1874, Fedorov met sixteen-year-old Konstantin Tsiolkovsky, whose pioneering work as a theoretical physicist would eventually form the bedrock of the Soviet space program and who would be described by NASA as "one of the fathers of rocketry and cosmonautics."[7] Upon meeting Fedorov, Tsiolkovsky dispensed with his university professors, who he now regarded as superfluous. Four years later, Fyodor Dostoevsky heard about Fedorov's work via one of the philosopher's pupils. Dostoevsky wrote to the pupil, asking: "Who is this thinker, whose thoughts you have conveyed? If you can do so, tell me his real name. He has intrigued me too greatly . . . And then I shall say that essentially I am in entire agreement with these ideas. I read them as if they were my own."[8]

Between 1881 and 1882, Fedorov met writer Leo Tolstoy and Vladimir Soloviev, a fellow philosopher. Soloviev wrote in a letter in 1881: "There are men here too. And God has allowed me to get to know two of them. Orlov is one, the other, and the main one, is Nikolai Fedorovich Fedorov. He is the librarian at the Rumyantsev Library. Remember, I told you about him. He has put together a plan of the common task of all mankind, having as its goal the resurrection of all people in the flesh. Firstly, this is not as insane as it seems. (Don't be afraid, I do not share and have never shared his views, but I have understood them so well that I feel capable of defending those views against any other credo that has an external goal.)"[9]

It's easy to see why Fedorov's work is still held in such high regard by the community of immortalists found in America today. He proposed fixing death through a series of technological solutions which seem a lot more plausible in modern times. To enable humans to live forever, Fedorov said human body parts should be replaced with artificial organs. This thought process birthed the transhumanist movement but was also extremely prescient. Modern medicine allows almost any body part to be replaced with artificial organs, and it's not uncommon for hearts, lungs, livers, and limbs to be switched out for mechanical stand-ins. This idea taken to the absolute extreme leads a lot of modern-day transhumanists and immortalists to believe the entire human body can be replaced by uploading the human brain to a computer.

To resurrect the dead, Fedorov wanted humanity to explore the cosmos to find particles of long-lost ancestors which would then be used to revive them. He also wanted to bring people back to life using their dead tissue, effectively proposing obtaining DNA for cloning.[10] But where to put the recently resurrected masses? Even in the nineteenth century, reanimating anyone who ever lived would have caused something of an overpopulation issue. This led Fedorov to his other area of influence: space flight. He believed that exploring the cosmos would lead to the perfection of the human race.

Fedorov's philosophy is now referred to as Russian Cosmism, but it almost didn't make it out of Russia at all. In the early era of the Soviet Union, the popularity of cosmism was crushed under the regime of Joseph Stalin. The spiritual approach to science was at odds with Stalin's vision of a Soviet Russia devoid of religion. "In the 30s, Stalinism begins, repression begins, when death becomes an instrument of regulation - it is impossible for cosmism that death is an instrument of social regulation. On the contrary, cosmism stands for the complete victory over death, and for it the social regulation is based not on death, but on love, on the common cause, on comradeship, on brotherhood," Anastasia Gacheva, of the Fedorov Museum-Library in Moscow, told me through an interpreter. The cosmist movement stayed largely quiet until the Soviet Union fell, and only then did Fedorov's work really get the level of attention some believe it deserves.

Anton Vidokle, an artist and founder of the art exhibition website e-flux, has studied Fedorov and Russian cosmism for many years. He believes Fedorov's era was well-suited to his ideas, even if they weren't widely spread at the time. "I think the pace of change at that time may have seemed to be even faster and more evolving than it does to us now," Vidokle told me. "I think people maybe were even more open-minded than we are now to the possibility of a really radical technological breakthrough. Suddenly there was a way to communicate with people on the other side of the world instantaneously, which seemed before like witchcraft or magic. So what would be so incredibly impossible about immortality or space travel?"

In the final half of the nineteenth century, Russia was on the brink of great social and political change, and this added to the feeling that anything was possible. Today there is a similar feeling of political upheaval as populism worryingly spreads across the globe, and a comparable rate of technological progress. However, Vidokle believes Fedorov would have a harder time getting his point across today. "We're a lot more cynical. I think that at the turn of the century and early twentieth century, before fascism, before World War II, before the Holocaust, there was a little bit more of a possibility of a kind of a positive future to imagine, before all of this mechanized nightmare, mass killings, before this machine became quite as visible."

Were Fedorov alive today, it would be easy to imagine him as some sort of Silicon Valley guru, advising the likes of Jeff Bezos and Elon Musk on their plans for the future. But Fedorov stood starkly against everything billionaires represented. He did not present his ideas as socialism because he thought that strain of thinking had no place for religion or spirituality, but he also didn't believe in the accumulation of wealth, according to Vidokle.

Fedorov makes for an ideal hero for today's immortalists because he addressed one of the core criticisms of the future they envision. Naysayers often accuse immortalists of attempting to defy nature, but Fedorov believed it was humanity's obligation to use technology to become one with the entire universe. When the US first experimented with inducing artificial rainfall using artillery projectiles in 1891, Fedorov sought to bring attention to the idea and contacted

Tolstoy to ask him to support Russian research. "It is the regulation, the governance of the forces of blind nature that constitute that great task which can and must become the common one," he said.[11] These leanings made Fedorov's message almost mystical. He believed in God but found some elements of religion to be too passive and wanted humanity to take a more active role in the future of the universe.

Cosmism itself is now enjoying a renaissance, decades after it first emerged. Many of the immortalists I met in Hollywood, Florida, were self-professed followers of Fedorov's teachings, and one member of the church even gave me a business card with Fedorov's name on it, explaining he was writing a book to spread the word of the Russian philosopher further. Fedorov's role as a prophet for the Church of Perpetual Life reinforces the religious structure immortalists have put in place. It is broad enough to welcome in other religious viewpoints, but contains just enough hallmarks of the major churches, like the regular gatherings, sermons, and almost ritual-like popping of supplementary pills, to capture the attention of those who have a religion-shaped hole in their lives.

The church is a physical reminder of the mystical aspect of immortalism. While gerontology, the study of aging, is a science, immortalism requires a level of belief and faith mostly seen in religion. Scientific breakthroughs give immortalists much more real-world hope than a religion, but they are still betting on being right in the same way a religious person might. This makes it even more interesting that the immortalists of Florida chose to label their pursuit a religion.

There are other immortalist groups besides the Church of Perpetual Life. On the opposite side of the country, another organization has been around for much longer. Although it avoids the moniker of religion, it has taken a much more spiritual approach to the problem of mortality.

People Unlimited, a California-based group campaigning for immortality, has a checkered history that brushes dangerously close to cult-like status. While some members of the cryonics community treat immortality as a dirty word, People Unlimited embrace it wholeheart-edly. But in the past, it's gone a little too far.

In 1959, Charles Paul Brown was studying to be a gospel preacher when a strange occurrence changed his life. In an event Brown later described as a "cellular awakening," his body glowed and a powerful vision of Bible verses flashed in front of his eyes. Each of the verses affirmed the idea that physical immortality was a real possibility. He said he experienced a "piercing through to the core of the cells and atoms of the body, which awaken the DNA." The experience left him bedridden for three months. When he recovered he declared him-self immortal. Brown spent the next five decades preaching to others about his immortality and advising them how they could be blessed in the same way.[12] He was joined by his wife Bernadeane Brown and, later, their business partner and friend James Strole. In 1982, Brown launched The Eternal Flame Foundation, where he shared his immor-tality with others through "cellular intercourse," which thankfully was less intimate than it sounded. Throughout the 1980s, the trio changed the name of their organization often, from People Forever to CBJ, which stood for Charles, Bernie, and James.

By 1994, the group, now known as the Flame Foundation, was prospering. More than thirty thousand people from around eighteen countries signed up to its mailing list, and an audit for 1992–1993 showed the three founders of the group each received salaries of more than $430,000. But around that time, doubt began to grow among its followers. Membership numbers were greatly reduced when a promi-nent member of the community, Donald Leon, died. Cellular inter-course had done nothing to save Leon, and community members were angry. In 1996, the trio incorporated a new company, the Scottsdale, Arizona–based People Unlimited. This new incarnation brought fame and appreciation—the three founders even spoke on Larry King. But increased notoriety resulted in added scrutiny. A host of articles ques-tioned the motives of the group; some claimed it was nothing more than a cult designed to manipulate and exploit its members. "In my opinion, they fit the criteria that establishes what I call the nucleus of a destructive cult," Rick Ross, executive director of the Cult Education Institute in New Jersey, said in 2014.[13]

When membership numbers dwindled again, the reduced spotlight allowed People Unlimited to operate without the same kind of oversight. Over time, the group's message softened in an attempt to bring more people to its cause. But in 2014, its origin story was dealt what would surely be a fatal blow—its founder died.[14] Brown had suffered from Parkinson's disease and heart failure and finally succumbed to the inevitability of death, proving his claim of immortality was false. Many would have predicted the end of the group after such a devastating blow, but People Unlimited lived up to its name and survived.

Today the organization is based in an industrial park in Scottsdale, very close to the headquarters of the cryonics company Alcor. Its YouTube channel publishes polished videos painting it as a self-help motivational group, urging its members to make the most of their lives and somehow become immortal along the way. The meetings themselves are energetic, to put it mildly. Prior to the pandemic, at a November Super Longevity weekend in 2019, attendees of all ages, including some with young children, would hug and dance in the aisles as Strole and Bernadeane whipped them into a frenzy. Speakers joined either via video call or in person and gave presentations; songs were sung on stage, stretching exercises were initiated, and there were even choreographed dances. "Everything will come our way that we need, we do not need to chase anything," Strole yelled to the crowd, who responded with shouts of encouragement. "I'm not here to live two hundred more years and be happy as hell and then say, 'I'm ready to die now,'" he told the crowd, to euphoric applause.

Jeremy Cohen, a PhD candidate and instructor at McMaster University in Canada, has spent a lot of time at People Unlimited events as part of his research into communities and new religious movements seeking extreme life extension and immortality. On a video call, he described his experience at the People Unlimited meetings.

A regular part of the events, Cohen told me, involves something called "expressions," where members are invited onto the stage to share their thoughts, hopes, and dreams. Cohen has participated in this process himself, but was once scolded for talking too much about the past and death. For Cohen, who studies death for a living and whose wife is in the funeral profession, that can be difficult. But in People Unlimited death is a taboo, an unspoken negative that shouldn't be worried about. He told me the dogma of the organization is that any death is avoidable, even if it's someone within the group. Cohen has heard members of the group even blame Brown for his own death as a way of explaining why he wasn't actually immortal as he claimed. But that tone doesn't sit well with all the attendees.

"There are a lot of members I've spoken to who are really uncomfortable with that kind of etiology of illness," Cohen explained. "For them, the idea that a member who just died, it's their fault that they got cancer, is really troubling and can create unnecessary anxiety and people to always be checking, 'Was that cheeseburger the thing that's going to do me in?'"

The group tends to favor spiritualism over technology, so is it fair to label it a religion or even a cult, as some have in the past? Cohen doesn't refer to them as a religious group in his research, mainly because the members and organizers don't describe themselves that way. The organization is incorporated, and structured as a business. But he does see similarities between their actions and others. The two original founders, Bernadeane and her husband Brown, both came from evangelical Christian backgrounds, and Brown has been compared to an evangelical pastor. But the modern version of People Unlimited appears to be moving away from that means of expression. Cohen told me they would not appreciate being labeled a religion, and he even believed they'd get a little mad if anyone brought it up to them. But he did note some similarities. "With People Unlimited, you have an actual community of people that are gathering on a regular basis. You could probably argue that taking supplements the way that people do is almost a ritual, and the way in which people talk about how they maintain their health has these ritual elements to it."

Over time, a new type of influence has taken a hold over groups like People Unlimited and even the Church of Perpetual Life. Where once there was cryonics, positive thought, and spirituality, now there is technology. People Unlimited is more at odds with this new way of thinking, and some members even think cryonics is a useless admission that immortality is yet to be achieved. A good number of them also don't believe in escape velocity (the point people need to live to before technological advances begin at such a rate that they will outpace death), as they believe the time where they can be immortal is already here, despite massive scientific evidence to the contrary. But over time, that attitude is changing, in part because of people like the man who invented the term escape velocity: Aubrey de Grey, who has become the driving force of the immortality movement the world over. Through de Grey's influence, the types of speakers attending People Unlimited events have morphed from hippy wannabes to scientific renegades, and the founders have been happy to go along with it. "I think because they see this as a collective fight and something that everyone should unite around, even if there are disagreements over the ways in which immortality will come," Cohen said.

But this new wave of science is useless without money, and for that, the quest to beat death has turned to America's biggest billionaire playground—Silicon Valley. As with the founding of the Church of Perpetual Life, de Grey was the man in the middle, connecting all interested parties.

6

THE VALLEY SHADOWING DEATH

Since the 1980s, wave after wave of technological change originating from Silicon Valley has crashed over the world. Each jump in progress has spawned new industries, fortunes, and even universes. A growing band of geeks steadily grew wealthier, and their influence expanded along with their bank balances. Behind each multibillion-dollar company was a flock of venture capitalists who readied their checkbooks when young startups needed them most and reaped the rewards when they grew into the monoliths that now prop up the American economy. Since the birth of the personal computer, the moment when high-technology made its way into the home, Silicon Valley has swallowed industries whole, one by one. The internet changed commerce forever, enabling all-conquering profit machines like Jeff Bezos' Amazon. Ride-hailing apps like Uber and Lyft quickly engulfed the transportation industry, while Airbnb and Seamless revolutionized hospitality. Technology transformed finance, logistics, media, and entertainment. It was only a matter of time before Silicon Valley turned its now all-seeing eye to the health care industry, America's most broken, and profitable, institution. Biotech companies have always fit snugly into the startup template. They begin as cash-hungry long shots, and when their treatments are approved, they pay gigantic dividends. When the men with the money sensed a quickening in anti-aging, they fell over each other to pump cash into young companies addressing just the kinds of fields that make immortalists so hopeful.

And so the world of immortalism crashed headlong into Silicon Valley and all its billions, guided by the man who has done more for the cause of immortality than anyone else. Aubrey de Grey, already mentioned in previous chapters, enjoys god-like status in the immortalist community. Over time he's publicized the goal of defeating aging and even made it somewhat fashionable. His rejuvenation theories, once scoffed at, were slowly accepted as fact by the scientific community, and he now sits at the center of a network patiently built over decades, in the middle of the science, the money, and the immortalists, his adoring fans.

De Grey has always appreciated the value of the media in his quest and has been interviewed for magazines, newspapers, websites, and documentaries countless times. He makes for a great spokesperson for such an eccentric community. Past articles noted his Rasputin-like beard, wild auburn hair, and tendency to crack open a beer at all times of the day. When we spoke on a video call, de Grey dialing in from his Silicon Valley base, I was relieved to see he lived up to all the hype. His beard was suitably wizardly, his red hair graying but still untamed, and not long into our call I heard the sound of a beer bottle hissing open at midday, California time. He talked like an idiosyncratic member of the old English aristocracy, rapidly and without pause, and at times I got the sense I'd signed up for a lecture rather than an interview.[1]

When de Grey was between eight and nine years old, his mother pressured him to practice the piano. The young Englishman resisted, and even at that tender age that instinct intrigued him and warranted further introspection. He concluded he didn't want to practice the piano because he wanted to improve the quality of life for the whole of humanity. He still doesn't know where that urge comes from, but it has driven him his whole life. "It led me to be very sure I never wanted to have kids, because for sure that's a very time-consuming thing that prevents you from doing other stuff," he told me.

After deciding scientists were the people who made the biggest difference to the world in the long run, de Grey began learning computer programming when he was fifteen and quickly found he was extremely adept at it. He went to the University of Cambridge to study computer science in the early 1980s, then worked for six or seven years in artificial intelligence research. De Grey always considered aging to be the greatest challenge of humanity but was content believing it was being addressed by the world's biologists, and he began fixing another issue, "the fact that people had to spend so much of their time doing stuff they wouldn't do unless they were being paid for it."

But at a graduate party in Cambridge, de Grey met the fruit fly geneticist Adelaide Carpenter, who he later married. His relationship took him into the world of biology academia, and he was shocked when he discovered aging was way down the list of priorities in the discipline. "It took me a couple of years to come to terms with that, really, but once I did I realized I had no choice, I just had to switch fields," he recalled.

De Grey first gained notoriety when he published his 1999 book *The Mitochondrial Free Radical Theory of Aging*, in which he argued immortality was theoretically possible for humans. At the center of his thinking was a concept called strategies for engineered negligible senescence, abbreviated to SENS. In 2005, *MIT Technology Review* announced a $20,000 prize for anyone who could successfully argue that de Grey's theories were more fantasy than science. To claim the prize, the entrants had to prove that SENS was "so wrong it was unworthy of learned debate." There were five submissions, of which three met the terms of the challenge. But the judges decided none of them met the criteria for victory and disproved SENS. [2]

"The scientific process requires evidence through independent experimentation or observation in order to accord credibility to a hypothesis. SENS is a collection of hypotheses that have mostly not been subjected to that process and thus cannot rise to the level of being scientifically verified. However, by the same token, the ideas of SENS have not been conclusively disproved. SENS exists in a middle ground of yet-to-be-tested ideas that some people may find intriguing but which others are free to doubt," Nathan Myhrvold, one of the judges and cofounder of Intellectual Ventures and former chief technology officer of Microsoft, wrote.[3]

In 2009, de Grey set up the SENS Foundation, a nonprofit and the world's first organization dedicated to curing aging. Through the charity, de Grey was able to place himself in a position to link the scientists working on rejuvenation—who could prove him right—with sources of investment. None of the labs that received money were required to declare they were working toward immortality, or even extended life, and some of the most respected scientists in the gerontology field received funding.

SENS is based in Silicon Valley, where the billionaires have deep pockets and don't shy away from a difficult challenge. De Grey thinks the Valley's forgiving attitude toward failure is the secret to its success. "That made Silicon Valley what it is today in IT, and more recently in biotech," he said. "And it continues to be an absolutely essential ingredient for anything where you're in the real vanguard. Anything that isn't really a thing yet but is on the way to becoming a thing. Of course, longevity is very, very much that."

It does help to have money, as well. More and more of Silicon Valley's billionaires have developed a personal passion in health and extended life over the past decade. Tad Friend's 2017 *New Yorker* article titled "Silicon Valley's Quest to Live Forever" most notably described the obsession. Friend's reporting from a symposium held in an aging expert's living room in Los Angeles documented celebrities and Silicon Valley elites gathering to grill biologists on their chances of making death optional.[4] A handful of the wealthiest people in the technology industry have spent huge sums of money on projects attempting to defeat aging. Some see this as an altruistic endeavor which can help the whole of humanity, others as the quickest route to living longer themselves, while a fair few consider it merely as a profitable industry of the future.

The technology industry's participation in the field of aging, both in a personal and professional capacity, has been relentlessly mocked the world over. The HBO comedy drama *Silicon Valley* featured moguls pumping the blood of the young into their veins to extend their lifespan, one of the many practices touted as the next big thing in life extension.

One of the characters who is heavily rumored to have invested in this field is Peter Thiel.[5] Thiel cofounded the payment giant PayPal and several other successful startups but is perhaps best known for his litigiousness and pseudo-libertarianism. He bankrolled the former wrestler Hulk Hogan's lawsuit that bankrupted the publisher of *Gawker* in revenge for an article written about Thiel years earlier that outed him as a homosexual.[6] A self-declared libertarian and a supporter of the Libertarian Party, he migrated quickly in 2016 to feed off Donald Trump's bare-faced nationalism and xenophobia.[7] In recent times, his name has been repeatedly linked to startups offering young blood transfusions similar to those seen on TV, which has only bolstered his reputation of having something of the night about him. In short, if ever there was a powerful reason to abandon life extension research, it might be the thought of Peter Thiel living forever.

Experiments in young blood transfusions have shown early promise. In tests on mice, older subjects injected with youthful blood were found to be more active, although any experimentation in humans has been less encouraging.[8] That hasn't stopped people profiting from the practice. California-based startup Ambrosia attracts the most attention in this field. The company, founded in 2016 by CEO Jesse Karmazin, began by charging patients $8,000 for one liter of youthful plasma. Karmazin leaned heavily on the prospect of immortality to sell its services. The startup is named after the mythical food that made Greek gods immortal, and the founder said in interviews the treatment "comes pretty close" to immortality.

In February 2019, the FDA weighed in on young blood transfusions, declaring the benefits unproven and side effects potentially harmful. "We're alerting consumers and health care providers that treatments using plasma from young donors have not gone through the rigorous testing that the FDA normally requires in order to confirm the therapeutic benefit of a product and to ensure its safety," FDA Commissioner Scott Gottlieb and Peter Marks, Director of the FDA's Center for Biologics Evaluation and Research, wrote in a statement. "We're concerned that some patients are being preyed upon by unscrupulous actors touting treatments of plasma from young donors as cures and remedies."[9]

Karmazin said the FDA did not contact him directly before or after issuing the statement and didn't take any action against Ambrosia. Regardless, he put his business on hold almost immediately after the statement was issued "under an abundance of caution." In August that year, it was reported the company had shut down entirely and Karmazin had moved on to another business, Ivy Plasma.[10] The website for the new company suggested it would be offering the same services as Ambrosia, but the plasma would not be sourced specifically from younger people. Karmazin later said the Ivy Plasma website was part of an effort to rebrand, but he soon decided customers wanted to buy their blood from Ambrosia, not Ivy Plasma. By October, the old website was operational again, and Ambrosia began to offer its services once more. Despite graduating from Stanford Medical School, Karmazin is not licensed to practice medicine and can't perform the transfusions himself, so instead he contracts doctors to carry out the procedures. As of 2021, the Ambrosia website is still accepting customers, although the prices have dropped, and one liter of young blood now costs only $5,000.[11]

Young blood transfusions, despite apparently finding a consumer base in Silicon Valley, remain on the fringes of longevity offerings, and as of now can be safely considered similar to snake oil. But the technology industry's march into life extension is not limited to crazed opportunists; some of the biggest names in the world are involved. Like Google.

The founders of the search engine giant, Larry Page and Sergey Brin, announced their intention to cure death in 2013, when they created Calico. Bill Maris, the CEO of Google's venture capital arm, did the initial legwork. His father died of a brain tumor when Maris was twenty-six, an event that forced him to confront the finality of death.[12] Maris built a reputation as a shrewd investor in young technology companies that went on to be massive, like Uber and the smart thermostat startup Nest. When he made the decision to build a company that would tackle death, he consulted Ray Kurzweil, one of the most revered figures in the immortalist community. Kurzweil first popularized the concept of the technological singularity, a single moment where progress explodes and artificial intelligence surpasses that of humans, leading to us merging with computers to become superpowered immortals. He is a renowned inventor and technologist who has produced many best-selling books. In 2012, Page personally hired Kurzweil to work at Google. Kurzweil is also a registered member of Alcor and will be cryopreserved if he dies before the singularity. He predicted in the year 2000 that cryonics would figure out how to reanimate patients within forty to fifty years.[13]

Kurzweil approved of the idea, but Andy Conrad, a geneticist who led Verily, the life sciences division of Alphabet, Google's parent company, told Maris how difficult his task would be to execute. Unperturbed, Maris pitched his idea to one of Google's top investors, John Doerr, in 2011, asking the billionaire why he'd ever want to die if he was so wealthy. Of course, Doerr lapped it up and took the pitch to Google's founders, Brin and Page. The duo soon declared the plan would be executed in-house at Google.[14]

Calico, which is short for the California Life Company, launched shortly after with $1 billion in funding.[15] Anti-aging advocates, gerontologists, immortalists, and other groups grew excited at the thought of such a gigantic company entering into this field of work. "Calico added a tremendous amount of validation to aging research," George Vlasuk, the head of a biotech startup called Navitor, told *The New Yorker*. [16]

But their hopes were soon dashed when it became clear Calico intended to keep almost all of its progress completely secret. The company vacuumed up a lot of talent from labs all over the world but has released barely any details about its work.

And even for those with the inside track on what was going on, the company has turned out to be a bitter disappointment. "They have totally fucked it up. I mean, they have royally fucked it up," de Grey told me. "Basically, just by not listening to me and deciding that I was actually a bit too crazy for their taste. And they've ended up completely blowing it."

De Grey insisted it would be "an extremely unlikely accident" if Calico ever contributed anything significant to the quest to end aging, simply because of the way it's organized. He said the company is set up to conduct discovery-based research, where researchers "find things out for the sake of finding things out, the way people do in academia," and then develop the means to turn proof of concept into a product at the end. But the middle section, where concept is converted to proof of concept, is completely missing. De Grey is clearly furious at how the company turned out. "It's fucked up. It's absolutely unforgivable, and it's all Larry and Sergey's fault," he fumed.

De Grey is also angered by the secrecy. He said it was to be expected from a company requiring absolutely no outside funding, but from a humanitarian perspective, it was inefficient. "But honestly, I don't care very much because they're set up so badly in the first place that there is a low probability that anything they are discovering is of any interest anyway, so they can just carry on wasting their money, as far as I'm concerned. The main problem right now is they are by far the biggest organization by budget, and so it's extremely tragic that so much money is being poured down the drain. But they may not be the biggest for very long."

Longevity enthusiasts and immortalists didn't have to wait too long until another set of tech billionaires threw their cash behind an anti-aging startup. In September 2021, it was reported that Russian-born billionaire Yuri Milner gathered scientists at his Silicon Valley mansion to discuss biotechnology that could make people younger. That meeting led to the creation of an anti-aging company named Altos Labs, which is developing biological reprogramming technology. According to *MIT Technology Review*, Altos Labs' list of investors includes the figure immortalists had hoped would enter the fray for many years, the world's richest man: Jeff Bezos.[17] The creation of this new mega-funded startup marked the latest round of billionaires seemingly unwilling to accept anything other than an extended life. Milner, aged fifty-nine, is estimated to be worth $5.9 billion, while Bezos, fifty-seven, has a net worth of around $200 billion and counting. Time may be running out for these two men, but their bank balances will not.

De Grey believes the influx of private sector companies into the anti-aging space is the most important recent development. He told me this increase in outside funding began no more than five or six years ago, and in earnest only a couple of years ago. Before then, the anti-aging industry was still seen as something of a joke—if anyone was selling anything that claimed to reverse or slow aging, it was a scam. "It was all about products that already existed but didn't work. Now it's the opposite. It's about products that don't exist but there is enough science and enough scientific authority behind them to allow investors to believe that they probably will exist fairly soon, and that they will work."

Research by CB Insights showed the number of investment deals in longevity startups jumped from less than five in 2013 to twenty-five in 2018.[18] Since then, the figures have increased even more rapidly. In 2019, the Bank of America issued a report stating technology was on the verge of bringing "unprecedented increases in quality and length of human lifespans" and predicted the market would grow roughly sixfold to $600 billion by 2025.[19] Further research from the Aging Analytics Agency showed that the United States dominates longevity funding. A study showed 3,475 longevity companies had attracted a total of $93 billion worth of investment in the US, compared to just 113 companies receiving $17 billion in China, the country with the second highest longevity investment.[20]

One such anti-aging investor is Sergey Young, the founder of the Longevity Vision Fund, a $100 million investment vehicle launched in 2019. He has set himself the goal of extending the healthy lifespan of 1 billion people and to personally live until he's two hundred. Young is one of a new breed of investor in this space, and his first longevity fund was the largest ever. "This is crazy, for you and me $100 million is a lot of money, but in financial industry terms $100 million is really peanuts," he tells me on a video call. "So we still need to realize that longevity is heavily underinvested and usually doesn't receive as much focus as you would expect."

When I spoke to Young, he was halfway through a promotional push for his new book, *The Science and Technology of GROWING YOUNG*, in which lays out his strategy to increase the average lifespan. Like every significant effort in longevity, de Grey is involved. He was on the scientific advisory board of the Longevity Vision Fund, and Young described him as a "beautiful soul" and a "great mind." But the two don't agree on everything, particularly around the topic of immortality. Young does not consider himself an immortalist at all. "I'm not a big fan of immortality, if you take death out of the human cycle, we're not going to be humans, or we'll be different types of humans. I'm not in that game," he said.

Young also doesn't believe in cryonics. "This whole cryonics thing is from forty years ago. It was the only brave school of thought, a breakthrough idea you can have back in 1980, but the world has changed since then. So we are not interested in cryonics at all. I'm interested in billions of people to be healthy, and have access to affordable and accessible version of health care, not preserving a couple of hundred bodies and for them to wake up in two hundred years from now and commit suicide if they can."

However, he told me he still has respect for the older crowd of longevity enthusiasts, including the immortalists. "We are united by one dream, to live longer, happier, and healthier on Earth," he said.

Many factors are fueling this rise in investment, but perhaps the most significant of them is the increasingly worrying demographics of major nations. The problem, to put it simply, is boomers. The boomer generation, as of 2021, is aged between fifty-seven and seventy-five. In the United States, as that generation gets older, the number of people aged sixty-four or older is expected to almost double from fifty-two million in 2018 to ninety-five million by 2060. The percentage of the population represented by these over-sixty-fives will rise from 16 to 23 percent.[21] This will bring huge economic and social challenges. The aging of the boomer generation could mean a more than 50 percent increase in the number of Americans requiring nursing home care, from 1.2 million in 2017 to 1.9 million in 2030. And the cost of social security and Medicare is also expected to increase, from 8.7 percent of the gross domestic product to 11.8 percent by 2050.[22]

The baby boomer generation is a ticking time bomb just beginning to explode. As this group ages, it will put a huge strain on health care systems around the globe, not helped in the United States by rising obesity rates. There is expected to be a steep rise in the number of Americans suffering from Alzheimer's disease—the figures could more than double, from 5.8 million to 13.8 million by 2050.[23] With these numbers in mind, it's easy to see why the world is starting to take aging research a lot more seriously. If rejuvenation is possible, and elderly people can take preventative medicine to revert their bodies back to a younger state, the boomer generation won't be so much of a problem.

Investors do not bet on a wild hunch or a belief system, and they were partially spurred on by many of de Grey's theories being proven more correct than most scientists originally believed possible. "Back when I was first talking about rejuvenation and about damage repair as the way to go, about twenty years ago now, I had a lot of trouble getting my expert colleagues on board with it. They really didn't understand a word I was saying at first. I was bringing a lot of new ideas and concepts from areas of biology they were unfamiliar with. It took a bunch of time. But over the past ten years, that's over. Everybody gets the damage repair concept," de Grey told me.

It should be made clear the startups attracting the big bucks from Silicon Valley are not touting immortality as their product. Most of the biotech companies in the aging space are focused on healthspan, not lifespan, a much more palatable concept for people handing out millions of dollars and expecting a return. De Grey is not shy in talking up his role in anything, but even after speaking to a handful of gerontologists, it seems his summary of recent events is largely accurate. So why is he still so divisive? There's a big difference between longevity, extended healthspan, extended lifespan, and immortality. Longevity is generally an umbrella term that includes the other three. Extended healthspan refers to making people less sick for the normal amount of time they spend alive. In an ideal world, someone with an extended healthspan would still die at eighty, ninety, or one hundred, but their demise would be quick, and they would be reasonably healthy and active for a large proportion of those years. Extended lifespan refers to the number of years we spend here on Earth and could possibly lead to a long, drawn-out affair where we live a lot longer but live miserable lives. Immortality is something different altogether, but de Grey insists it is very much possible.

While biologists broadly agree on de Grey's rejuvenation theory, they have never accepted the concept he named back in 2004: longevity escape velocity. This way of thinking suggests that once we are able to obtain a twenty- or thirty-year postponement of death, the job is done. At that point, he explained, we can be "very nearly certain that we will be able to continue improving our therapies fast enough to stay one step ahead of the problem. And therefore, that is functionally equivalent to having completely solved aging and staying youthful indefinitely." This is an extremely important part of the immortalist handbook. It gives them hope that they only have to hold on a little longer. But scientists can't accept something so obviously based on faith.

"They still don't think it sounds like science. And that's okay, and that's kind of correct, because it isn't science," de Grey said. "We're not saying 'this is how we're going to do this,' which is what you could say is science. What we have instead is simply an appeal to the typical trajectory of other technologies in the past." De Grey says although it's tough to predict when the initial fundamental eureka moment will happen, once it's made, similar to Kurzweil's singularity, the refinement of that breakthrough will occur at a rapid and predictable rate.

Before I spoke to de Grey, I asked some members of the biology field what they thought about him. Most were unflattering in their responses, calling him a "crackpot" and a "crank," and some stated they didn't think de Grey believed in immortality but rather used it as a means to an end. One scientist told me he was an incredibly good salesman for the ideas he peddles and begrudgingly accepted de Grey had never personally attempted to make money out of them. I asked de Grey why some members of the scientific world spoke about him in this manner, and he gave me a typically flawless answer—one I had trouble proving, disproving, or even believing. According to de Grey, most academics rely on government funding for their research, and in this competitive field they can't do anything which would give the authorities reason to rule them out of the running. One such reason could be being seen colluding with someone like de Grey. He told me he knows most of the scientists in the field, is perfectly friendly with them, and is happy for them to distance themselves from him as much as they need, providing they are doing the right type of research to advance the cause of longevity. He's content with his position connecting money with science.

"I am the guy in the middle with the biggest network because I've been prominent for a long time. I've viewed being the nexus as a big part of what I can do over the years, which means that I can do it better and better as the years go by, and that applies to the private sector as it does within the nonprofit world. I spend my life making introductions between investors and founders, or investors and other investors, or whatever. As such, it's very gratifying for me that I'm continuing to be able to make a difference. Even though on the science side of things I can still make a contribution, but I'm not as necessary as I used to be," he said.

De Grey may find his ability to make a difference severely hindered in the future, as he was fired from his position as Chief Science Officer of SENS in August 2021. Earlier that month, two members of the longevity community accused him of sexual misconduct. Celine Halioua, now CEO of Loyal, a biotech company attempting to extend the lives of dogs, claimed de Grey pressured her at a dinner to have sex with donors. Laura Deming, the founder of one of the most prominent longevity investment vehicles, The Longevity Fund, said de Grey harassed her via email when she was as young as seventeen years old.[24]

Both women made the claims in public blog posts, and SENS hired an independent law firm to investigate the accusations. De Grey, however, was soon found to have interfered in the investigation by trying to contact one of his accusers through a third party. As a result, he was removed from his position even before the investigation was completed.[25]

When the law firm published the results of the investigation, almost all of the accusations were upheld. The report by Van Dermyden Makus Law found that de Grey did send two emails of a sexual nature to Deming, "with the purpose of developing a romantic and/or sexual relationship."[26] One of the emails read:

Heh . . . an admission for you—you probably know (it's public) that I have a fairly adventurous love life, and I'm not coy in talking about it, but I've always taken care to avoid letting conversations stray in that direction with someone so young as you, and I confess that that has always felt quite jarring given that I could treat you as an equal on every other level. Maybe those days are over . . .

At the time of receiving the messages, Deming was seventeen and eighteen years old. [27]

The report also confirmed that de Grey pressured Halioua to "use her sexuality" to solicit donations to the SENS foundation at a dinner at the University of Oxford. In a bizarre defense, de Grey attempted to claim he hadn't done this to Halioua because he'd done something similar previously and learned his lesson. However, he continuously insisted that everyone should be "using all the weapons [they] have, including weapons that are not just intellectual," in the battle against aging. Aside from damning him in the eyes of the investigators, this viewpoint also shed some light on the authenticity of his own media-friendly appearance. In an email to the unnamed person he admitted to pressuring into using their own sexuality to advance the cause, he said: "I have a mission in life, and I have no compunction whatsoever in furthering it by means that have nothing to do with my intellect, whether that be my ability to feign a reasonably aristocratic accent or my own physical attributes."[28]

De Grey admitted to sending the emails to Deming and apologized, although he denied they were sexual in nature. He also denied Halioua's claims or that he attempted to sabotage the investigation. At the time of writing, he was adamant that he would clear his name. In social media posts during and after the investigation, he refrained from placing any blame on his accusers, but his denial drew hundreds of comments of support, and resulted in angry attacks on both Deming and Halioua. [29]

De Grey is not the only big name in the immortalist community, of course. Another is the renowned geneticist David Sinclair. He boasts much more gravitas in scientific academia than de Grey, but also often throws around the word immortality. Sinclair, born in Australia, moved to the United States in 1993 when he was twenty-four to become a postdoc at the MIT lab of Leonard Guarente, who was studying aging in yeast. Aging research was still considered to be fairly niche at the time. But Sinclair was determined to change that. After three years at MIT, he made a groundbreaking discovery explaining a mechanism of aging in yeast and raised hopes the same process could be manipulated in humans. It was a turning point in Sinclair's career. He soon left MIT and set up his own lab at Harvard Medical School, where he became an assistant professor of genetics. He built on his previous work with sirtuins, a family of proteins found in all living beings. In yeast, activating these dormant proteins enhanced health and extended life.[30]

Sinclair set out to find a substance that could mimic the effects of calorie restriction in yeast and believed he'd discovered it with resveratrol, a molecule found in red wine. That breakthrough kicked Sinclair's career to another level, and suddenly wealthy investors were extremely interested in the work he was doing. In 2004, with the aid of biotech entrepreneur Christoph Westphal, Sinclair founded his first company, Sirtris Pharmaceuticals, which would attempt to create drugs based around the resveratrol molecule. His lab studies continued, and a paper published in 2006 made him the most well-known aging researcher in the world. His study showed that overweight mice fed resveratrol stayed healthier and aged more slowly than counterparts which had not been given the molecule.[31] The paper made the front page of *The New York Times*, and Sinclair was soon giving interviews all over the world. It was at this point that Sinclair's claims grew bolder and bolder. He told *Science* magazine that resveratrol was "as close to a miraculous molecule as you can find."[32]

Sinclair's respect went beyond the field of aging and into the mainstream. He became rich when Sirtris went public in 2007 and was bought one year later by the pharmaceutical giant GlaxoSmithKline for $720 million. But despite his success, many of Sinclair's peers either doubted his research or disapproved of the publicity he generated. After his initial study on resveratrol, two former colleagues at Guarente's lab published a paper saying they were unable to replicate Sinclair's results and suggested his conclusions were false. A few years after that, a pharmaceutical company named Amgen also raised questions over the same paper. In 2010, the pharma giant Pfizer released a paper stating not only was Sinclair wrong about resveratrol, his theory on sirtuins was also incorrect. Sinclair was not happy and disputed the paper.[33] But the bad news kept coming. The same year as the Pfizer paper, GlaxoSmithKline canceled a Sirtris trial in humans because of potential side effects.[34] Then, just five years after buying the company, the pharma behemoth closed down Sirtris altogether.[35]

Sinclair had overpromised, and his company never delivered a product. The Sirtris fiasco warned investors off aging companies for a while, but breakthroughs like Sinclair's were always going to bring them back. One scientist in the field of aging told me Sinclair had "oversold" his research, and his claims that immortality might be possible were motivated by his desire to sell his various products.

Despite this, Sinclair, along with the likes of de Grey, have ushered in a new era for longevity and the battle against aging, where Silicon Valley investors provide the cash and legitimate scientists the know-how. The immortalists cheer from the sidelines, many watching every move and reading every scientific paper with hawk-like vigilance.

The goals of the biotech companies, the scientists, and the majority of investors are not completely aligned with the congregation of the Church of Perpetual Life. They all want to address aging and reverse its effects, but beyond that they're building toward different futures. For now, though, the immortalists are just happy to see the progress, and they look to their heroes, like de Grey and Sinclair, for inspiration. In 2019, Sinclair released a book co-authored with journalist Matthew LaPlante. *Lifespan: Why We Age—and Why We Don't*

Have To was a *New York Times* bestseller. In it, Sinclair discusses the hallmarks of aging, a series of processes that form the core underlying mechanics of how our bodies age. "Address one of these, and you can slow down aging," the authors wrote. "Address all of them, and you might not age."

7

KNOW THYSELF

The signs of aging are obvious to most of us. Grey hair, aching joints, impairment of vision or hearing, and the dreaded week-long hangover after a night out all make it clear we are decaying at an ever-increasing rate. But while those things make us feel old, what's actually happening in our body is a series of complex, interconnected processes. Over time, scientists have gotten a grip of these procedures and put them together to form the "hallmarks of aging." To scientists, these hallmarks represent a chance to tackle the underlying cause of a great deal of disease and suffering. To immortalists, they may hold the key to a never-ending life.

The nine hallmarks, as they were called in a 2013 paper published in the journal *Cell*,[1] are not the easiest to understand. Regardless, I'll list them here: epigenetic alterations, loss of proteostasis, deregulated nutrient sensing, mitochondrial dysfunction, cellular senescence, stem cell exhaustion, altered intercellular communication, genomic insta-bility, and telomere attrition. Most of those descriptions mean abso-lutely nothing to the layperson, but they are important enough to be worthy of further exploration.

First, it's crucial to have a vague understanding of how our bodies work on a cellular level. The human genome, often spoken about but rarely understood, acts as what is commonly described as an "instruction book for the human body." The genome is made up of a long sequence of DNA strands and contains all the information needed to build and maintain a human.[2] DNA strands are wound around spools of proteins called histones, and these are quite important. Histones and DNA have chemical handles, levers, and switches attached to them which allow certain genes to be turned on and off.[3] Skin cells and brain cells are vastly different from each other but are both made up of DNA. Their differences are created by the on/off buttons for the genes. Flip a switch here, turn a handle there, and you've got a completely different cell performing an entirely new task. The handles, levers, and cranks make up the epigenome, and this is crucial for the first hallmark of aging. As we age, the epigenome changes, and some of the levers are lost, added where they're not needed, or moved around.[4] As you'd imagine, this causes havoc among cells and can even turn them cancerous.[5] Scientists discovered this hallmark by studying yeast, worms, and flies. This research found there is one particular group of proteins that influence the epigenome: sirtuins, which brought Sinclair global fame. In past trials, mice made deficient in one the seven mouse sirtuins showed signs of accelerated aging, while superabundant levels of the same sirtuin made them live longer. Interestingly, it's not just age that affects the epigenome—diet, pharmaceutical, and lifestyle factors can all change those levers.[6]

So we know genes can be turned off and on by the epigenome, which can go haywire with age, but what do the genes do? Their primary job is to provide the information to make proteins, the heart of the cell's biology that regulate almost all its chemical reactions and provide structure.[7] These proteins are folded into complex shapes like origami in order to perform their jobs. But as we age, our origami skills deteriorate; proteins are damaged, and they begin to misfold. When that happens, not only do they cease performing their jobs properly, they also clump together and become toxic. This clumping causes a host of problems, including Alzheimer's disease. When these proteins are well-balanced and behaving properly, it's called proteostasis. Cells have elaborate and complex systems designed to keep proteins in order, including specialized molecular devices that repair and refold them. Scientists established the key role proteostasis plays in aging by proving misfolded proteins increase with age and are found in the brain and muscle of Alzheimer's patients. Researchers have also managed to extend the life of mice by enhancing protein quality control through gene alteration and drugs.[8]

The inner workings of a human cell contain the secrets of further hallmarks of aging. Mitochondria, often called the powerhouses of the cell, produce energy. But they also create free radicals, known as Reactive Oxygen Species (ROS), that damage nearly every molecule they come into contact with. For a long time scientists saw mitochondria as the main culprit behind the aging process and sought ways to eliminate them from the body. But more recently the scientific consensus about this has been challenged. Studies are now suggesting that reducing ROS has little impact on health. In fact, increasing ROS may be beneficial. The latest thinking suggests that ROS send signals to the body warning that cells are under stress, and this could kick regenerative functions into gear; perhaps ROS production needs to be kept in a "Goldilocks" range—not too much, not too little.[9]

The average human cell contains the string of three billion DNA letters that make up the genome. If the genome is faulty for whatever reason, your body may not run so smoothly. Past research has estimated that the DNA in each cell is damaged up to one million times per day by external factors like radiation or pollution and internal sources like oxygen-free radicals. And while our DNA does have processes in place to detect and repair that damage, as we age the repairs become increasingly imperfect, and problems with the genome begin to build up, which eventually can cause cancer. In both humans and mice, compromised DNA repair has been linked with accelerated aging.

The fifth hallmark of aging refers to a set of very basic rules that govern all animals. When nutrients are in abundance, animals—including humans—grow and reproduce. When the supply of nutrients becomes limited, evolution has taught our bodies to focus on maintenance and repair. Studies suggest if we were able to trick the body into thinking nutrients were scarce—with drugs like rapamycin, or simply starving ourselves—the body's cells would focus on regeneration and potentially slow the aging process. This has been partially proven in mice and other species, and is one of the most important hallmarks for immortalists looking for ways to increase their lifespan. Neal VanDeRee's intermittent fasting is an attempt to tap into this.

The next hallmark involves a controversial topic covered in more detail in a later chapter: stem cells. Our bodies have a powerful ability to regenerate and heal themselves, and that process is almost completely reliant on our stem cells, the source of new cells in virtually every tissue in the human body. When stem cells are needed, they replicate, but that ability to divide declines with age, meaning we can lose our regenerative powers as we get older.

So far, each hallmark has focused on the processes that lead to the disrepair of our cells. But communication between the cells and tissue is also a crucial factor in maintaining health as we age. Communication occurs through a number of methods, including through hormones, but can be blocked by inflammation in the body. When we're still young, inflammation is usually a response to an injury and eases as the body heals. But as we age, a low level of constant inflammation can appear, unrelated to injuries. This type of inflammation isn't just uncomfortable and potentially debilitating, it's also damaging to the surrounding tissue. One way of easing chronic age-related inflammation could be to improve communication between the cells. The young blood transfusions which have made Silicon Valley look so weird are often touted as one potential solution to the inflammation problem.

Telomeres are often brought up by immortalists and longevity advocates as one of the secrets to extending life. They have three main uses that we know of. At the end of each strand of DNA, telomeres act as a protective cap. In the past they've been compared to aglets, the plastic tips at the end of shoelaces that stop them getting frayed. They also help organize each of the forty-six chromosomes within the nucleus, the control center of cells. Finally, they allow the chromosome to be replicated correctly during cell division. Every time a cell divides, telomeres become shorter, and eventually when they become too short the cell takes action. This usually triggers the cell to die but can sometimes make them dangerous. Research in mice has shown that when the telomerase enzyme is reduced, the mice show signs of premature aging, and when their telomeres are given a boost, their lifespan is extended. However, the role of telomeres in human aging is still unclear. Some believe the length of telomeres is a good predictor of lifespan, but others think it is responsible for the signs of aging, like greying hair, rather than the aging itself.

The final hallmark of aging concerns the mortality of the cells themselves. When they reach the point where they can no longer replicate, they are considered senescent cells. Instead of dying or disappearing, the cells hang around secreting molecules into their surrounding area. As we age, these senescent cells accumulate. For a long time, it was debated among the scientific community whether senescent cells made us age faster or if they were some kind of protection against the development of cancer. More recently, research in genetically engineered mice showed that if senescent cells were removed, there were clear health benefits, including longer life.

The hallmarks of aging have become something of a constant in aging research. But some major players in the field don't see them as complete. Steven Austad is a senior scientific director at the American Federation for Aging Research, a co-director at the University of Alabama's Nathan Shock Center of Excellence in the Basic Biology of Aging, and a Distinguished Professor in the Department of Biology— all of which suggest he knows a thing or two about aging. He told me there is nothing new or novel about the hallmarks, but they do act as a benchmark against which to compare new research, even if they may not be complete. "I know of at least three different people now who are writing about updating those. But I think, in terms of summarizing what we know about what goes wrong with aging, they're okay. They're a little bit redundant, they overlap. Some of them are processes, some of them are things. But it's reached a point in the field where everybody has to nod to the hallmarks before they do much else," Austad said on a call.

Like this book, Austad's journey into aging featured an early encounter with an opossum. He initially trained in evolutionary ecology and was conducting field research with the animals when he came upon a curious discovery—they age incredibly rapidly. By the time an opossum reaches nineteen months to two years old, it is already approaching the end of its life, assuming it hasn't been flattened by a car in a sad Florida suburb. This short lifespan is tiny in comparison to that of a house cat, which is a similar size but lives much longer. The plight of the opossum encouraged Austad to study aging. He was particularly interested in the evolutionary question of why we age, but he never thought his chosen field of study would attract the attention of those who believe they can be immortal. "I was probably in the field for ten or fifteen years before it ever occurred to me that humans would have interest in this because they wanted to live longer," he said.

Austad is upbeat about the progress made in the field of aging. In 2000 he was quoted in a *Scientific American* article saying the first 150-year-old person "is probably alive right now." A fellow expert on aging, Jay Olshansky, disagreed, and the two made a wager. In September that year, they put $150 each into an investment contract and agreed that the money and any returns would be paid out to the winner or his descendants in 2150. Austad will win the bet if a human has lived until 150 and maintained their mental functions when they reached that milestone.[10] The venture received national attention, and Austad was even contacted by a man who had seen the news and wanted to make a wager of his own with the expert—that he would live longer than Jeanne Calment, the oldest documented human, who died at age 122. Austad said he was tempted to take the money but realized he didn't want to be rooting for someone to die. Incidents like this, however, made him appreciate the passion of those who believe in immortality.

Now, like other researchers in his field, Austad fights a strange battle. He sees there is genuine promise in the science aiming to address the nine hallmarks, and remarkable progress is being made at a breakneck speed right now, but there's still a concerning pattern of people taking any small breakthrough and describing it as the secret to eternal life. "I think there's some real promise. Not for living forever, of course, not for immortality. But for prolonging health I think there's some real promise in the area, but people have taken it to ridiculous extremes," he told me. "You're constantly fighting this rearguard action against this type of claim, while at the same time trying to point out that there is legitimate research with legitimate promise. And just by debunking these extreme claims doesn't mean you're debunking the whole idea that you can improve health and extend health. It's a balancing act."

One of the more promising areas of research has come from the final hallmark listed above, the senescence of cells. Senolytics was one of the first scientific areas to attract attention—and dollars—from technology investors. Over time, evidence accrued that senescent cells, the cells which have ceased to divide and then hang around causing mischief, are a key factor in the aging process and a potential cause for some of the deadliest diseases linked with aging. They are also known, however, to form some kind of protection against tumors forming in the body. Now, a race has begun to develop drugs capable of eliminating either the right type or the correct amount of senescent cells in order to prevent certain diseases or reduce the impact of aging, potentially lengthening the lifespan of humans in the process. A number of scientists have made significant progress in the area of senescence, none more so than Dr. Judith Campisi.

Campisi took an unconventional route to the aging industry. After attending an all-girls Catholic high school in New York City, she had no idea what to do next. Nobody in her family attended college and money was tight, but she enrolled in a local college despite not knowing what to study. Each of the course descriptions in the college paraphernalia showed the percentage of males and females in each class. Campisi chose chemistry, one of the classes with the most boys. She later said although she knew she was good at the subject, her main motivation was "teenage hormones." At the end of her two-year program, she went through several jobs in several fields, including pharmaceuticals, working as an editorial assistant at a small newspaper, and pumping gas. None of them stuck, so she took an extended road trip with a friend. Around that time, she decided to go back to school to pursue chemistry further. Campisi completed a four-year degree first, then went straight to graduate school, and later earned a PhD from the State University of New York at Stony Brook. This was followed by a postdoctoral fellowship at the Dana-Farber Cancer Institute in Boston, where she worked in the lab of Arthur Pardee, a renowned expert on the cell cycle.

Campisi jumped headlong into cancer research, a field she knew little about. When she secured her first faculty position in 1984 at Boston University Medical School, she took the advice of her mentor Pardee and picked a project well away from the mainstream. Oncogenes had recently been discovered as a key driving factor behind cancer, and everyone was rushing to start research into the topic. But with a small lab and a crowded field, Campisi decided to study why we don't get cancer, or tumor suppression. She believed this path would be less competitive and allow her to make more of an impact in the science community, a belief that was proven correct. The study of tumor suppression also led her to the field of aging.[11]

Many of the diseases caused by aging, such as heart disease, kidney failure, and neurodegeneration, all involve the gradual degradation of the body, where age takes hold and organs begin to fail over time. But there is one disease that doesn't follow that pattern. Cancer involves extreme mutation of the cells brought on by damage to the DNA. Once a cell is cancerous, it can mutate in hundreds of different ways to avoid the body's processes that would either repair it or force it to die permanently. As one of the ways to guard against cancer, the body shuts down cells which have ceased to divide and are open to damage—the senescent cells mentioned in the hallmarks of aging.

Researchers initially believed these senescent cells were crucial in the body's fight to suppress tumors, but Campisi discovered they were also damaging the tissue around them, contributing to aging. In 1996–1997, two editors from *Cell* and the *Journal of the American Geriatrics Society* asked her to write papers on this theory of aging. It took five years to prove how the theory works in a mouse. Campisi's study appeared in the Proceedings of the National Academy of Sciences of the United States of America, and in 2008, her team described the secretion, called SASP—the Senescence-Associated Secretory Phenotype—in *PloS Biology*. That later paper became one of the most cited in biomedical research.[12]

From there, a whole new area of biotechnology was born, where companies raced to create the first drug to selectively eliminate senescent cells. "I'm very optimistic about senolytic drugs," Campisi told me on a call. "There are still big gaps in our knowledge, big, big gaps in our knowledge, but I think they are on the horizon, they're being developed, and they will be used. But these are not immortality drugs."

When her research shifted into aging, she began to notice the frenzy around any related studies, and the tendency of some groups to link everything to immortality. When I spoke to Campisi about her experience with immortality-seekers, she was patient, informative, and utterly exhausted by people claiming we can live forever. "When Larry Page first started Calico, he declared that the mission of Calico was to defeat death. I said, 'What?' As long as I've been working in aging, not so much senescence but *aging*, I realized that there are first of all people who confuse aging and death, and secondly there are people who really believe that physical immortality is real and a possibility," Campisi said.

The confusion between the study of aging and the halting of death has been going on for decades, according to Campisi. The idea of cells dividing indefinitely and organismal immortality stretches back to early in the twentieth century, when French biologist Alexis Carrel, a transplantation surgeon who won a Nobel Prize for his work in that area, announced a discovery from his work with in-culture chick embryos. He noticed the cells appeared to divide indefinitely when in this state, and he wrote a paper proposing that organismal mortality was linked with multicellularity. He thought if we could understand why the chick embryo cells divide indefinitely, we might discover why organisms are mortal.[13] "If you think about it, what was this guy thinking about?" asked Campisi. "If you dump hydrochloric acid on these cells, I guarantee you they're going to die. And so it was this confusion between replicative capacity and organismal mortality."

And the confusion didn't stop there. Leonard Hayflick, an American anatomist, faced an uphill battle to convince the world Carrel was wrong. In 1962 at the Wistar Institute in Philadelphia, Pennsylvania, Hayflick demonstrated that a regular human fetal cell population divides between forty and sixty times before entering a senescent state, directly contradicting Carrel's assertion that cells are immortal.[14] Hayflick also noticed the same did not apply to cancer cells, which did seem to multiply forever if left unchecked. He was the first person to suggest that senescent cells were perhaps associated with anti-cancer measures, and he turned out to be correct. He also linked that mechanism with aging—"based on nothing," according to Campisi—and again was found to be right.

Campisi is quick to urge caution with senolytics and says the drugs still have a long way to go. A lot of research right now is focused on how to make them more selective, and there has been promising research with mice. "We made a transgenic mouse in which we can eliminate senescent cells at any point in the lifespan. Then you cross those mice to disease prone mice, and you can show that eliminating senescent cells either delays the onset or lessens the symptoms or in a few cases even reverses a surprisingly large number of age-related pathologies. But the mice still die, and they still die pretty much on time," Campisi explained.

By altering the genes of these mice, Campisi's lab has mimicked what senolytic drugs are expected to do—to kill senescent cells at any point in the lifespan of a human. But killing the cells isn't the only way to attack the problem. Senescent cells drive so many age-related diseases not because they simply exist, but because of their secretion of molecules. This secretion finds its way into the tissue and causes low-level chronic inflammation. Senomorphic drugs have the potential to halt this secretion, and are encouragingly made of natural compounds. This gives scientists like Campisi the hope that the issue can ultimately be addressed with supplements and dietary intervention rather than the Big Pharma–produced senolytic drugs.

Campisi's work has led to the private sector startups de Grey puts so much faith in. She cofounded Unity Biotechnology in 2011 with the specific aim of developing senolytic drugs. The company immediately attracted investors from Silicon Valley's wealthiest, raising over $200 million from the likes of Bezos, Thiel, and notable venture capitalists.[15] Unity went public in 2018, raising $85 million through its Nasdaq listing at a market capitalization of $700 million.[16] But in August 2020, the company's shares dropped 60 percent. A clinical trial involving the lead drug candidate, intended for patients with osteoarthritis, produced disappointing results. Unity also cut 30 percent of its employees.[17]

Campisi added two major caveats to the progress of her research. The first was that no matter what, it remained highly unlikely any of the results would drastically extend the human lifespan. She believes humans have a maximum lifespan of around 115, give or take ten years, although she's prepared to be proved wrong. "Now, does that mean ten years from now or one hundred years from now we won't find a way to break through that barrier? I can't say no forever. We're not soothsayers," she said. "But based on our current knowledge, it's extremely unlikely. I usually follow this up and say even though I consider myself a good scientist—I never say never and never say always—I can guarantee one thing: you will die one day."

Campisi's area of expertise inevitably brought her into the same orbit as de Grey. The SENS Foundation funded some of Campisi's work at the Buck Institute. She has known him for years and sits on the SENS Research Advisory Board.[18] She told me de Grey wears two hats—one for the public and investors, where he makes outlandish claims about living for thousands of years, and the other for the scientists he supports. "When I talk to Aubrey about that work, he's rational. He doesn't know as much, he's not a trained scientist . . . but he's quite rational," she said. "He puts these hats on depending upon his audience. What does he really believe? I don't know, I've never gotten him drunk enough."

Despite Campisi's pleas, immortalists still see senolytics as one of the most promising areas of research that could address one of the major hallmarks of aging. But it's still hard to stop death if you can't see it coming. If immortalists are to reach escape velocity and live forever, they need to have a good understanding of their current health and how many years they might have left. Knowing your chronological age is really helpful for throwing birthday parties and applying for a passport, but in the world of the immortalists, only your biological age matters.

Theoretically, an accurate biological age would tell you roughly how much longer you will survive, or at least how many good years you might have left. Unnatural deaths can't be foreseen, of course, but most people who live comfortably will die of old age, even if that's not what is written on their death certificate. Prior to the COVID-19 pandemic, around one in four deaths in the United States were due to heart disease; that's 659,041 people in 2019.[19] Cancer was just as lethal, accounting for 599,601 deaths the same year.[20] But research as far back as 1990 suggests that even if we were to cure cancer, heart disease, and diabetes, only a handful of years would be added to the lifespan of the average American's life.[21] When a person's body ages to a certain point, the general decay makes ideal circumstances for these kinds of diseases to emerge, so even if cancer were beaten, the problem of aging remains. Put more simply, when your body reaches a certain biological age, it's just a matter of *what's* going to kill you, not *if* something is going to kill you.

Forecasting that point of no return is difficult. Through the study of epigenetics—the small indicators of aging on the cellular level—scientists have developed a clock which can supposedly tell a person's biological age. The epigenetic clock takes data from the epigenome to predict how far along your body is in the aging process. The first such clock was developed in 2011 by Steve Horvath, a biostatistician at the University of California, Los Angeles, after he analyzed hundreds of epigenetic markers.[22] The process involved measuring the specific patterns which are linked to aging and disease and comparing the results against what would be expected for a person of the same age as the participant. At the end, a person is told whether they are aging faster or slower than expected, and by roughly how many years.

Horvath initially had a tough time getting his results published amid skepticism over his claims.[23] But once the science was widely recognized, a handful of companies began selling kits and services based on Horvath's clock. Customers typically pay around $500 to send saliva or blood to a lab and receive results explaining how old their body is.

This may seem like a vital tool for an immortalist looking to reach escape velocity, but some doubts remain. Although the kits are based on the same science as Horvath's, they are completely unregulated by the FDA and aren't independently evaluated. The tests are not accurate predictions of how long someone will live, and anyone paying for them would surely know that. For one thing, we don't know what kind of accident or illness is ready to jump out on us, and secondly, the technology is not that accurate. So it's not immediately clear what an immortalist would gain from the average epigenetic clock. Unlike genetic testing, the results don't tell a person what their chances of developing a certain disease is. All they are told is how much older or younger their bodies are than other people their age.

Even if a person is older than expected, the solution almost all of the time is to eat healthier, sleep better, and exercise. It doesn't take $500 to realize that will help everyone, regardless of their biological age. Epigenetic clocks are not just a potentially massive waste of money, there are other more nefarious and dystopian uses of them that would impact society. Some of these clockmakers have attempted to sell them to insurance firms, offering them the means to roughly gauge how old their customers' bodies are before deciding on their premium costs. They also represent an opportunity for mass data collection, and employers could even use them to ensure prospective new employees were suitably healthy to become an effective long-term hire.[24]

Some experts have raised significant doubts over the validity of the epigenetic clock concept. Leonard Schalkwyk, Professor of Human Genetics at the University of Essex in England, and Jonathan Mill, Professor of Epigenetics at the University of Exeter, wrote an article in 2020[25] comparing data gleaned from epigenetic clock models against their own DNA methylation results. They found that epigenetic age doesn't move at a steady pace and performs differently depending on which tissue is examined.

They argued that our epigenetic aging slows as we get older, particularly as we enter old age. "Ultimately, our work shows that researchers need to be careful when using the epigenetic clock to estimate how old people are. Age acceleration really does appear to be age dependent, and care should be taken when interpreting any age acceleration associations," the pair wrote. "The epigenetic clock is a useful tool for researchers, but given the limited nature of the DNA methylation profile that the clock is based on, taking it at face value could lead to misleading results."[26]

Austad was also dismissive of any test that claims to tell someone their biological age. "There are many ways that people are saying they can do this. Some of them are frankly bogus, and some of them have some promise. But there is an assumption underlying all of this, not very well validated, which is that *you* have a biological age, rather than your heart has a biological age and your kidney may have another biological age and your brain may have another biological age. So there's some interesting work going on in that area, but I don't think I would say anyone should take these biological age metrics on a personal level all that seriously," he said.

Epigenetic clocks are just one method claiming to determine the speed of a person's aging process. A number of companies offer blood work and testing which list biomarkers—most of which are linked to the nine hallmarks of aging—so customers can plot their best approach to slowing or even reversing aging. Among those offering this service is the Life Extension Foundation, a company run by Bill Faloon, one of the founders of the Church of Perpetual Life. On the company's website, one of the main sections is Lab Testing, where well over one hundred different types of tests are listed.

"Are You Healthy? These Tests Reveal the Truth," reads the banner across the top of the page. Rudi Hoffman, the cryonics insurance salesman, is one of their customers. On one of the days I called him, he had just completed one of his blood tests, where he sends off a vial of blood and gets back five or six pages of biomarkers. He is then able to call the Life Extension Foundation and have a health consultant go through the results with him to explain where he's going wrong and what he needs to do to stay healthy for longer. Fortunately, the solution to any of the deficiencies found in the test are located on the very same website—in the hundreds of vitamins and supplements on sale there.

It's a familiar story. The private sector moved in on the telomere craze in the mid-2010s, offering tests to those seeking to understand the length of the protective caps on the end of their DNA strands. Telomere Diagnostics, a company founded in Menlo Park, California, began offering $89 tests to determine the length of telomeres in 2016. Customers mailed in a drop of blood and received a calculation of their age in "TeloYears," which worked in much the same way as epigenetic tests. For a little extra, users could also sign up to receive advice from an expert on improving diet, sleep, and stress levels in the hopes their telomeres would lengthen. But experts in the telomere field were far from convinced.

Mary Armanios, MD, of the Telomere Center in the McKusick-Nathans Institute of Genetic Medicine at Johns Hopkins University School of Medicine wrote a paper in 2018 titled "Telomeres in the Clinic, Not on the TV" which cast severe doubt on the legitimacy of the tests offered by private companies.[27] She argued the products present an oversimplified view of telomere length health by saying short telomeres are bad and long telomeres are a sign of youthfulness. Armanios called into question the quality of the testing, saying the assays used to measure telomere length in direct-to-consumer tests have been found to be "highly variable" and wanting when it came to "reproducibility and robustness." She also pointed to problems with interpretation, as many of the private company tests only consider the median value as normal, which means anything even slightly shorter than that is considered an aged telomere level, and anything longer is youthful. Telomere length in the human population is more nuanced than this, Armanios argues. "The direct-to-consumer telomere testing thus risks causing unnecessary anxiety, with some believing they are 'biologically aged' and further leading them to pursue untested products," her paper stated.

As if this weren't bad enough, the tests and their interpretation do not consider the growing body of evidence suggesting long telomere length is not linked to youthfulness, but to a risk of several forms of cancers. The conclusion of the paper is damning: "Recognizing the clinical indications in which telomere length testing matters for patient care decisions exemplifies molecular medicine at its best. Distinguishing these indications from commercial testing is critical. While the former may be lifesaving, the latter may be considered a form of molecular palm reading." (Telomere Diagnostics switched its entire focus when the pandemic hit and abandoned its TeloYears products, instead using its laboratories to offer coronavirus testing.)

Despite pushback from the scientific community, new devices and tests constantly appear. The AgeMeter is a nonintrusive method of tracking physiological biomarkers for aging. It looks a little like a chunky iPad and tests for numerous signs that a person is getting older, like memory, reaction time, hearing, agility, decision speed, and lung function. The device is mostly marketed to health care providers, but is available for individuals to buy at the modest price of $2,500. The AgeMeter website features a testimonial from noted geneticist George Church and a fairly vague quote from David Sinclair explaining the need for such a device. It is far more straightforward than epigenetic clock offerings, but it's easy to see how it appeals to the neurosis of those concerned with aging.

As de Grey told me in the previous chapter, the earlier products offering immortality were easily identifiable as fakes, but those on the fringes of life extension are more ambiguous. It's a trend seen in this area of science in general, according to Austad. He told me that twenty years ago there was a very sharp distinction between what was completely bogus and what was genuine, but now that line has blurred. "I have people all the time asking me who can I get to prescribe for me some drug that they read about in the press," he said. "It puts me in an awkward position because I don't want to say there's no science behind that. But I can say there's no science that suggests that humans are ready to try these things yet."

Try telling an immortalist that.

8

DIY IMMORTALITY

The Church of Perpetual Life's cryonics symposium brought together the biggest names in the cryopreservation business, but that was only a sliver of the entire immortalist community. To see the whole crowd on display, I attended the immortalist version of Coachella—RAADfest. For those seeking to add years to their lifespan, the event is an essential date in the diary, when they can catch up on the latest biological research, find inspiration from motivational anti-aging speakers, and spend their hard-earned dollars on the next key tool to halt death.

Previous iterations of the annual event have been held in Las Vegas and San Diego, but in 2020 COVID-19 forced the three-day conference online for the first time, as the pandemic sent the immortalist community into isolation, justly worried the deadly virus would end their hopes of living forever. Even so, the speaker list featured some of the biggest names in the business, including de Grey and the founder of the Church of Perpetual Life, Bill Faloon.[1] As I perused the daily schedule, some of the topics up for discussion immediately caught my attention. The United States Transhumanist Party was giving an update on its progress, there was a talk on how to control aging in pets, and (perhaps most mind-blowing, given the immortalist crowd appeared to be made up mostly of the elderly) another presentation with advice on how to reverse sexual aging. From the very first minute of the event, it did not disappoint.

Before the conference got going, I became engrossed in the live chat running alongside the video stream. The virtual attendees began talking among themselves quite cordially, telling each other where they were tuning in from—and it was truly a global audience. But as the scheduled start time came and went, the digital crowd grew increasingly unruly and irritable, getting angry with the organizers. After what I felt was a very short delay, the event began. The day opened with a singer named Audrey Archer, who performed a song inspired by the fight for immortality. Although not exactly to my taste, it went down well with those in the live chat, and some of the lyrics gave me a handy preview for what was to come. "They can say it all sounds crazy, they can say we've lost our minds. I don't care if they call us crazy. We can live in a world that we designed," Archer sang, to much cooing in the live chat.

When the entertainment was done, the founders of RAADfest took to the stage—two characters we have already met, Bernadeane Brown and James Strole, the brains behind People Unlimited. While People Unlimited did not formally organize the event, it was produced by another of Strole and Bernadeane's ventures, the Coalition for Radical Life Extension, which seeks to bring together ideas from across the life extension spectrum, from cryonicists to mind uploaders to pill-popping hippies.

At RAADfest, Strole and Bernadeane ruled over their host of digital acolytes with beaming smiles and inspirational speeches. When they first appeared on screen, the chat descended into fawning comments about how young they looked, and it was clear both of them had made considerable effort with their appearances. Bernadeane, the older of the pair at around eighty years old, wore tight black jeans, a white shirt with a black blazer, and a black tie draped loosely around her neck. She sported a metallic bob haircut and wore heavy dark eyeshadow. Strole, much taller, wore a sharp suit and tie and boasted a full head of shocking white hair. I found myself agreeing with the other attendees—neither looked their age.

Strole was calm and measured, speaking in silk-tongued motivational quips. "Don't make yourself incidental in this movement. We're going for a mass movement that changes the tide of death in the world," he told the virtual audience. Bernadeane was less restrained and much more militant in her remarks, which were clearly not rehearsed. "We're making it possible to really have the right to live free of death," she told viewers.

When the two founders finished pumping up the crowd, the microphone moved to the event's emcee, Joe Bardin, the communications director of both RAADfest and People Unlimited. He was a polished and charismatic host, and when I spoke to him after the event, it was clear he was an effective advocate for the cause. Many years ago, he heard Bernadeane and Strole speak, and although he didn't embrace the idea of immortality initially, a girl he had a crush on did, so he went back. "That kept me coming back a few times until I could kind of get my mind engaged. Personally, I just didn't really understand. I hadn't really put it all together, but [now] I don't know if this will make sense, but for me, the repetition of mortality, it's just crushing," he told me.

Bardin believes that people should consider their lives eternal already, rather than wait for a technology to save them in the future. When I mentioned the different types of immortalists and life extension enthusiasts I'd already met, he told me those wanting extremely long lives but not immortality were kidding themselves:

"I think Ray Kurzweil famously said, you're not going to get to [when] you're eighty or ninety or ninety-five or one hundred and five and suddenly feel like you don't want to live longer. And Jim Strole thinks the whole thing's ridiculous. He says if you get to two hundred and you're feeling good, first of all, you'll have done something amazing and you'll have surpassed all the social norms and you're feeling good. You're not going to want to stop.

I'm an immortalist, but I think in the long run, anybody who's really into longevity, it's all going to just blend together, and even wellness. Right now, wellness is just a totally different cohort of people, and that's why we can't market to them. It's a waste of our money, what little money we have for marketing. But the reality is if you're sixty or seventy and you're into wellness, what's the difference? There is no difference."

Bardin has been involved in RAADfest from the beginning. He said the initial idea was to create a platform which wasn't just for scientists, entrepreneurs, or "the PhD crowd," but to make the information accessible for a general audience as well. The organizers gather the most important personalities in the world of life extension and some years the event is devoted to a specific theme. For example, stem cells were big at the 2019 conference, Bardin told me, and previous years focused more on supplements or particular drugs.

The first major speaker was a man who would probably prompt arguments on any other stage but this one: Dave Asprey. The man behind Bulletproof Coffee has attained semi-priesthood status among his followers. He is wealthy, intelligent, and successful. And over the course of his thirty-minute presentation, I became worried some of his claims were not just false but, frankly, dangerous.

Asprey describes himself as a biohacker and is perhaps the most well-known among that growing cohort of transhumanists. Biohacking refers to people doing whatever they must, usually with technology, to get the most out of their bodies. This could be something simple, like exercising more often, taking a cold shower in the morning, or meditating. But the practice extends all the way to taking brain-boosting drugs, trying out experimental medical procedures, and having pieces of technology installed under their skin. The ultimate goal of biohackers is to either drastically extend their lifespan, become super-intelligent, or both.

The Hollywood movie *Limitless*, which starred Bradley Cooper as a man who takes a drug that makes him incredibly smart and productive, is a bible to most biohackers, some of whom believe the film could become reality. Asprey hasn't just tapped into this market, he's placed himself right in the center, from where he influences trends, attends events like RAADfest, and of course peddles his own range of biohacking products.

Throughout his talk, he gave the occasional disclaimer that he is not a qualified professional in the fields he was lecturing in, yet he handed out advice as if he were anyway. His first presentation of the day (he gave more than one) discussed boosting the immune system, and inevitably COVID-19 cropped up quickly. Asprey impressed the importance of exposing the immune system to regular challenges and predicted that the need for "super immunity" will soon rise exponentially. Some attendees in the chat took this to mean they shouldn't be wearing masks in a pandemic, and a brief but fiery debate erupted over the need to wear personal protection when an airborne virus is circulating. The libertarian side of immortalism was on full display, but Rudi Hoffman, the self-styled recovering libertarian who had a talk later in the event, waded into the chat to shut the anti-mask talk down.

Asprey, who spoke at an incredible speed, moved on to an herb called andrographis. He claimed it worked on COVID-19, something that turned out to be not entirely ridiculous. Studies have suggested the natural remedy may ease some of the symptoms which arise after infection by the virus,[2] and Thailand approved its use in treating patients.[3] But the evidence, and use of andrographis, never became widespread, and scientists have stated herbal remedies lack the necessary clout to treat coronaviruses.[4]

But it was Asprey's next suggestion that concerned me.

He told the audience to look into ozone therapy, and rectally administered ozone therapy in particular. Ozone refers to the same part of our atmosphere that protects the Earth from the sun's radiation. It is harmful to breathe, but some reports have suggested it can help treat diseases like cancer, arthritis, HIV, SARS, some heart diseases and can activate the immune system. However, the FDA disagrees vehemently. In 2019, the agency released a statement warning against the use of ozone as a medical therapy. It said ozone is a toxic gas and has no known useful application in either supportive or preventative medicine.[5] So, just to recap: Asprey told a conference of attendees hanging on his every word to take a toxic gas and literally blow it up their own asses.[6]

I asked myself what motivates someone to suggest a thing like that, or give one of these talks at all. The answer, of course, is money, mixed with status. Asprey is an incredibly successful entrepreneur, mostly due to his Bulletproof Coffee product. Earlier in his life, he enjoyed a prosperous career as an IT executive in Silicon Valley, but success came at a cost. He became overweight, reaching three hundred pounds at his heaviest, and fell ill as a result. In 2004—a satirist could not have invented this—he traveled to Tibet to learn how to meditate and improve his well-being. While trekking in the Himalayas he was offered a cup of tea infused with yak butter, and later he said the drink made his brain feel better than it had in a long time, despite the high altitude. Asprey was so affected by this yak milk–flavored tea he attempted to make his own version when he returned to California. He switched yak milk for grass-fed cows, as yaks were hard to come by in the Golden State. He also abandoned tea and went for coffee instead, and added a purified form of coconut oil. In 2009 he shared his discovery in a blog post, and three years after that began selling his Bulletproof Coffee online.

Customers have to buy the drink in three parts—the coffee, the butter, and the oil. Asprey used his venture capital connections to secure a meeting with Trinity Ventures and asked them for $50,000 in funding to buy more coffee supplies. They gave him $9 million instead.[7] Gradually, the coffee's popularity grew, and it blew up when Whole Foods, the grocery store chain, agreed to stock all three parts of the product. Bulletproof Coffee steadily gained celebrity fans and a cult following. Now, the Seattle-based Bulletproof 360 company has attracted more than $68 million in investment and has expanded into selling other food and lifestyle products, including t-shirts, books, and protein bars.[8]

Asprey's story reads directly from the privilege playbook, a true hero's tale in Silicon Valley's age of excess. The rich white man, unhappy that his overindulgence from a well-paying job left him unhealthy, traveled to an exotic location (somewhere with fewer white people) to find spiritual enlightenment and a new way of living. But he didn't find a charitable outlook or a zen-like philosophical balance, he found a new product to sell and a ticket to multimillionaire status. At that point, Asprey felt comfortable enough to declare himself an expert on all things nutrition and began lecturing the world on how to eat, drink, exercise, and live their lives.

He didn't stop at selling people the coffee; Asprey devised a whole diet to go with the drink. The regimen involves eating foods high in fat, low in carbohydrates, and moderate amounts of protein, all of which was underpinned by Bulletproof Coffee. The plan also recommends intermittent fasting, the type of dieting VanDeRee was also using and something which will be covered in more detail later in this chapter. Not all nutritionists and dietary experts are convinced. Aisling Pigott, a spokesperson for the British Dietetic Association, was highly critical of the diet in an interview with the BBC in 2019. "Bulletproof Coffee is not something I'd ever recommend, because it's introducing extra calories and extra fat in a way that isn't providing any other nutritional value," she said. "There is no benefit to adding butter to your coffee. With a Bulletproof Coffee–based breakfast you're missing out on what you're getting from a food-based breakfast—there is no protein, vitamins, or minerals."[9]

Julia Belluz, a senior health writer for *Vox*, went even further. "The Bulletproof Diet is like a caricature of a bad fad-diet book. If you took everything that's wrong with eating in America, put it in a Vitamix, and shaped the result into a book, you'd get *The Bulletproof Diet*. The book is filled with dubious claims based on little evidence or cherry-picked studies that are taken out of context. The author, Dave Asprey, vilifies healthy foods and suggests part of the way to achieve a 'pound a day' weight loss is to buy his expensive, 'science-based' Bulletproof products," she wrote.[10]

Belluz found a lot of the research Asprey quoted to back up his claims was based on tests done on rats and mice, and not humans. In 2014, the British newspaper, *The Daily Telegraph* scrutinized Asprey's citations for the book and found them to be either seriously dated or completely unreliable. "The one about cereal grains, for example, begins with a quote from the Bible and is written by a man called Loren Cordain, otherwise known as the author of *The Paleo Diet*, a health plan that involves eating only foods that were available to humans during the Paleolithic (or caveman) era, and has been widely discredited. Another paper—'Switching from refined grains to whole grains causes zinc deficiency'—is a report of a 1976 research project featuring a study group of just two people. A third study—'Diets high in grain fiber deplete vitamin D stores'—is a 30 year-old study of 13 people. A fourth— 'Phytic acid from whole grains block zinc and other minerals'—is based on a 1971 study of people in rural Iran eating unleavened flatbread. Another is about insulin sensitivity in domestic pigs," the article read.[11]

So how did Asprey's views on health, become so popular? *The Bulletproof Diet* follows a very successful template, an easy way to capture the attention of people desperate for some kind of personal epiphany. It makes readers believe they've stumbled on a well-hidden secret that will put them ahead of the crowd, of their friends, and of their enemies, and comforts them with the belief that everything they've done in their lives up to that point is completely wrong. That narrative allows people to go all in on the diet, believing it to be everything they've ever wished for, a surefire miracle cure to make their bodies fitter and healthier. It's a thought process that underpins the entire biohacking movement, and at the heart of it is Asprey, the self-proclaimed original professional biohacker.

Intermittent fasting forms another crucial part of Asprey's regime, and he talks about it regularly, either through his blog or at events. Unlike ozone gasses up the rectum, fasting does have some scientific basis to back it up. The trend is a type of caloric restriction, where a person goes without eating for an extended period of time. Fasting has played a major part in religions for centuries, although it was never done to reap health benefits. In recent years some studies have suggested the practice could extend the human lifespan: caloric restriction has been shown to cause weight loss and prolong healthy life in a variety of species, including worms and nonhuman primates.[12] However, the side effects can be difficult to overcome, and can include fatigue, muscle wasting, and loss of libido.

These challenges were tackled by many, including Valter Longo, of the University of Southern California (USC) Longevity Institute, a pioneer in what he called fasting-mimicking diets. In a 2008 study, Longo found that fasting for two days protected healthy cells against the damaging effects of chemotherapy, while cancerous cells stayed sensitive to the treatment. This prompted Longo to create the first fasting-mimicking diet as a way to allow cancer patients or mice in a lab to enjoy the benefits of fasting while still being able to eat.

"The oncologists did not want to fast the patients, and the patients did not want to fast," Longo said in a USC article. "We went to the National Cancer Institute, and they came up with a call for a fasting-mimicking diet, essentially saying: 'Let's develop something that people can eat but [that], to the body—whether it's a mouse or a person—is going to be like water-only fasting, meaning that it will cause very similar changes, as if they were not eating at all.'" Longo then demonstrated that fasting for five days per month for three months caused positive changes in risk factors of age-related diseases in humans. But five days of restricting calories per month is still a big ask for most humans, and studies showed that up to 30 percent of subjects attempting the diet dropped out.[13]

A breakthrough arrived in 2012, when Satchidananda Panda at the Salk Institute for Biological Studies found mice who were given a high-fat diet for eight hours per day were healthier and leaner than mice allowed to eat the same quantities whenever they wanted. This led to the development of Time Restricted Feeding, which eventually morphed into intermittent fasting.[14] The diet usually requires going twelve to sixteen hours, or more, without eating. There are other forms, like alternate-day fasting and alternate-day modified fasting, but they all have an identical goal—to trigger the same response in the body as basic caloric restriction. That desired reaction is called metabolic switching, where cells use up their stores of fuel and then convert fat into energy, which appears to improve cellular health, thus providing better well-being at later ages. That's the theory, and it's backed up by a good amount of promising research and science. But as with most biohacking schemes, the long-term effects are yet to be fully studied in humans, and many agencies and organizations around the world think it's too early to declare intermittent fasting a surefire way to extend your life.

Participants are almost certain to experience short-term side effects like grouchiness, irritability, light-headedness, and difficulties concentrating—what normally happens when you go a long time without eating.[15] However, most people are said to get accustomed to the plan within around a month, and those effects go away if they stick with the diet that long.

This kind of dieting raises other concerns, though. Intermittent fasting has been endorsed by a host of celebrities, but its popularity has spawned questions over its societal impact. An article in *Quartz* in 2019 asked why when men brag about not eating for most of the day it's called optimizing, but when women talk about extreme diets they are accused of having an eating disorder.[16] This type of dieting is not right for everyone, and fasting for long periods of time could lead to an obsession about eating and an unhealthy relationship with food. As ever, the most sensible advice on the topic appears to be do what you think is best for your own body, and always talk to a physician before doing anything drastic like starving yourself.

These diets highlight the gaping inequality in the United States, and the world. While millions struggle to work out where their next meal is coming from, this band of biohackers led by Silicon Valley gurus like Asprey egg each other on to eat less and less in order to maximize their comfortable lives. Around 13.7 million households in the United States—about 10.5 percent of all households in the country—experienced food insecurity at some point during 2019, according to US Department of Agriculture data. For around a third of that number, access to food was so limited their calorie intake was reduced and eating patterns affected. And that was before the pandemic hit. An estimate by researchers at Northwestern University suggested food insecurity more than doubled in 2020, affecting 23 percent of households.[17] Were Asprey to show up at any of those households lecturing about the benefits of calorie restriction for better health, it's fair to assume he'd get thrown out pretty quickly.

For an immortalist, calorie restriction can only take you so far toward eternal life. The gains of such a diet are minimal on their own and are most commonly paired with a strict regimen of supplements. Nearly every immortalist I met, with the curious exception of de Grey, popped pills at a rate that would embarrass a dodgy cycling team. Over the counter supplements were a hot topic at RAADfest, and every time a presenter mentioned their routine, a handful of people would ask questions in the chat about dosage, effectiveness, and where they could get their hands on the pills. Ray Kurzweil, one of the biggest heroes in the transhumanist and immortalist worlds, reportedly takes over one hundred different types of minerals and vitamins a day as part of his quest to reach the singularity. He used to claim he took over 250 supplements and employed someone specifically to sort through them each morning, but he has apparently cut that number down.[18]

Nutritional supplements are commonly used, and most doctors recommend taking a multivitamin once a day to keep the body ticking over. Every year, Americans spend around $35 billion on vitamins, minerals, botanicals, and various other supplements,[19] and research from 2019 claimed 77 percent of people in the country take a supplement of some kind.[20] Biohackers, and most immortalists, take way more than one per day, and some of the pills they're ingesting are doing more than boosting their Vitamin C intake. Their supplements come from a wide range of sources, including obscure roots and plants, and each is said to address at least one of the issues raised in the hallmarks of aging.

Some of the most popular anti-aging supplements contain a molecule linked to a number of longevity-inspired benefits. Nicotinamide adenine dinucleotide (NAD) plays a key role in the cellular production of energy. It's often written as NAD+, the name of its oxidized form, and has had rejuvenating effects in nonhuman trials. The molecule is essential for a host of metabolic pathways and is also involved in DNA repair. As people and animals age, NAD+ levels decline. Studies have shown boosting the amount of NAD+ can extend the lifespan of yeast, worms, and mice and kickstarts the mitochondria, the powerhouses of the cells.[21] Spurred on by this research, a host of companies began offering supplements containing NAD+ precursors like nicotinamide riboside (NR) and nicotinamide mononucleotide (NMN).

At the time of writing, the front page of the Life Extension website, the company cofounded by Bill Faloon, featured NAD+ heavily. There's nothing wrong with this; dietary supplements are very lightly regulated by the FDA, which allows companies to sell them even before they have passed clinical trials proving they are safe and effective for humans. There has been research conducted into these types of supplements—one clinical trial, which was funded by two of the largest companies selling them, ChromaDex[22] and Elysium,[23] showed adults taking them for six to eight weeks boosted the NAD+ levels in their blood without serious side effects. But no research proved beyond doubt that NR or NMN can improve human health, an issue that plagues the supplement world. There is very little evidence that most supplements, whether addressing longevity or not, actually make any kind of difference.

I contacted the Office of Dietary Supplements (ODS) at the National Institutes of Health to ask if there was any encouraging research at all. "There is no evidence that dietary supplements can reverse aging or increase lifespan. But the term 'longevity' could encompass many things, such as improving cognitive function, enhancing immunity, or reducing the risk of chronic disease," Carol Haggans, a scientific and health communications consultant at the department, told me via email. She said there have been a few studies examining the effects of some of the ingredients mentioned above for supporting cognitive function, but most show no benefit. Haggans listed one study for NAD+ which she said studied potential cognitive improvement but showed no effect. There were several conflicting results from a few small studies examining resveratrol's effect on age-related cognitive decline, and melatonin has mainly been studied for sleep deprivation, but "there have only been a few studies for cognitive function, and most show it's not helpful."

Sometimes, they aren't just ineffective, however; they can also be damaging. The most famous case of a supplement gone wrong was ephedra, a substance naturally occurring in plants that was marketed as an appetite suppressant and energy booster. The FDA took it off the market in 2004 after 155 people died.[24] Ephedra remains the only natural supplement removed from stores by regulators.

The potential for long-term or less severe damage is mostly left unchecked. Even vitamins can be harmful: beta-carotene is believed to increase the likelihood of developing lung cancer in smokers,[25] and excess Vitamin E was found in trials to increase the risk of prostate cancer.[26]

In recent years, cancer researchers sounded the alarm over NAD+. Studies suggested cancer cells rely on the molecule to sustain their rapid growth, and limiting the supply may be a potential method to kill them. "It might still slow down the aging part, but it might fuel the cancer part," Versha Banerji, a clinician-scientist at the University of Manitoba, told *Scientific American*. "We just need to figure out more about the biology of both of those processes, to figure out how we can make people age well and also not get cancer."[27]

More cold water was poured on the enthusiasm for NAD+ in February 2019, when a *Nature Cell Biology* study reported the molecule may have a role in cellular senescence, one of the other hallmarks of aging. Rugang Zhang of the Wistar Institute and his colleagues found that in cells entering senescence, rising levels of an enzyme which produces NAD+ encourage the release of the damaging molecules that can cause inflammation and even cancer. Zhang warned, "We should be cautious and bear in mind the potential downside of NAD+ supplementation as a dietary approach for anti-aging."[28]

Haggans added that the safety of supplements depends on the ingredients and their doses. "Vitamins and minerals, like magnesium, have a recommended intake and an upper limit, so we know they are safe at doses within these ranges. Other ingredients, like herbs, don't have recommended intakes because they aren't essential nutrients, so in many cases, less is known about their safety. Companies are responsible for determining that the dietary supplements they manufacture or distribute are safe, but federal law does not require dietary supplements to be proven safe to FDA's satisfaction before they are marketed." The risks associated with supplements may prove minimal, but with no regulation they are being taken every day by Americans who really have no idea what the side effects may be in the long term.

Biohackers are also fond of nootropics, the supplements intended to increase alertness, concentration, and even intelligence. But while some of them may make minimal improvements in cognitive function for a short amount of time, there is no telling what they are doing to a person's other organs.

I asked Dr. Luigi Ferrucci, the scientific director of the National Institute of Aging, how supplement distributors were able to sell their product. He told me the ambiguity and lack of accountability helped them.

"The effect is not measurable, there is no way that somebody can tell you that's not true," he said. "And so I laugh when I see those advertisements, I think it's as old as the philosophy of human beings—the idea that if you could make a pact with the devil, you will have beauty, eternal health, and incredible longevity." Ferrucci told me he thinks the FDA's approach to supplements is getting better, and the regulator is realizing the supplements market is "a bit tricky" and "a little bit dirty" as well.

"If you want the supplement to be prescribed by a doctor through a prescription, you have to go through FDA approval. And if you go through FDA approval, your capacity to sell it as a supplement is gone, you can't have both. That means that if you sell something that's really effective, you want to go through the FDA because you want it to be paid through Medicare and other insurance. But if you want that and go through the FDA, you lose your ability to sell it as a supplement. This in the long term is going to clean the field a little bit."

The anti-aging supplement field is incredibly murky. Most are not dangerous, just a waste of effort and money and completely ineffective. Tamar Haspel wrote in *The Washington Post*: "That's the dietary supplement conundrum. Most of them do nothing, so you shouldn't take those. But the ones that actually do something are the ones that pose danger, so you shouldn't take those either. If something really can enlarge your penis, imagine the havoc it can wreak in your liver."[29]

In March 2020, Asprey's Bulletproof 360 company came under the scrutiny of the FDA, and the regulator found that his promotional articles, and his method of storing supplements, were not up to scratch. The entrepreneur was sent a warning letter following a visit to his facility, in which investigators found "serious violations" of regulations governing the manufacturing, packaging, labeling or holding of dietary supplements. The reprimand also focused on certain products the company had claimed helped defeat aging. The letter quoted an article titled "13 Anti-aging Supplements to Turn You Into Benjamin Button," which pushes readers to take Curcumin, an ingredient in the company's Curcumin Max product.

"Your products are not generally recognized as safe and effective for the above referenced uses and, therefore, the products are 'new drugs,'" the letter read. "New drugs may not be legally introduced or delivered for introduction into interstate commerce without prior approval from FDA."

The bold claims on the Bulletproof 360 website had switched the definition of Curcumin Max from supplements to new drugs in the eyes of the FDA. While the letter was just a warning, it does at least suggest some kind of policing is under way in the dubious business of dietary supplements.

Three months later, the FDA sent another letter to Asprey, stating that it had "determined that you are unlawfully advertising that certain products prevent or treat COVID-19." Among the many alleged cures Asprey mentioned in his article "What I Do to Protect Myself From Coronavirus, and How I Plan to Kick It if I get It," was andrographis, which he mentioned in his talk. Asprey was reminded it was illegal to advertise a product that can prevent, treat, or cure a disease unless he possesses "competent and reliable scientific evidence," and was told to "immediately cease making all such claims."

Without regulation, the supplements market must seem like easy money for those practicing the age-old trick of selling so-called elixirs of life. RAADfest appeared to be full of these people. The event boasted a series of sellers, all peddling wares which promised to help immortalists and longevity advocates on their way to radically extended lives. Even if supplements really did work, it seemed their impact would be minimal for anyone attempting to reach the promised land of longevity escape velocity. And the fact that de Grey himself didn't take any seemed to indicate they weren't a route to immortality. But with no laws to stop them and a steady and receptive customer base, supplement peddling is here to stay. However, iffy pills are trivial compared to some of the offerings in the more experimental fields of anti-aging and regenerative medical technology.

9

REGENERATION

Unfortunately, Asprey didn't stop at telling the RAADfest audience to take dangerous gases rectally. He also focused heavily on a controversial and promising area of medical science—stem cell therapies. Like any good biohacker, he'd already tried it himself.

Stem cell treatment is a young branch of medicine. It had a shaky start. First the treatments were caught up in America's culture wars, then exploited, and now they occupy a much-disputed part of American discourse. Despite this, the science is some of the most exciting in medical technology.

Stem cells play an extraordinary role in the human body. If the genome is the instruction manual from which the body reads, stem cells are the raw materials it uses to build itself. There are two types of these stem cells. One version, pluripotent stem cells, are first found in human embryos and can become any type of cell in the body. When the minuscule beginnings of a human body needs a new blood cell or a new skin cell, these stem cells are happy to oblige. Because of this tremendous ability, embryonic stem cells are of great interest to doctors, scientists, and anyone looking to turn the clock back. The other group, adult stem cells, are quite limited by comparison, and can't transform into any cell the body may need. The scientific understanding of both types has built up over decades, but our knowledge still has some way to go.

Stem cells were first discovered in the 1960s by a pair of Canadian scientists, James Till and Ernest McCulloch, based at the Ontario Cancer Institute, who found the hematopoietic stem cell, which forms blood. These are adult stem cells, and although they can transform into different kinds of cells, they appear to be limited to the part of the body they are found in. For example, a hematopoietic stem cell would not be able to become a cell unassociated with the blood. Till and McCulloch followed up their discovery with a series of studies defining the hallmark properties of a stem cell and prompted the research which theorized that some cells are capable of self-renewal.[1]

The next major success came in 1981, when British biologists Martin Evans and Matthew Kaufman identified and isolated embryonic stem cells in mice.[2] Researchers quickly realized these cells had some astonishing properties and soon managed to culture them from mouse embryos. But it took another fourteen years to achieve the same feat in monkeys.[3] James Thomson, at the University of Wisconsin-Madison, made that breakthrough, and followed it up three years later in 1998 when he used donated embryos that were left unused in fertility treatments to isolate and grow human embryonic stem cells in the lab.[4]

That discovery caused something of a furor among religious groups, particularly in the United States. This means of research usually involved destroying an embryo, and critics argued that an embryo was a human being, somehow reaching the conclusion that scientists were committing murder. America's religious right, frothing at the mouth, put pressure on politicians, and in 2001 President George W. Bush caved and restricted government funding of research on embryonic stem cells.[5] The clampdown was not as severe as it could have been, however, as the new rules allowed existing research to continue, and not all stem cell lab work was affected.[6] In other countries, such as

Germany and Italy, the creation of stem cells via Thomson's method was banned altogether. But scientists unfettered by the demonization of stem cell discovery continued their work, and it wasn't long before biologists in Australia, Singapore, Israel, Canada, and the United States reported they had converted embryonic stem cells into other cells of the body, including immune cells, neurons, and beating heart cells.[7]

But there were further setbacks to come. The scientific community wanted to derive stem cells from embryos made by a process called somatic-cell nuclear transfer, the same method which had birthed Dolly the sheep, the first cloned animal unveiled to the world back in 1997. The intention was to use this "therapeutic cloning" to provide an unlimited supply of stem cells with the same DNA as the cell donor, which would be extremely useful for all kinds of medical interventions. In 2005, the science world rejoiced as South Korean scientist Woo Suk Hwang claimed to have isolated stem cells in this manner. However, it was soon discovered the researcher's claims were fraudulent, and it was eight more years before therapeutic cloning was finally achieved.[8]

A year after Hwang's false claims, scientists reported a genuine breakthrough. Shinya Yamanaka was based at Nara Institute of Science and Technology in Japan when he began an ambitious research project. It was long thought specialized adult cells could never return to their immature state, but Yamanaka set out to prove this wrong. In 2006 he successfully identified a small number of genes in the genome of mice that controlled the state of a cell. When he activated these genes, he could reprogram mature skin cells into immature stem cells, which could then grow into any kind of cell in the body.[9] Yamanaka's work ensured a steady supply of embryonic stem cells for scientists and eliminated the need to kill an embryo in the process. In 2007, Thomson achieved the same feat but with human cells, giving scientists a clear path to limitless supplies of stem cells while avoiding any kind of ethical debate. From there, breakthroughs and miracle cures arrived quickly: eyesight was restored, diabetes cured, and kidney transplants eased. All this is thought to be just the beginning for stem cell therapies. But the astonishing progress made in the field didn't only inspire other scientists, it also caught the eye of opportunists looking to sell a miracle cure.

Asprey doesn't sell stem cell therapies, but he loudly advocates for unproven treatments in the field. He is also a customer, having traveled to a number of different countries to have stem cells—farmed from his own body—injected into himself. FDA warnings effectively banned the treatments in the United States initially, scattering these companies across the world to countries with less stringent regulations. As a result, stem cell tourism emerged. Companies popped up in Russia, China, and some Latin American and Caribbean countries.[10] But within the past ten years, would-be stem cell entrepreneurs noticed the FDA was not enforcing its regulations in the United States, and stem cell therapy operations began to open domestically. Rather belatedly, the authorities realized they had been slow to respond and began cracking down. But many companies offering unproven stem cell treatments still operate in the United States. A quick Google search of "stem cell therapies" reveals hundreds of options, most of them offering treatments that scientists and researchers say are not even possible.

Dr. Sean Morrison is the director of the Children's Medical Center Research Institute at UT Southwestern and a Howard Hughes Medical Institute investigator. Morrison served as the President of the International Society for Stem Cell Research between 2015 and 2016, and has actively pursued public policy to regulate the stem cell industry further. When I spoke to Morrison by phone, there was a tired note in his voice, as if he'd covered this topic many times before. For genuine researchers in the field of stem cells, the phony companies trading off their work can be draining.

"It's hard to see people harmed by people who are just engaged in fraud," he said, "Those of us who really understand the biology and understand the science, I think it's important for us to stand up and to tell the public about what's true so that people can make more educated choices. And in parallel to encourage regulators to be more aggressive about enforcing regulations, to put these people out of business who are trying to rip off desperate patients," Morrison told me.

Despite his frustration, Morrison hopes the new push to eradicate these companies in the United States can be successful. "I think what you're going to see in the coming years is the FDA is going to further significantly ramp up their enforcement activities. The Federal Trade Commission is starting to enforce regulations on misleading advertising, and one of the most important things that's happening is that state attorney generals are starting to sue these companies for misleading advertising. I think once you see some successful cases where there's really substantial penalties as a result of these state cases, I think it will have a chilling effect on the industry," he said. "The people in the industry recognize that the industry is not going to last much longer, that there's enough different government agencies onto them that they're not going to be able to do this much longer. But I think they're just trying to make as much money as they can as long as they can, knowing they're going to get shut down in a couple of years."

Tom Miller, Iowa's State Attorney General, took on stem cell companies operating in his state. In July 2020, his office sued Regenerative Medicine and Anti-Aging Institutes, an Omaha-based stem cell therapy center, for allegedly trying to lure older customers with incorrect advertising. The lawsuit alleged the company made "deceptive and misleading claims" in its adverts and in more than ninety live events held in Iowa between April 2018 and September 2019. According to the suit, the company's salespeople used high-pressure tactics to persuade potentially hundreds of people to pay for unproven procedures with costs from $1,400 to more than $27,000. "Stem cells hold great potential to treat or even cure diseases, but some providers are exploiting that promise to make misleading and unfounded claims," Miller said. "The defendants are an example of the 'unscrupulous providers' that the FDA and others have warned consumers about."[11]

The case wasn't confined to Iowa. The same owners were reportedly running similar operations in Nebraska, and the Attorney General in that state filed a similar lawsuit. Regenerative Medicine's advertising was very typical of these types of companies. "Today's regenerative medicine offers a revolutionary treatment that helps to heal your injured tissue," some of the adverts claimed. "If you suffer from injured or degenerative conditions in your back, knees, hips, shoulders, or have arthritic joints or suffer from neuropathy or respiratory diseases like COPD, Stem Cell Therapy can help get you out of pain and discomfort!" A TV commercial which aired in Iowa also made the claim that "stem cell therapy has the ability to reverse your COPD."[12]

The advertising was designed to lure potential customers to the live events, usually held in hotels, where the potential of stem cell therapies would be inflated further. These "educational seminars" featured some outrageous claims. According to the lawsuit, one slide of a presentation read "Anti-Aging: Mesenchymal Stem Cell infusions turned back the hands of Father Time about three years! Would you like to get back three years?" Scientific studies, also presented to attendees, were often taken out of context or didn't support the claims made in the presentations.

Meanwhile, the founder, Travis Autor, was teaching his employees how to milk every last drop out of desperate people. He once explained to his sales staff during a company training session that "the more these studies I can quote and stuff—it gives me more authority . . . that I know what I'm talking about." He also acknowledged during training sessions that most or all of his customers were older people, the lawsuit alleged, and he told sales staff to sell treatments to healthy people and to "upsell them" on higher doses of stem cells. [13]

"Once somebody has, you know, agreed to 9,000 or to 15,000 (dollars), getting another 1,000 is easy. It really is," Autor allegedly told his employees. "So, the psychology of sales: Once a person commits to a large purchase, they get a huge endorphin rush in the pleasure spot of our brain, called the brain reward cascade system. And the endorphins are released, and we are like 'ah . . .' . . . Um, so, when a patient gets to 15,000 dollars and they get that rush, we're gonna offer them a second ability to have that rush again."[14]

This was not Autor's first stem cell center. He previously operated similar facilities in other states, including Arizona and Idaho. He held a chiropractor license that was revoked in 2009 in a settlement with the state of Washington amid allegations of double billing, having sex with a patient, and smoking marijuana during his lunch breaks.[15] Autor, who changed his name from Travis Broughton after the Washington incident, is an all-too-common participant in this netherworld of stem cell therapies. He has questionable medical credentials, moves around a lot, and appears to target vulnerable patients. These companies will do almost anything to package their offerings as miracle cures. One particularly egregious practice is to target ex-military to boost the company's reputation. Morrison said he has been told of former Navy Seals being offered stem cell treatments for various combat-related injuries, none of which are viable from a scientific standpoint. Companies hired an individual to recruit fellow retired soldiers to take the treatments, drumming up business and providing the founders with a badge of honor that ex-military personnel placed their trust in them.[16] Some stem cell companies feature discounts and promotional offers aimed at military veterans.[17][18]

Company websites feature written and video testimonials from all types of people with glowing reviews. Patients are happy to provide these endorsements, partly because for most people the treatments appear to work initially.

"People that are so highly motivated that they go to these clinics so want to believe that the therapy works that there is a very strong placebo effect. And this has been documented in scientific studies," Morrison told me. "And so these companies know that there's a small fraction of their patients that are going to claim miraculous cures, but ultimately the disease process continues unabated, and when these people die later nobody hears about it."

According to Morrison, the psychological trauma suffered by cheated patients is an often-underestimated consequence of fake stem cell therapies. And these therapies are not cheap, often costing tens of thousands of dollars, and they're not covered by health insurance. There are also huge problems with the way some companies are run, which can cause a patient leaving a facility sicker than when they entered. "One of the things we've learned is that the people that are willing to ignore FDA regulation and sell fake therapies and lie to people are also willing to ignore good manufacturing procedures. We've had multiple cases now of fake stem cell therapy companies selling products that were contaminated with pathogens. So once people got injected with them, they ended up sceptic and in intensive care units," Morrison said.

In 2019, *The Washington Post* reported that at least seventeen people were hospitalized in the same year after a company called Liveyon sold vials of a solution derived from umbilical cord blood—a source of stem cells, according to its marketing material. Liveyon said its product was "as miraculous as the birth of a child itself" and claimed it "stimulates regenerative healing." The product was not approved by the FDA or supported by any kind of research. Twelve cases involving Liveyon, according to a report from the Centers for Disease Control and Prevention (CDC), highlighted the dangers of bacterial infection. Patients suffered swollen spinal discs, infected bones and joints, and abscesses in their backs. Three of the twelve spent a month or more in a hospital recovering.[19]

Further complications are caused by the delay between patients receiving stem cell therapy and when they become sick. In 2019, a report in the *Canadian Medical Association Journal* described how a thirty-eight-year-old man developed a benign tumor on his spinal cord that doctors believe was caused by an experimental stem cell treatment he received twelve years earlier. The man was not named, but his struggles were laid out in detail in the report. When he was twenty years old, he injured his spine in a trampolining accident. After surgery and rehabilitation, he still suffered paralysis in his arms, legs, and torso. Bereft of options, the desperate man traveled to Portugal to undergo a stem cell procedure involving cells taken from the inside of his nose being injected into his spine. The goal was to reduce his pain and potentially make him walk again. But he never gained use of his arms or legs, and his pain actually increased. Twelve years later, a team of doctors found a tumor on the upper part of his spine and matched samples taken from the mass to the type of cells transplanted from the inside of his nose. Only part of the man's tumor was removed, and while it wasn't considered cancerous, radiation was used to halt its growth.[20]

Unfortunately, the use of experimental stem cell therapies in the United States has also proven fatal. In 2010, a doctor named Zannos Grekos performed a stem cell treatment on a sixty-nine-year-old woman. Grekos extracted blood and bone marrow to obtain the cells and infused them near damaged tissue. Soon after, she suffered a stroke, was hospitalized, and died when she was taken off life support. According to the Florida Department of Health, the bone marrow was "grossly filtered," meaning it was essentially impure, and bone particles and other fragments became lodged in her right carotid artery.

Officials in Florida, where Grekos was based, imposed an emergency restriction order preventing him from using stem cells in any treatment. But the ban was lifted on appeal, and in 2012 another of his patients undergoing stem cell treatment went into cardiac arrest and died. In 2013, the Florida Board of Medicine revoked Grekos's medical license, a decision that was upheld by a Tallahassee court in 2015.[21] In 2021, I Googled Grekos and found him listed as the Chief Science Officer at Regenocyte, a stem cell therapy company he founded well before he had his license revoked.[22] I called Regenocyte, and a concerned woman on the other end asked me what my problem was. Not wanting to descend into a made-up sob story, I asked if they were still operational, and where any procedure would take place. She told me they were indeed still accepting patients, and while the office was based in Florida, the stem cell therapy would be carried out in the Dominican Republic.

The market for unproven stem cell therapies is alarmingly deregulated, and it's no wonder a handful of operators are making serious money offering treatments that amount to no more than snake oil. They are profiting from the hard work of scientists making genuine and exciting breakthroughs in a very promising field. For the injured, sick, or elderly, it's easy to see how growing desperation would lead them down a path toward these fraudsters. But immortalists have no such excuse. Of those I spoke to, Rudi Hoffman was one of the few who'd actually attempted stem cell therapy, and that was to ease the pain during his recovery from cancer. He described disappointing results.

The question of how to find a safe and reputable stem cell therapy provider emerged during RAADfest and the speakers, including Asprey, told viewers they needed to do their due diligence and make sure the company was legitimate before taking the plunge. But that recommendation didn't seem fair. If there are genuine stem cell clinics out there, they're almost impossible to distinguish from those which are fraudulent and dangerous. So how would an immortalist choose a stem cell treatment capable of getting them that little bit closer to escape velocity?

"There's no evidence that any kind of stem cell therapy available to humans would lengthen a healthy person's lifespan," Morrison told me. "There are certain stem cell therapies, particularly related to the blood system, that can cause people to live longer if they have a failure of immune system function or a certain kind of leukemia. But in a normal person, a stem cell therapy that could lengthen your life? There's no evidence for it."

Other scientists have gone even further than Morrison. "I believe strongly that it isn't ethical to charge patients for unproven therapies like these and raise what are likely to be false hopes," Paul S. Knoepfler, a stem cell researcher at the University of California, Davis, told *The New York Times* in 2019.[23] In labs around the world scientists are attempting to discover if genuine stem cell therapies can have anti-aging capabilities, but the results so far have been modest. "In my view, the kinds of incremental improvements that we might derive from that research is on par with what you can already achieve by living a healthy lifestyle. If you don't smoke, if you don't eat too much, if you exercise, if you take care of yourself, you can already accomplish what people are doing through that research," Morrison said.

Meanwhile, the scientists and researchers conducting genuine work in the field grow increasingly dismayed at the effects of the murky industry. Anthony Atala is a bioengineer, urologist, and pediatric surgeon, as well as the founding director of the Wake Forest Institute for Regenerative Medicine. He told me he has always been happy to follow the FDA regulations and sees them as vital. "It's just a matter of dotting your Is and crossing your Ts, and yes of course it requires more work to put this stuff through the FDA, but it's for good reason," he said. "They really want to make sure what you're doing is safe, and you can't argue with that. When you put stuff into patients, you have to make sure you're not going to harm the patient. We keep pushing these technologies through and advancing these technologies. It takes more time, you're doing more work, but at the end of the day you're doing the patient a service because you're providing something you know is safe. And also, you're doing yourself a favor because you're not taking shortcuts that will come back to haunt you when things don't go well."

Many immortalists are impatient for stem cell therapies to receive approval from regulators—they believe they are fighting against their own biological clock to secure eternal life. This puts them at loggerheads with government agencies like the FDA and nudges them closer to the types of libertarian leanings mentioned by Hoffman. Some libertarians believe the FDA should be abolished, and this fits well with a growing hunger for experimental medicine. One of the key elements of a recent push to undermine the FDA, according to Morrison, was the Right to Try Act, which was signed into federal law by Donald Trump in 2018.[24]

The law gives terminally ill patients the right to try experimental drugs which have not received approval by the government. Previously, terminally ill patients would need to apply to the FDA for access to drugs which had not been clinically tested and approved, and most of these applications were granted. Now they can bypass that system completely and only need the approval of their physician and the drug manufacturer. The law also protects doctors and companies from any legal ramifications if anyone gets hurt or killed. Those utilizing the law will still need to prove they have exhausted all other approved treatments. The bill was pushed through with support of the president, who talked up the idea in a State of the Union speech and told patients and families during the bill signing ceremony: "America is a nation of fighters. We never give up, right?" The Right to Try was opposed by several groups, including the American Cancer Society.[25]

FDA commissioner Scott Gottlieb, a doctor and cancer survivor, expressed concerns to Congress the year before the bill was passed. "The clinical trial process is crucial to the development of innovative new medical products that can improve or save patients' lives." He said there needed to be a balance between giving patients investigational treatments and ensuring that new therapies were safe and effective.[26] The passing of the law barely changed anything for patients, anyway: 99 percent of requests to the FDA since 2009 were granted within a few days or even, in some emergency cases, instantly via phone.[27] The purpose of the bill appears to be an attempt by politically motivated groups to erode confidence in the FDA and any kind of regulation of the health care sector.

"Right to Try will either be irrelevant or it will harm people," predicted Morrison. "But it swept across the country, and there were a lot of people who found it benign. It sounded good—give people access to any therapy if they have a serious disease. But the reality is most people don't have the capacity to evaluate whether a therapy really has the chance to benefit them or not. There are a lot of people lined up who want to rip off desperate patients."

Stem cell therapies attract the desperate like no other medical breakthrough, and for good reason. These therapies should be a cause for great optimism and hold the potential to cure many terrible diseases, despite being relatively new. For many immortalists, they represent a dangerous temptation. There are hundreds of predatory stem cell therapy clinics operating in the United States today, and they're all waiting for the next mark to step through their doors and ask about anti-aging solutions. It's all propped up by the likes of Asprey, who described his own experience with stem cell therapies in a blog post where he lists the "anecdotal benefits of stem cell therapies." They include smoother skin, longer life, flexibility, and (most bizarrely) a bigger penis.[28] "You can get up to 20 percent more length and girth from the P-shot (stem cell injections into your bits), no kidding. But you have to use a medical grade pump for 30 days after the procedure to create micro-tears in the corpus cavernosum so the stem cells cause them to heal," Asprey wrote. I sent Asprey's stem cell article to Morrison, who said the claims were "typical of unproven stem cell therapy companies that have been the subject of enforcement actions by the FDA." He also mentioned that one of the people recommended in the article as a therapy provider, Kristin Comella of US Stem Cell, was the subject of an FDA enforcement action that led to an injunction in federal court in June 2019. The company was banned from manufacturing or distributing adipose-derived stem cells (the kind of product Asprey mentions in the article).

Disturbed by what I found in this area of regenerative medicine, I wanted to look at technologies even further in the future to see if the same problems plagued any other scientific field where immortalists had a vested interest. I started with gene therapy.

10

THE IMMORTAL JELLYFISH

In 1988, Christian Sommer, a marine biology student in his early twenties, discovered immortality. This may be a shock to read so far into the book—but, of course, there is a catch. Sommer was conducting research on hydrozoans, small sea-dwelling invertebrates whose appearance alternates between that of a jellyfish and soft coral, depending on where they are in their life cycle. His work took place in a picturesque setting—he spent a summer in Rapallo, a small city on the Italian Riviera, and went snorkeling off the cliffs of Portofino every morning. As he snorkeled, he scanned the seabed for hydrozoans, scooping them up with plankton nets. One of the obscure species he found was the *Turritopsis dohrnii*. He put these hydrozoans in a petri dish with his other specimens and observed their reproduction habits. After a few days he noticed the *Turritopsis dohrnii* were acting strange and couldn't come up with an explanation. Eventually, Sommer realized that these tiny hydrozoans appeared to be immortal.[1]

Sommer observed that this rare species of invertebrates was capable of aging in reverse, growing younger until it reached its earliest stage of development. At that point, instead of mercifully dying like Brad Pitt as Benjamin Button, the *Turritopsis dohrnii* began its life cycle all over again. Sommer didn't immediately appreciate the significance of his discovery, and it was nearly a decade before scientists in Genoa released research detailing the strange abilities of the hydrozoans. The paper, titled "Reversing the Life Cycle," described how the species would transform itself back to a polyp, "thus escaping death and achieving potential immortality."[2]

The authors of the paper were first to label *Turritopsis dohrnii* the immortal jellyfish, but the world didn't erupt with wonder as one might expect. There were no demands to harvest the creatures for the good of mankind, and outside of the academic world, the paper was hardly noticed. Over time, interest increased, and progress has been made studying the species. It was discovered that the rejuvenation of the jellyfish is caused by either environmental stress or a physical assault, and during the process the cells undergo the same transformation as human stem cells—cellular transdifferentiation, where one type of cell is converted into another. Other discoveries emerged slowly, some more alarming than others. In the past few decades, immortal jellyfish have spread throughout the world's oceans, hitchhiking on cargo ships to travel huge distances. *Turritopsis* have proven they are able to flourish in any ocean in the world. Immortal and on the charge, perhaps one day these jellyfish will inherit the Earth.[3]

The *Turritopsis dohrnii* is believed to be the only species which boasts biological immortality, but there are others with extremely long lifespans. Most of these can be found in the sea. Sponges—which are actually alive and classified as animals—live for an extremely long time. Estimates vary, but numbers have reached thousands of years, and one species, the *Monorhaphis chuni*, has apparently lived to be eleven thousand years old. Quahog clams are similar to sponges in that they have little or no personality but extremely long lives. One such clam, named Ming, died at the age of 507 when it was dredged up from Icelandic waters. The normal lifespan of the species is said to be around 225 years. And there are deep sea fish, like the orange roughy, which are believed to live to up to 175 years old.[4] On land, there are fewer longer-living species, but there are still a few surprising animals capable of surviving well past one hundred. They include Jonathan, a 189-year-old Seychelles giant tortoise, the oldest known terrestrial animal.[5] Jonathan is still alive as of 2021 and, despite losing his sight and sense of smell, reportedly spends his days eating, sleeping, and mating with his long-term lover Frederik.[6]

Tortoises survive so long partly because they live very slow, incident-free lives. Turtles, the umbrella species under which tortoises sit, are masters of survival and are built to survive even a lack of oxygen. They are the most evolved and complex animal that can do so, and are able to forgo oxygen for well over a year. For contrast, humans can only survive without oxygen for around two minutes before their brains are irreversibly damaged. In order to live without fresh air, turtles drop their metabolism rate to close to zero. They bring their energy production down to nothing by changing an enzyme which turns off their mitochondria, forcing the body to secrete proteins that protect cells. When faced with a lack of oxygen, turtles initiate an organized shutdown of fifty thousand processes in their bodies. They also don't panic. Turtles turn off their stress-response proteins, allowing their bodies to focus on reshaping the cells to deal with no oxygen.[7] In comparison, human cells panic badly when they are deprived of oxygen. They turn on stress kinases, signaling proteins to respond to a potentially challenging situation. This process uses up a lot of energy, overloads the system, and can ultimately lead to death.

Jellyfish, clams, sponges, turtles, and tortoises are not remotely similar to humans, making it difficult for immortalists to learn any handy tips from them. But inspiration can be taken from mammals. Bowhead whales are a good example: they live longer than scientists would expect of an animal with its enormous size. They are the second-largest mammal still around, and their two hundred–year lifespan is double what scientists would assume given their vast proportions. Researchers have found that the whales have an extremely accomplished DNA repair process, which slows down the accumulation of damage in their genomes.[8]

Scientists usually look for similar qualities in species which are smaller. Mice, flatworms, and fruit flies are used in the majority of research as they are easy to work with, and there are plenty of genetic tools available that can be used on them. There is also an increasing interest in species which live longer compared to similar creatures. While a house mouse lives to just two or three years old, the naked mole-rat, a similar-sized rodent, can live for over thirty-five years.

These mole-rats, as their name suggests, are never going to win any beauty prizes. But while their looks may let them down, their durability is something to be admired. The burrowing rodents, which are native to East Africa, are highly cancer resistant. Only a handful of cancer cases have ever been observed in captive naked mole-rats, and scientists have rounded them up in ever-increasing numbers to find out why. In 2020, research from the University of Cambridge found the secret behind their cancer immunity is the cell's microenvironment—the system of cells and molecules surrounding a cell—rather than the durability of the cell itself.

"The results were a surprise to us and have completely transformed our understanding of cancer resistance in naked mole-rats. If we can understand what's special about these animals' immune systems and how they protect them from cancer, we may be able to develop interventions to prevent the disease in people." Dr. Walid Khaled, one of the senior authors of the study from the University of Cambridge's Department of Pharmacology, said.[9] Naked mole-rats also have other interesting traits. They are the only cold-blooded mammal, they lack pain sensitivity to chemical stimuli in their skin, and, like the turtle, they are able to withstand very low levels of oxygen.

Science is yet to establish exactly why some animals live longer than others, but it's clear their genetic makeup is crucial. The same is true in humans who live longer than average. The oldest person to have ever lived is Jeanne Calment, a French woman who died in August 1997 at age 122. Before she died, Calment became something of a celebrity. She was written about countless times and often threw out some zingers when interviewed. She once told a reporter, "I wait for death . . . and journalists." She was reportedly still cycling when she was one hundred, only gave up smoking at 117, and was said to have had a mental capacity equivalent to people far younger than her. Eventually, time did catch up with her: by 1996 she was using a wheelchair and was mostly blind and deaf.[10]

Calment's story took a strange turn about two decades after she died. In 2018, a Russian mathematician named Nikolay Zak published a paper with an extraordinary claim—that Calment was a fraud. He alleged that Jeanne Calment had actually died in 1934 and her daughter Yvonne had assumed her identity in an attempt to avoid inheritance taxes. Zak came to his conclusion after digging through her biography and finding inconsistencies. Unsurprisingly, France did not take the accusations lying down and defended its national treasure while attacking Zak. But the thirty-six-year-old stood his ground. He published an extended version of his paper the next year, compiling evidence such as physical differences between the young and old Calment and discrepancies in the testimonies she gave while living in a retirement home. The people of Calment's hometown Arles formed a group to disprove Zak's claims and offered the sensational argument that Calment was considered so unpleasant by her neighbors, there was no way they'd have kept the secret on her behalf.

The debate continues today. Those seeking to disprove Calment's claim say her DNA should be tested to find out whether she was Jeanne or her daughter. Others want to get hold of her DNA for other reasons. They believe that someone who lived so long should be studied in more detail, to extract any secrets relating to longer life. Aubrey de Grey is among that crowd—it was his journal, *Rejuvenation Research*, which published Zak's paper initially, and there has been speculation he promoted the theory as a means to force the release of Calment's DNA and blood samples, rumored to be held in a private genetic research center in Paris.[11]

If Calment truly did live to 122 years old, it's clear her body was built differently than most. She avoided the diseases which usually finish us off—heart disease, diabetes, and cancer— for longer than anyone else, despite seemingly living a less than healthy lifestyle. This supports theories that healthy living and biohacking can only take a person so far, and that our death is already foretold in our genes. But there is hope for immortalists. Science is slowly making progress to ensure living longer isn't a genetic lottery, partly by taking inspiration from plants, animals, and humans that live extraordinarily long lives.

One of the most promising areas is gene therapy, which is already used to treat some diseases. In 2021, a new type of treatment utilizing the genes of algae partially restored a man's eyesight. The man, who hasn't been named, suffered from retinitis pigmentosa—where light sensing cells on the surface of the retina die—and was completely blind. The treatment first involved gene therapy, where genetic instructions for making proteins called rhodopsins were taken from the algae and given to cells deep in the retina at the back of the patient's eye. When light hit these new proteins, it sent an electrical signal to the brain, but not one that could be deciphered. They only respond to amber light, so the man wore goggles with a video camera on the front and a projector on the back. This getup captured what was happening in the world and fired a version onto the back of the eye in the right wavelength for the proteins. The patient then waited months for the levels of rhodopsins to build up in the eye, and for the brain to learn a new way of interpreting sight. He first realized the treatment was working when he went out on a walk with the goggles and saw the white stripes of a pedestrian crossing. He has since been able to grab and count objects on a table in front of him. [12]

Many consider gene therapy one of the most exciting areas of medicine, and immortalists have not missed the potential they hold for their cause. The practice itself has had a rocky history, but now appears to be entering into a new age of breakthroughs.

In 1972, Theodore Friedmann and Richard Roblin published a paper titled "Gene Therapy for Human Genetic Disease?" in the journal *Science*.[13] The two American scientists outlined the potential of inserting DNA sequences into a patient's cells to treat genetic disorders. Each of our cells contains thousands of genes that provide the information for production of proteins and enzymes that make bones, blood, and muscles, which support most of the body's functions. Issues arise when a whole or part of a gene is defective or missing. This can occur from birth or a gene can mutate during a person's lifetime. When that happens, it disrupts how proteins are made and can cause major health problems or diseases.

Genetic diseases were once seen as completely incurable, but the 1972 paper proposed a solution: gene therapy. However, the two authors urged caution on the development of the technology and opposed any attempts at gene therapy in human patients.[14] The scientific community took note and waited eighteen years, conducting a lot of research before launching the first gene therapy trial in 1990. Ashanthi DeSilva, a four-year-old girl suffering from a rare genetic disease known as severe combined immunodeficiency, underwent a twelve-day treatment involving gene therapy. DeSilva's condition meant she lacked an enzyme called adenosine deaminase (ADA), rendering her immune system almost completely useless. This put her at risk of dying from infection and forced her to live in isolation.

To boost DeSilva's ADA levels, doctors introduced a functional copy of the gene that encodes the enzyme into the immune system. As you might imagine, it's not easy to insert a gene directly into a person's cells. It has to be delivered via a carrier, known as a vector. The most common gene therapy vectors—and what was used on DeSilva—are viruses because they can identify certain cells and carry genetic material into the genes of that cell. In order to make it safe, researchers remove the disease-causing genes from the virus and replace them with the genes that would help. When the viral vector containing the gene therapy was introduced, DeSilva's immune system improved, and she was able to live a normal life.

The DeSilva case was celebrated around the world, kicking off numerous other trials in the field during the 1990s. But just nine years later, that progress was brought to a sudden halt when a clinical trial went tragically wrong.[15]

In 1999, Jesse Gelsinger, an eighteen-year-old suffering from the genetic condition ornithine transcarbamylase deficiency, signed up for an experimental gene therapy trial at the University of Pennsylvania. The disease, which was caused by a genetic mutation, stopped his liver's ability to break down ammonia, causing the toxic substance to accumulate in the blood. The trial introduced a functional copy of the missing gene to Gelsinger's liver cells, using a modified common cold virus as a vector.

But four days after the treatment, Gelsinger suffered a catastrophic immune reaction and died. His death shocked the field and received widespread media attention. The FDA criticized the design of the trial and suspended the University of Pennsylvania's entire gene therapy program, which was one of the largest in the world. The regulator also launched investigations into sixty-nine other gene therapy trials underway in the United States. In the fallout, gene therapy was accused of moving too fast, and viral vectors in particular were called into question. Researchers in the field were rocked, and progress slowed considerably. When it did rebound, the comeback was gradual.[16]

In 2003, China approved its first gene therapy, called Gendicine, which treated head and neck cancer. Russia then gave the green light to Neovasculgen, a therapy for peripheral artery disease, in 2011. The next year, the European Commission approved Glybera, a gene therapy treating lipoprotein lipase deficiency, an ultra-rare disease. Although it was heralded at the time as a great success for Europe, Glybera was a commercial failure. The therapy came with a one million Euro price tag, making it the most expensive treatment in the world. By the time it was withdrawn in 2017, the treatment had been prescribed to just one patient.[17] The United States didn't approve such a treatment until 2017.[18]

Immortalists are among those seeking to speed up the introduction of gene therapies, believing the treatment could be used to reverse the effects of aging. Frustrated that the science was moving too slowly, one anti-aging advocate and entrepreneur took drastic steps to ensure gene therapies to reverse aging were at least being tested on humans.

In 2015, forty-four-year-old Liz Parrish traveled to Bogotá, Columbia, to receive dozens of experimental gene therapy injections, with the goal of turning back her biological clock. Her journey to Bogotá began in 2013, when she learned that her nine-year-old son was diagnosed with type 1 diabetes. Parrish, who was already a keen researcher and advocate for stem cell therapies, was outraged by the amount of time and money it took for experimental treatments to reach patients, despite scientific breakthroughs in key areas in regenerative medicine. She traveled to medical conferences and badgered experts in the hallways, asking if their treatments could be applied to children. Eight months after her son's diagnosis, Parrish traveled to Cambridge, England, for a SENS Foundation conference hosted by Aubrey de Grey.[19]

Among the presentations on gene editing, tissue regeneration, and calorie restriction, one word kept coming up—telomeres. As discussed in an earlier chapter, telomeres are a key part of the hallmarks of aging. Their full purpose was discovered in 1984 by Elizabeth Blackburn and her student Carol Greider. They identified telomerase, the enzyme that lengthens each strand of DNA before it is copied, compensating for the way cells shorten when they divide. Blackburn went on to establish the link between telomere length and cell health. Her research in the early 2000s with psychologist Elissa Epel studied the telomere length in mothers of children with chronic diseases and found that stress can prematurely age a person's cells[20]—a worrying discovery which may make most of us assume we'll die tomorrow.

At the conference, experts told Parrish she had to talk to one person, Bill Andrews.[21] By that point, Andrews was a key researcher in telomeres. His work at the biotech company Geron led to the discovery of the gene that controlled the production of telomerase—TERC. His team also found the protein component hTERT. The company tested turning off the production of telomerase in cancer cells and were able to kill them by accelerating their aging. In 1995, Geron published its discovery in *Science* and filed patent applications. The company faced a choice—should it begin work on a cure for cancer by reducing the number of telomerase in cancer cells, or focus on curing aging by adding or inducing it in healthy cells? Geron, despite being named after gerontology, the study of aging, chose to put its efforts into cancer first.

Andrews, shocked by the decision, left in 1999 and started his own company, Sierra Sciences, which would take the same breakthrough and apply it solely to aging. His new company took off, backed by major investors. It seemed only a matter of time before a telomere drug made its way to market. But the 2008 financial crisis changed everything. Funding evaporated, and Andrews' march to immortality halted.[22]

When Parrish called Andrews in 2013, his company was struggling along on a meager budget. The pair got on well and hatched a plan to speed up the development of longevity drugs. Early in 2015, Parrish founded her own company, BioViva. In her frantic pursuit of treatments for children, her quest had turned toward anti-aging. She realized that by curing aging, everyone—including children—would suffer less. Parrish made her first public appearance as CEO at People Unlimited and told a receptive crowd of immortalists that she wanted to cure aging, and do it fast enough so they could all benefit.[23]

I spoke to Parrish on a two-hour Skype call in 2021, as the COVID-19 vaccination program was well underway in the United States. By this point she was double-vaccinated and keen to push on with her mission. She was a passionate speaker, extremely driven, and I quickly detected both stubbornness and charm—two things that will get you far in an investor's boardroom.

In 2015, she raised enough cash to fund the Bogotá experiment, and already knew she would be patient zero. (A video of Parrish's procedure is now available online.[24]) Prior to the treatment, she made jokes to the doctors. "I'm supposed to go in the corner, grab my face and shake around, and turn around and be young, right?" she laughed. "It's not going to happen like that." Wearing a white medical gown, she sat back for hours while a doctor and nurse administered more than one hundred injections in her triceps, thighs, buttocks, face, and below her kneecaps. By the time she was done, past midnight, she had created medical history as the person to receive the most potent dose of gene therapy ever, all in the quest to fight aging.[25]

The aftermath was messy. The company put out a press release two weeks later with the headline "BioViva Treats First Patient with Gene Therapy to Reverse Aging."[26] There was no mention that Parrish was the patient, but she later told me she was wary about putting out the press release at all. A reporter contacted BioViva for a story about the ethical issues of the treatment, claiming nobody could really know the risks and give informed consent, and Parrish felt she had to get ahead of the game. She announced to the world that she was patient zero via Reddit.

Parrish and BioViva were bombarded with attention, some good, some bad. Being patient zero brought a lot of pressure. "There are a lot of expectations. People are constantly looking at me and saying, 'Do you look younger? Do you feel younger?' I'm a guinea pig." At the time the news broke, Parrish was particularly disappointed with the media reaction. "Some misinformation comes out and then people write it, and it's not true, and then everybody else just keeps writing the same crap," she told me. "So the biggest battle is getting the truth out there instead of just some crap that some writer initially wrote about it. The most frustrating thing about trying to do something good in the world is you're constantly misquoted and misrepresented based on someone else's biased opinion when it's supposed to be science. You get written into history based on what somebody wanted to write."

The criticism didn't just come from the press, however. George Martin, a gerontologist and member of BioViva's scientific advisory board, resigned soon after, and George Church, another advisor, stressed the importance of proper clinical trials.[27] Among the longevity and immortalist crowds, however, Parrish became an instant hero. Finally, someone was taking the initiative in the mission to beat aging. A year after the treatment, BioViva issued a follow-up press release with the results. The company had compared blood drawn from Parrish before and after the procedure and found her white blood cells' telomeres had increased in length by 9 percent. However, this was just one person's results, and no study was published. There was not enough data to measure, and the news was dismissed as inconsequential by the scientific community. [28]

One person remained silent throughout. Bill Andrews had made the therapy Parrish was given in Colombia, but was not quick to either praise or condemn her. He later told *Outside* magazine he was "a chickenshit" and took full blame for what happened. Despite being so involved in the production of the therapy, he had declined to take any kind of part in the experiment itself, mainly because he didn't want to jeopardize his career if something went wrong. Although Andrews praised the bravery of Parrish, he said he couldn't even tell if she had "used a legitimate protocol" and added, "We don't have anything we can really measure."[29]

When I spoke to Parrish, long after she and Andrews had gone their separate ways, she acknowledged his abilities and research in the field of telomeres but appeared to still be unhappy at the way he approached the experiment. "I did it because I thought we might be able to help seven billion people. He doesn't do it because he wants to live forever and he wants to make sure that all the kinks are worked out in that therapy." Since the experiment in 2015, Parrish has been a ubiquitous figure on the immortalist speaking circuit. She spoke at the first RAADfest and was also there when I tuned into the online version during the pandemic. During her talk, she appeared to be the sensible voice in the room, looking to temper expectations rather than let dreams of immortality run wild.

"Just trying to increase healthspan with the limited resources this industry has, it's a lot of pressure and people need to be tempered," she said. "They need to realize that it's good to say you want it, but it's more than just wanting it. You can't just have a tantrum. It takes a lot of work, and we are in the midst of a lot of work." For Parrish, that work includes battling against the current system of regulation, which she believes is holding back crucial medical technologies.

When we spoke, she was writing her thesis for an MBA on a new regulatory system she is proposing called Best Choice Medicine. Parrish wants to make it easier for gene therapies and other regenerative medicines to enter human testing trials. "It's medicine that performs better in animal models than anything that we have available to humans through a regulated market. These gene therapies are already performing better, hitting more points of metabolic disorder and dysfunction that happens with aging in animal models, and yet we continue to do animal models, and no humans get access to this?" she told me. "That's what we were saying when I took the gene therapies in 2015. We were saying no, we have to jump, at some point you have to jump, and if you don't jump you die of the same predictable diseases."

Parrish's model is not quite on par with the libertarian suggestions of some immortalists. She has no ambitions to destroy the FDA and is driven by a genuine desire to remove as much suffering as possible from the world. Some of her points are hard to argue against. She wants terminally ill patients to have access to therapies immediately after the patient is diagnosed, giving biotech companies the chance to test their treatments on humans rather than animals and patients an unlikely chance of a miracle cure. "The only way we're going to create better drugs for humans is to get them in humans. We can continue to extend the lifespan of rats and mice now and we can move into cats and dogs—people think that's the logical next step. I would say the logical next step is humans," she said.

I wanted to speak to scientists in the gene therapy field to see how they felt about the rate of progress, so I contacted George Church, who was listed as an advisor on BioViva's website.[30] Church is something of a legend in the scientific community. He teaches genetics at Harvard Medical School and MIT, heads up synthetic biology at Harvard's Wyss Institute for Biologically Inspired Engineering, and is director both of the US Department of Energy Technology Center and of the National Institutes of Health Center of Excellence in Genomic Science. His list of achievements is just as impressive as his job titles. He developed the first direct genomic sequencing method in 1984 and helped initiate the Human Genome Project that year. In 2005, he helped launch the Personal Genome Project. Church has founded and advised numerous biotech startups and is seen as a major contributor to CRISPR technology, which edits genes.[31]

Unsurprisingly given his résumé, he is well connected and respected in the gene therapy space. On a video call, Church, who sports a bushy beard and glasses, patiently explained his thoughts and smiled warmly toward the end of his answers. He told me Parrish was not the only person he knew who had conducted self-experimentation attempting to advance science. He said he encourages these pioneers to use a double-blind placebo crossover trial, where there are two samples, one a placebo and one the real thing. The researcher then injects themselves, not knowing if it's the real thing or not, and a few days or months later injects the other sample. That means at some point they get both the placebo and the real thing, but they don't know what order they had them in.

Church described this as a cheap and easy way to make self-experimentation results more useful, but also said there was some value in the work Parrish and others had done. "If you have enough resources, it's totally obvious what you should do—a full-fledged clinical trial. But it helps to do these little things because at a minimum it shows it's not toxic. And if it's nontoxic, a whole variety of people will want to try it out, and then you'll find out if it's toxic in a wide variety of people," he said. "It's hard to show efficacy, that's the other thing you have to do, you have to very carefully do baseline. And if you know you're getting the experimental over the control there are going to be all types of placebo effects. I know one of these people that self-administered lifted a refrigerator and said, 'Wow, I can lift a refrigerator,' and hurt his back. So you're tempted to try things you don't normally try and then report it anecdotally, so it's much better if you don't know which treatment you're getting."

Church told me he doesn't consider himself to be working toward immortality or even longevity but focuses entirely on age reversal. He said human longevity was out of the scope of most laboratories, "even though they claim they're working on it." In age reversal, one of the more exciting companies to spin out from Church's lab is Rejuvenate Bio, a startup cofounded by Church himself. The company wants to reverse aging in dogs by adding new DNA instructions to their bodies.[32] These kinds of treatments have shown promise in worms, flies, and mice, and Church sees dogs as the next step. He believes any treatment that would make dogs live longer would be hugely popular and fund the next stage: clinical trials in humans. However, he doesn't believe this would lead to immortality in the truest sense of the word.

"Age reversal is somewhat related to longevity, which is somewhat related to immortality. The problem with immortality is it's vague about infinity. When you start dealing with infinities, it's not the real world. Even the universe is not probably immortal. And it's not even that old yet, it's only about 13.7 billion years old. So if we put that extreme version aside, it's likely that if you can reverse aging you can get another ten, twenty, forty years, although it will take a long time to prove that. If you get forty years, then you might be able to get another forty years, and so forth."

Church sees two main pathways to reverse aging. One is the silver bullet approach, to find a way to address aging at a cellular level, which would help avoid the "whack-a-mole" effect of fixing one problem, only for another to quickly appear. He told me evidence of winding back the biological clock gives him hope this may work. "You have to hit all the organ systems and all the biochemical pathways, probably, to avoid the whack-a-mole. Evidence that you can avoid the whack-a-mole is that at the cellular level or tissue level, we've shown that for both humans and mice and a few other mammals that you can reverse the clock significantly, you can go from an eighty-year-old human cell that is senescent to something that is close to zero years old."

The other approach is to address each part of the puzzle separately.

"I don't really care which it is, I think our technology is capable of doing it either way," Church said. "A lot of people love the one single silver bullet, but many of my inventions are complicated enough that I know the advantages of complication . . . Not everything can be $E=MC^2$ or F=ma, there are some truly interesting complicated things, including our body. But I don't think it's so complicated that we necessarily have to control all twenty-five thousand genes. There's going to be a few leverage points that may be sufficient."

Although Church works with animals, he hasn't found much inspiration in a lot of the longer-living species mentioned at the start of the chapter. He said the jellyfish was basically a yeast, and too far away from humans to really learn anything useful. The bowhead whale is more interesting to age-reversal scientists, as it's similar metabolically and developmentally, according to Church. But even long-lived humans like Calment offer few hints at the secrets of reversing aging. "We've sequenced them, and we hoped we would learn something, but it's very challenging because there are three million differences between each of them, and each other, and us as well. It's underpowered statistically. We were hoping something would jump out at us, it might still . . . I don't think we've learned that much from supercentenarians yet."

Church works on the very cutting edge of science and told me he has always been attracted to technologies that operate on an exponential curve. It's a concept similar to Kurzweil's singularity, but more grounded in hard evidence. These scientific breakthroughs are a crucial aspect of de Grey's longevity escape velocity theory, but it can be difficult to predict exactly when they'll take off.

"Certain things are simple engineering, and you can kind of project the curve, but I don't think aging reversal is one of those just yet," Church told me. "We're going to be going into clinical trials for a number of age-reversal therapies, but our mice and dogs are not living particularly longer, which I think is what people will care about. So I don't think we're quite there yet, but it's exponential so it's going to be fast. I wouldn't be surprised if it happened in our lifetime, if we got really good aging reversal technology and a bunch of other medical breakthroughs that impact the poorer parts of the world."

Parrish and Church know and respect each other, but their differing attitudes show the chasm between scientists and immortalists. Parrish believes the finishing line is in sight and will do anything to reach that point faster, including self-experimentation. She is frustrated by the delays put in place by organizations like the FDA and wants answers now. Church is much more philosophical about his own area of study. He would like to see his own life extended by a breakthrough in his lab, but he appears to be quite calm about the issue either way. When I spoke to Parrish about stem cells and some of the comments researchers in that field had made about the unproven companies offering questionable cures, she was quick to reproach me for siding with the scientists.

She argued that they were out of touch with patients, and unable to see the damage diseases were doing to everyday people's lives.[33] It was a populist view, which made me slightly uncomfortable, perhaps because for a while I wanted to agree. But the scientists brought me back to Earth every time, insisting patience was the key, not outlandish statements claiming eternal life was just around the corner. None of the major research labs working in stem cells, gene therapy, or other age-related fields appear to have immortality as their stated goal. Their mission is to extend healthspan, and while it does overlap with the aims of immortalists, it's drastically different.

Over the course of my conversations with immortalists and during the talks I'd attended, two major topics were consistently brought up in an attempt to fill the major gaps on the path to immortality. One was nanotechnology. The other was uploading the human brain to a computer.

11

THE DIGITAL RESURRECTION

If **modern science fiction** is to emulate *Astounding*, the magazine which predicted the dropping of the atomic bomb, then it's highly likely mind uploading will become reality. A host of books and films have imagined worlds where it's possible to store the contents of a human brain on a computer. Spurred on by these fictional worlds, transhumanists and immortalists have sought to accomplish the most gore-free form of everlasting life.

When I spoke to Alexei Turchin, a Moscow-based researcher and author of several papers on the prospect of digital immortality, I asked if he was comfortable with me recording the conversation for my notes. It was a redundant query. Turchin, a keen transhumanist, keeps a record of almost every conversation he has and regularly films a video diary. He's not feeding an out-of-control ego or auditioning for a role in the latest reality TV show, he's creating a record of his personality so he can be digitally resurrected in the future.

Cryonics is the most popular and widely available backup option for immortalists, but the community has always retained an interest in digital immortality, a solution with similarly optimistic outcomes and a far less gruesome means of preparation. This method of resurrection involves making a digital copy of a human brain, storing it somewhere safe until after that person dies, and then using powerful new technologies to return them to the living, either in a synthetic body or in a digital form residing in some sort of metaphysical world.

Turchin first contemplated immortality at school when a classmate died suddenly. He wanted to tackle death immediately, but concluded he had all the ideas but lacked any means to take action, so put his ambitions on hold. He graduated in 1997 from Moscow State University, where he studied physics and art history. While there, he discovered transhumanism and joined the Russian Transhumanist Movement in 2007. In 2012, Turchin cofounded the world's first political party based around transhumanism, the Longevity Party. He began writing roadmaps to reach immortality, with each using different means to reach eternal life. Plan A was regular life extension, Plan B was cryonics, Plan C was digital immortality, and Plan D was quantum immortality. Digital immortalists, like cryonicists, largely acknowledge their goal is a long shot, but they're willing to put in the work anyway to improve their odds.

Turchin records several hours of conversation between him and his wife every day and tries to log as much video footage as possible. The couple recently had their first child, and while this major life event took a toll on their documentation efforts, they still try to fit in sessions whenever they can. Aside from the audio and video recordings, Turchin also keeps a regular diary and writes down any dreams he has. All of this, he hopes, will help future scientists rebuild his personality accurately when he's brought back to life.[1]

Both Turchin and his wife are also signed up to be cryogenically preserved by the Russian cryonics organization KrioRus, where Turchin's mother's brain currently resides. But he knows how much can go wrong with cryonics, which is why he sees digital immortality as so crucial. He told me the frailty of cryonics organizations could scupper his resurrection plans, either because they'll run out of money and pull the plug, or the cryopreservation won't be conducted properly and there'll be nothing left of him to be brought back to life. "It is like a vicious circle here, a small amount of money creates problems with technology and the public view, and then it's not easy to attract money. It's a small business, but it is growing because they have cheaper prices," Turchin said of KrioRus.

His hesitation to trust the cryonics provider is understandable, given the company's current turmoil. Turchin said the organization is similar to Alcor but a lot cheaper and so has less sophisticated technology. He also told me the organization had suffered a split around two years ago, when the couple who cofounded KrioRus ended their relationship. Now there is a battle for control with a hostile acquisition, a move to a new headquarters, and confusion as one side owns the website while the other faction owns the facility.[2] This type of infighting, and the fact that the concept is not too popular in Russia, worries Turchin. "We concluded that the main problem is that people do not want to live long, so the avenue of immortality is not very strong in the general population. People prefer to die. It is changing now, but it is changing slowly. Even billionaires and governments depend on the popularity of ideas, so they can't do unpopular things or it will be bad for PR relations, so that is why going to Mars is a better sounding idea than resurrecting the dead."

But together, the two methods give him some hope. "I think that the combined chance is like 10 percent, maybe smaller," Turchin said on a video call from his slightly chaotic home office. "Digital immortality has a small chance, but combined they have better chances because the data that will be lost in the freezing restoration for the brain could be filled with digital immortality data, somehow collaborated with my previous recordings to check it's okay."

To ensure he maximizes his chances of being digitally resurrected, Turchin stores his recordings on several different devices, including optical discs, flash drives, hard disks, and M-Discs, which come with a long-term guarantee. He also buried some of the recordings at his summer home using a hermetically sealed bag to ensure they don't decompose.

All this assumes scientists of the future will develop a technology capable of resurrecting people. Turchin believes the success of these technologies rests on the successful construction of a super sophisticated artificial intelligence. In one of his papers, titled "Classification of Approaches to Technological Resurrection," he examined artificial intelligence's role in digital resurrection and concluded that AI will play an essential role in all forms of digital immortality, where people's minds are uploaded to a computer.[3] Initially, this option will only be available to those who've meticulously documented their lives, but as AI evolves and becomes stronger, more humans could be resurrected. The most sophisticated iteration of this AI will be a machine the size of a planet powered by a Dyson Sphere, a theoretical device which would harness the entire energy of the sun.

Turchin predicts this technology would be capable of examining the entire recorded history of humanity and resurrecting everyone in some kind of collective digital simulation. Turchin admitted this relies on the dual assumption that humanity would be capable of building an all-powerful AI and that it wouldn't turn out evil and attempt to wipe out the species entirely.

If all that fails, the final plan is quantum immortality, a bizarre theory that sounds like it was written for a comic book. Many scientists believe parallel worlds could be created every second by *Sliding Doors*–style moments, when every mundane choice we make creates new branches of reality. Each of these worlds would be slightly different but largely the same, and immortalists see them as a loophole to immortality. If new worlds are constantly created with slightly different realities, there will be a world where cryonics, digital immortality, and superpowered AI all worked and were developed successfully, and in some parallel realm, immortality has been achieved. It's not clear how that would benefit their current and present version of themselves, still struggling with the prospect of death. They would be alive in some reality, but their consciousness in this one would still die. Turchin's plans are wildly ambitious, as he himself acknowledged, but the seeds of a digital afterlife have already been sown, and a fledgling industry has begun to emerge.

. . .

In the late 2010s, a handful of startups offered grieving relatives the chance to talk to the dead. Their apps drew comparisons to a 2013 episode of the British dystopian sci-fi TV show *Black Mirror* titled "Be Right Back." The protagonist of the episode, distraught at the death of her boyfriend, installs an app which mimics his personality and allows her to pretend she's still communicating with him. As with most *Black Mirror* episodes, this ends badly, and highlights how quickly the concept can become creepy. But it didn't put off the entrepreneurs testing the capabilities of chatbots and AI.

In 2015, a Belarusian man named Roman Mazurenko, still in his thirties, was hit by a car in Moscow and died. After hearing about the death of her close friend, Eugenia Kuyda began reading through the thousands of text messages they'd exchanged since they'd met in 2008. The texts were of a distinctive style—Mazurenko used very specific phrases and was mildly dyslexic—and they provided a shred of comfort and familiarity as she mourned the loss of her close friend. At the time, Kuyda, an entrepreneur and software developer, was working on a messenger app called Luka, which used AI to chat like a human. Inspired by the *Black Mirror* episode, she modified her app to act more like the one in the TV show, so she could create a digital ghost of Mazurenko.

Kuyda gathered messages from friends and family and used them to create a bot that could parrot human language, making it possible for her to talk to a mocked-up version of her deceased friend. The app talked a lot like Mazurenko and was able to recall many of his memories and regurgitate them. Kuyda posted the chat logs of friends talking to the bot, and they were surprisingly human in their flow and language. Buoyed by the success of Luka, Kuyda made another app called Replika, which asked users a series of questions until it could mimic their personalities, then provided a digital version of themselves to talk to. The app was extremely successful and was downloaded millions of times. [4]

Kuyda isn't the only person to have created a chatbot to cope with the death of a loved one. James Vlahos, a journalist and AI enthusiast, developed Dadbot, a chatbot which allowed him to converse with a digital version of his father. In 2016, John Vlahos was diagnosed with lung cancer. When his son heard the news, he began recording his conversations with his father, with the intention of writing a book about him when he died. He built up 203 pages of transcripts from their conversations, containing memories, anecdotes, and recollections of his father's career, marriage, and interests. Vlahos used those transcripts to create his bot, a software that runs on his phone and allows him to talk to a digital representation of his late father. Buoyed by the success of Dadbot, Vlahos set up Here After, a company that offered the same type of software to the world.[5]

But the idea of chatbots mimicking dead people never really took off.

In 2020, Microsoft was granted a patent that would allow the company to make a chatbot based on images, voice data, social media posts, electronic messages, and personal information of a person. "The specific person [who the chatbot represents] may correspond to a past or present entity (or a version thereof), such as a friend, a relative, an acquaintance, a celebrity, a fictional character, a historical figure, a random entity etc.," the patent stated.[6] The application was filed in 2017, and since then it seems Microsoft changed its ethical approach to the deployment of artificial intelligence. In a tweet in 2021, Tim O'Brien, Microsoft's general manager of AI programs, said he "confirmed that there's no plan for this," and replying to another user agreed the patent was "disturbing."[7] But while giants like Microsoft don't fancy building bots, some deep-pocketed individuals are going all in on mind uploading.

. . .

Martine Rothblatt didn't take a conventional route to success. She dropped out of UCLA after a year to travel and visited Europe, Iran, and Kenya before ending her trip in the Seychelles. There she stumbled on a NASA tracking station and asked an employee to give her a tour of the facility, which helped guide spacecraft to distant planets. The experience completely changed her perspective and life goals. She returned to UCLA and graduated in communication studies in 1977, writing her thesis on international direct-broadcast satellites. Rothblatt worked in the global telecommunications sector and spent time at PanAmSat, where she helped take on and defeat the global satellite monopoly Intelsat. In 1990 she founded two companies of her own, Geostar and Sirius. The latter, a satellite radio business, was hugely successful and went public in 1993. Rothblatt left soon after when her daughter was diagnosed with pulmonary hypertension, a potentially lethal disease at the time. She dropped everything and began researching possible cures.[8]

"I finally discovered a pathway that could get me to a medicine that could halt the progression of our daughter Jenesis' illness. And so, I decided that I had a new purpose in life. My previous purpose was to help humanity expand off the earth and into space, but my new purpose was to save my daughter's life. And I didn't care about anything else—I didn't care about eating, I didn't care about anything—I was going to do whatever it took to save my daughter's life," she said in an interview with *The Washington Post*.[9]

Rothblatt founded the PPH Cure Foundation and later started United Therapeutics, a biotechnology company. Her daughter was given the treatments she needed, one of which was developed and sold by Rothblatt's company. She is still alive today. Around that time, Rothblatt underwent sex reassignment surgery, having been born Martin Rothblatt. United Therapeutics is now a highly successful biotech company, and in 2013 Rothblatt was the highest paid female

CEO in the United States, earning $38 million.[10] The company focused on transplantable organs and developed a system which enabled lungs that were previously discarded to be made ready for transplantation. But Rothblatt's ambitions stretched even further, as she used her fortune to advance the immortalist cause.

Between 2002 and 2004, Rothblatt helped set up three organizations with similar goals under the umbrella company the Terasem Movement. The first two nonprofits both sought to ensure that scientific advances related to longer lives, like cyber consciousness and nanotechnology, were used responsibly. They also made steps to enable immortality through the digital storage of personal information. Two programs, named CyBeRev and LifeNaut, collected and stored information from people interested in having their digital selves preserved for eternity.

They worked separately until they merged in 2021, the data from CyBeRev slowly being incorporated into the records of LifeNaut. Both projects have created what they call mindfiles, which consist of the digital reflections and biographical information of an individual, and are stored for free by the organizations. The files are kept secure on a hard disc in an off-site location, on the cloud via Amazon, and copied onto M-Discs. Individuals go through a set of questions to submit information for their mindfiles, and can be coached through the process by a staff member at the newly merged entity, Terasem Movement Foundation, Inc. These mindfiles aren't just stored, they're also beamed into outer space via a radio signal in the hope that either alien lifeforms or people from the future who can travel faster than the speed of light are able to intercept the signal and receive the information. LifeNaut also offers individuals the chance to send a DNA sample to be stored for the future as BioFiles.[11]

Bruce Duncan sits at the head of the Terasem Movement and is responsible for the safe upkeep of the mindfiles and BioFiles. He is based in the organization's headquarters in Vermont, and has been there since studying at the University of Vermont. He was working on a project in his main area of interest, international peace studies and conflict resolution, when he read Rothblatt was looking for someone to help set up her new startup and pursue her dream of mind uploading. Duncan said he was probably picked for the job because he had shown self-reliance in the past, and his skill with conflict resolution would come in handy for an organization Rothblatt was determined to make completely transparent and open.

"I have found that this project challenges you in so many ways. It's at an intersection of lots of different disciplines, questions, implications—ethical, moral, even spiritual challenges," he said on a call. Duncan is also in charge of the upkeep and development of the foundation's other major project, BINA48 (Breakthrough Intelligence via Neural Architecture, 48 exaflops per second) a robot designed to look like Rothblatt's wife, Bina.

BINA48 is the foundation's first attempt to create a physical representation of its ultimate goal, to install the memories and personalities of a person inside a robot. The machine was built by roboticist David Hanson and has thirty-two facial motors under its rubber skin but only has a head and shoulders, no body.[12] It has a microphone to hear, and voice recognition software allows it to listen to the world around it and participate in conversations. BINA48 uses two cameras to see and deploys facial recognition software to remember faces of people who visit frequently.[13] Watching videos of the robot talking, even ignoring the fact it has no body, it's impossible to pretend BINA48 is real. The facial movements seem awkward, and the voice sounds like the default diction of a computer rather than a human. Despite this, its conversational skills are impressive.

Around 2014, an artist named Stephanie Dinkins saw a video of BINA48 in action and was surprised that one of the most advanced pieces of technology she had seen depicted a black woman. "It shocked me because I didn't understand how the black woman was the beacon for the technology," said Dinkins, who is African American, in a later interview.[14] "I immediately wanted to see if I could meet the robot and talk to it, just to contextualize it within the idea of the technology, and then its relationship to humans as well." Dinkins spent time talking with the machine and began an art project called Conversations with Bina48. She described many aspects of the robot as inauthentic when she first started talking to it in 2014. When she asked BINA48 about racism, the answer "fell flat," according to Dinkins. She concluded that although the robot was modeled on a black woman, it was influenced by the mindset of the white men who had created it. BINA48 was picking up on social interactions and other cues from its real-world conversations, constantly learning from the world around it. But if the initial algorithms used to build the robot failed to take into account anything outside the worldview of its makers, then it's unlikely a robot could teach itself life experiences of people from different backgrounds.

"I started to critique the idea of what the algorithms are doing and what kind of data is being used, where the data is being culled from, why, and what that means for humans. If the algorithm is using data that is biased—data that contains historical biases or the biases of the people making the software—how do we extricate that once it is encoded into the system?" asked Dinkins.[15]

Dinkins brings up a major worry for advocates of digital immortality. The data collected from people before they die will have to be run on software, and that software will be filled with algorithms and assumptions based on the real world. If biases are evident in those algorithms, then the whole identity of a person could be lost. Artificial intelligence is still in its infancy, but it has already experienced what *The New York Times* referred to as a "white man problem."[16]

In the past, artificial intelligence systems used in image recognition software have classified black people as gorillas and rejected an Asian man's passport photo because it deemed his eyes to be closed. There have been many other incidents, not least in predictive policing algorithms deployed in cities including Chicago and New Orleans, which give police the opportunity to pick out people who are supposedly predisposed to committing crime, which some have argued leads to profiling.[17] The most obvious solution to this problem is to ensure that the teams putting together the AI systems are as diverse as possible and are capable of understanding and dealing with societal differences.

But that's not going so well. A report released in 2019 showed that at Google and Microsoft, two of the biggest technology employers and major players in the AI world, the proportion of technical employees who are either black or Latinx rose less than one percentage point from 2014. Apple doesn't do much better—the share of black technical workers at the company has remained at 6 percent over that same timeframe, while Amazon does not report its tech workforce demographics at all.[18] With those kinds of statistics, it's hard to see a future where the major technology players will be in a position to offer any kind of artificial intelligence technology made by a group representative of the whole world.

At Terasem, Rothblatt and Duncan, at least, took Dinkins's findings to heart and addressed her concerns. "She raised challenging questions about why BINA48 isn't better about speaking to her perspective of an African American female living in the United States," Duncan said of Dinkins. "We invited her back to give BINA48 an update by having a conversation with Bina the human about Bina's experience of growing up black and female in the United States in the late '60s. We took that information and transcribed it and integrated it into BINA48's current mindfile. So she now speaks in a more sophisticated and specific way about her identity, about her experience of bigotry and prejudice."[19]

Duncan doesn't speak like a mad scientist trying to bring a robot to life, and for good reason. Terasem is built on a moral code as much as a technological ambition, and seeks to ensure that any progress is achieved in the most ethical way possible. He became particularly passionate when talking about the importance of identifying the driving forces behind an idea and said anyone chasing a goal like digital immortality should constantly ask themselves what the world would be like if they succeed, and if they would want to live in the future they are creating.

"Just because you can doesn't mean it's going to be a good future. You might want to use some wisdom, some compassion, some intellect to discern if it's a viable path forward for you, your community, your region, or humanity as a whole," Duncan said.

The Terasem Group isn't just two foundations joined into one. It's also a religion. In 2004, Rothblatt and those close to her set up the final project—the Terasem Movement Transreligion (TMT). The TMT has locations in Florida and Vermont and is a not-for-profit religious organization. The goal of the religion is to build a collective consciousness made up of the immortal extension of its followers, known as "joiners." It has four core beliefs.[20] The first is Life Is Purposeful, which asserts that the purpose of life is to "create diversity, unity and joyful immortality everywhere." The second is Death Is Optional, which is fairly self-explanatory but leans heavily toward digital immortality. "Nobody dies so long as enough information about them is preserved. They are simply in a state of 'cybernetic biostasis.' Future mindware technology will enable them to be revived, if desired, to healthy and independent living," the religion's website states. The third tenet is God Is Technological, which suggests that as we implement new technology that is increasingly powerful, we are "making God," and the ethical use of nanotechnology will "ultimately connect all consciousness and control the cosmos." The final belief is a more basic one—Love Is Essential, which tells its followers that love makes the happiness of others essential to our own happiness, and "love must connect everyone to achieve life's purpose and to make God complete."[21]

This is the third religious or quasi-religious organization detailed in this book. The Terasem religion differs from People Unlimited and the Church of Perpetual Life as it has a set of very specific tenets and a clear goal. It does not have a hazy hero story, like Dave Asprey's

Bulletproof Coffee endeavors or those of mainstream religions, but seems to be born out of concern that technological progress, if done wrong, could end really badly for all of us.

Whether backed up by a religion or not, the digital uploading method of preservation has some serious flaws. There are many, many different elements that make us what we are, and most of them are not recorded at all. For example, a person's personality and future actions could be massively impacted by being picked on by a particular child at school. Even if you were to gather all the data, recordings, and writing that person has ever done, that life event would probably not be adequately archived to recreate the impact it had on shaping someone's life. If you go further into science fiction, through alien intervention or time travel, perhaps it would be possible to gather all the data needed to digitally recreate someone, but both of those possibilities go against the current understanding of the universe.

Digital resurrection would be far more probable if it were possible to scan the human brain and extract memories that way. It's a slightly terrifying thought, but some believe one day we can take slices of the brain and gather information. Turchin includes brain slicing in his roadmap to digital immortality. He says in this method, the brain would not have to be kept in the same conditions found in cryonics. "Lenin's brain was sliced after his death, and they are still preserved in Moscow, so it could be scanned and brought back to life. But Lenin had brain disease so his brain is damaged anyway," Turchin told me.

But even if a brain or a slice of brain was preserved perfectly, scanning it would be immensely difficult, and to properly restore a brain either to a digital simulation or some kind of robot, we would need to know exactly how our brains work, and figure out where consciousness comes from, something that neuroscientists, philosophers, and psychologists have been brooding over for a couple of centuries. A big part of that process is to map the human brain, a task which so far has proven well beyond our capabilities. In 2019, the Allen Institute for Brain Science in Seattle, Washington, successfully mapped one cubic millimeter of mouse brain, which was roughly the size of a grain of sand. In that tiny part of brain, there were 100,000 neurons and one billion connections between them. To complete this task, researchers had five transmission electron microscopes running continuously for five months, collecting more than 100 million images of 25,000 slices of mouse brain, each of which were just 40 nanometers thick.[22]

After that, software developed especially for the task took around three months to put the images together in a 3D volume. The total amount of data collected during the scans was two petabytes, the equivalent of two million gigabytes.[23] While the Allen Institute's results were impressive, it was all for a mere sand grain portion of a mouse's brain. It's thought a whole mouse brain could be mapped within the next decade, such is the pace of progress in this field, but the human brain is so much more complicated—it contains about 86 billion neurons, connected by at least 100 trillion synapses.

The task is incredibly difficult, but theoretically not impossible. And one man wants to make sure we're prepared for when we do master that ability. Robert McIntyre has been fascinated by the information contained in a person for as long as he can remember. When he was in high school, he was given an assignment in a humanities class asking him what he wanted to do with his life. He wrote he wanted to figure out how to access the information in the brain and digitize it, something he felt would create an unprecedented opportunity for humanity. I spoke to McIntyre on a long phone call, the first hour of which he spent grilling me to decide if he wanted to be interviewed at all.

McIntyre went to college at MIT, determined to help find the key to the data held in our heads. But as he searched through journals and papers from the field of neuroscience, he realized science was so far from accomplishing that goal it was almost a hopeless ambition. McIntyre switched his focus to AI, hoping to create tools that would speed up progress in his lifelong obsession.[24]

"Computer science is the closest thing to magic that we have in this world. You write something down and it's like a little spell, and it actually does something useful that's cool," he told me.

After graduating, he returned to MIT to study in its master's program for artificial intelligence, but before that took a year off to work on the thesis that would form a large part of the degree he hadn't started yet. He lived in a barn for a while, then moved to Kansas to be with his father. They would go on walks in the desert regularly, always strapping revolvers to their legs in case they encountered rattlesnakes or other dangerous wildlife. On one of these walks, his father asked McIntyre what he would do if AI wasn't an option. He thought about the question for a while and realized he was only studying AI to speed up progress in unlocking the brain, but if he were to put his efforts into preserving brains, he could buy time for the whole world. The two got really excited about this prospect and drove into the nearest town to download papers on cryobiology. But again, the amount of progress made in the field disappointed McIntyre. "It kind of put a whole damper on our spirits because we were like, 'Well, geez, that seems really tough,'" he recalled.[25]

McIntyre returned to MIT to pursue his masters in AI. He won the prize for the best thesis that year and was asked to return for a PhD, but by this point his head had been turned again. During his studies for his master's he discovered an organization called the Brain Preservation Foundation (BPF), run by Kenneth Hayworth, an expert neuroscientist and brain preservation and mind uploading advocate. McIntyre began volunteering his time at the BPF, attending meetings and helping with the website. Hayworth was keen to establish that methods of preserving the brain weren't nonsensical, so he organized a $100,000 challenge prize. The first team to preserve a mammalian brain in a way which could be proven would last at least one hundred years and maintain the synaptic connections would take the prize fund. The competition laid down the gauntlet to two specific groups—the neuroscientists who'd been using aldehyde chemistry to preserve brains, and the cryonics enthusiasts who claimed they'd been freezing them to reanimate later on.

Two competitors emerged: Shawn Mikula from the Max Planck Institute in Germany who was working on plasticizing whole brains, and a company called 21st Century Medicine, run by one of Mike Darwin's former colleagues, Greg Fahy. The latter company licensed some of its technology to Alcor, and McIntyre described their techniques as "the idealized versions" of the work the world's largest cryonics company had conducted in the past.

The cryonics team had a problem from the start—their brains shrunk. "The problem with their idea is you get all this shrinkage because the cryoprotectants don't cross into the cells fast enough for them to be loaded efficiently, and so the cells will shrink. A brain can shrink to two-thirds of its original size or so, or even 50 percent of its original size, depending on the loading protocol used. When you look at that under a microscope, it looks all swirly and it's hard to really notice synapses. So a neuroscientist like Ken Hayworth would say it's not traceable to my eyes, so it wouldn't qualify for the brain preservation prize," McIntyre said.

The 21st Century Medicine team argued the brain was still intact, it was just smaller, but there was no way to confirm significant damage hadn't occurred. Mikula, meanwhile, used aldehyde cross-linking to preserve the brain initially, but his second stage, where he tried to make sure the brain could be stored in that manner for a really long time, was producing cracks and wasn't really working.[26] As part of his volunteer work, McIntyre researched the two techniques to make a YouTube video and realized that between the two of them, they had an answer. "You fix it with the aldehyde, which preserves it instantly, and then you take all the time you'd ever want in the world to slowly add cryoprotectant so they don't osmotically crush the cells, and then you vitrify the thing and you're good. You turn it into a gel with aldehydes, and then you turn that gel into a glass by vitrification, and then your brain is preserved," he said.

Instead of returning to MIT, McIntyre approached 21st Century Medicine and told them he could win them the Brain Preservation Prize. The company gave him a lab and two years to complete his task, and after some initial issues with the cryoprotectants, he won the $100,000 in just nine months.[27] While McIntyre was pleased with the results, his method was not suitable for cryonics or organ preservation, the two areas of interest for the company. His technique met the requirements of the prize, but while it stored the brain perfectly, it could never be reanimated.

Then McIntyre started his own company, Nectome, in 2015.

"I didn't really know what I was doing. I basically spent some time trying to figure out what a business plan would be and talking to people about this and trying to figure out how I could do it, and do it well and what the next steps would be to properly validate this," he said. After around six months, he got a government grant to look into brain preservation and did some contract work to keep the company alive. Not long after, he broke into the Silicon Valley investment community and secured funding.

But in 2018, McIntyre's company got into trouble. An *MIT Technology Review* article reported Nectome's solution was 100 percent fatal, claiming McIntyre's solution would require assisted suicide to make it work. While this was certainly something McIntyre was contemplating at the time, it was also something of an error in communication on his part. The reporter wrote that the brain also had to be "fresh" and that McIntyre had contacted lawyers associated with the End of Life Option Act in California, which allows doctor-assisted suicide in some cases.[28] In the fallout, an MIT biologist ceased working with the company and the university released a statement distancing it from Nectome entirely. Social media didn't help, when users incorrectly decided that the name Nectome was Latin for "I have been killed."[29] The name does, in fact, come from the term connectome, which refers to that elusive map of all the brain's neurons and connections. Perhaps McIntyre had gotten carried away, perhaps it was a simple communication issue.

Aubrey de Grey told me he once gave a TED Talk on how to be a successful heretic, and all but two of his pointers were about communicating properly. "I think it's fair to say that Robert did not adhere to my principles back then. And it didn't work out well for him as a result. At some level, if you're trying to be a pioneer and make a difference, you're going to piss people off. If you're not pissing anybody off, then you're probably not making a difference. At one level it kind of goes with the territory, but on the other there are ways to optimize," he told me.

By the time I caught up with McIntyre in 2021, he appeared to have learned some key lessons from his earlier encounter. He hadn't just developed a deep suspicion of journalists, he'd also dialed back any claims of reanimation in the future. Now he says his main goal is to preserve brains so future technology can read and decipher the information inside them. McIntyre compares this lofty goal to a new stage of human evolution, where information can be passed down generations more effectively. He doesn't believe there is any kind of brain preservation field right now and dismissed the efforts of cryonics as inconsequential, given how few people had actually signed up to it. He compares his work to that of the San Diego Frozen Zoo, a group of scientists who in 1972 began freezing the DNA of endangered animals.[30] When they started, there was no reason to assume anything they froze would be useful at all in the future, but as technology improved their actions became incredibly prescient. "It's a generally useful fact that if what you want to do is preserve stuff, generally the technology that enables you to preserve the stuff comes way before the technology to be able to read the stuff or manipulate the stuff or really do anything useful with the stuff," McIntyre explained.

Nectome's approach has been criticized by some members of the neuroscience community, but backed up by others. There's no way of knowing if McIntyre's technique, which uses glutaraldehyde, actually preserves all the information inside the brain, like memories. But it's also almost impossible to disprove. McIntyre believes there is clear evidence that the brain's memories would survive the preservation procedure and would be readable by the technology of the future. He pointed to people who had been dead for hours after drowning in icy lakes. When their bodies were warmed up, they returned to life, with their memories still intact.

McIntyre also described deep hypothermic circulatory arrest, a surgical technique that involves cooling the body and stopping blood circulation and brain function for up to one hour. The procedure is a carefully managed clinical death which enables surgeons to carry out tricky interventions. After the surgery, despite being dead for an hour, patients do not suffer long-term memory loss, suggesting memories are in some way physically imprinted in our brains. "Either neuroscience is catastrophically wrong about how memory works, or we can preserve memories," he insisted.

Toward the end of our conversation, which lasted well over two hours, McIntyre can't help but mention the ambitions he has for the future. "I hope neuroscience as a profession itself recognizes the ultimate goal, or the ultimate crown jewel, of neuroscience would be mind emulation with uploading. Simply because if you really understand something then you can build it. And until you can build it, you don't really understand it." He is under no illusions that this will be achieved any time soon but can't understand the hesitance in making it a realistic goal.

"I think neuroscience is stuck there because it doesn't want to get made fun of, because these ideas are kind of kooky. And I think that's a shame because what really inspires people is this grand vision, and I don't think the grand vision is crazy. Obviously it's not crazy—if you know what you're doing, it's absolutely true that an architecture can be made that runs a human mind, you have one in your skull right now, and the only thing that separates us from that is mastery."

McIntyre is now attempting to prove that even very tiny amounts of data can be extracted from brains he's preserved. He's working on animal brains but has also done work on human brains donated for scientific research.[31] He hopes he'll be proven correct, like the San Diego Frozen Zoo, and his work will be celebrated in the future as a great act of human conservation. There's no way of knowing the outcome until we make some serious advances in our technological capabilities.

And one of the areas which promises to usher in the kind of future McIntyre and others predict is nanotechnology, a much-hyped field with a confusing number of definitions.

12

A RACE TO THE BOTTOM

Most people first hear about nanotechnology through cinema. Science fiction screenwriters lean heavily on the concept to explain away some of the more far-fetched undertakings seen on screen. The mass-murdering robot in *Terminator II* used nanotechnology to shapeshift, *Star Trek*'s evil Borg civilization relies on nanobots to assimilate its victims, and various Marvel superheroes have utilized the technology to keep themselves alive long enough to sell more merchandise. In film and TV, nanotechnology represents the future, a far-flung place where cars fly, aliens invade, and—sometimes—people live forever. But in fact, nanotechnology has been used here in the real world for a very long time.

The Romans developed technology way ahead of their time. They built transport infrastructure, water delivery systems, and even heated baths, all considered advanced for a civilization of that era. Astonishingly, they also dabbled in nanotechnology. The Lycurgus Cup, named after the king depicted tangled in vines in the vessel's glass, has some fascinating properties. When light shines through the front of the cup, it appears jade green. But when the cup is turned around, it glows a blood red. The British Museum acquired the artefact in the 1950s,[1] and it baffled scientists for decades. In 1990, researchers took broken fragments of the chalice and put them under extremely powerful microscopes. What they found was incredible. The Roman artists who created the cup had impregnated the glass with tiny particles of silver and gold, which were ground down until they were just fifty nanometers in diameter. To achieve the color-shifting effect, the mix of particles—which were less than one-thousandth the size of a grain of salt—needed to be exact. The complexity proved the Romans had mastered the art of infusing nanoparticles into objects, even if they probably didn't know exactly how it worked.[2]

The Romans weren't the only early civilization known to use nanotechnology. The windows of late medieval churches were found to display the same properties. They shone a magnificent luminous red and yellow as the sun passed through them thanks to the gold and silver nanoparticles meticulously placed inside the glass.[3] But the coolest early use of the technology came from the Middle East. Europeans were first introduced to Damascus Steel when the Crusaders attempted to retake the Holy Lands, beginning in the eleventh century. Swords made of this material could slice a silk scarf floating to the ground. They were extraordinarily strong, and flexible enough to bend from hilt to tip. Many of the Crusaders learned this the hard way—it was often them being cleaved in two midair instead of a piece of clothing.

The swords were immediately recognizable by watery, wavy marks in the steel, and any Crusader close enough to see it was already at risk of losing a limb.[4] Armorers from across the region, including Persia, closely guarded the secrets of Damascus steel, and many legends and myths emerged speculating on how the swords were made. Most focused on the way the metal was quenched, the process of cooling it rapidly after heating it to extreme temperatures. Some of the rumors were wild. One suggested the swords were quenched in dragon blood, while a person in Pakistan, who said they'd had a sword in their family for generations, insisted its makers in Afghanistan cooled it in donkey urine. Medieval smiths in Europe believed the urine of either a red-haired boy or a three-year-old goat fed only ferns for three days were the secret ingredient. Writing found in Asia Minor told a grislier tale. It said to temper a Damascus sword, the blade must be heated until it glows "like the sun rising in the desert," then cooled until it was royal purple by plunging it into the body of a muscular slave so their strength was transferred to the steel. It seems the red-haired boys got off lightly.[5]

The popularity of the swords eventually died out in the eighteenth century, some say because of the rise of firearms, and no European smith was ever able to fully replicate their method of production. But in 2006, the mystery was finally solved when Marianne Reibold and colleagues at the University of Dresden discovered the smiths were inadvertently using nanotechnology.

All Damascus swords were forged from the same small cakes of steel which originated in India and were labeled "wootz." Steel is made from iron and carbon. Typically, there will only be a tiny amount of carbon to strengthen the metal. If the carbon content reaches 1–2 percent, the steel becomes a lot harder but is also brittle enough to shatter easily. Wootz had an abnormally high carbon content of around 1.5 percent, so really should have been useless for swords. Even so, the Damascus swords were both malleable and tough.

Reibold and her team analyzed a Damascus sabre created by a famous blacksmith named Assad Ullah in the seventeenth century. They dissolved a tiny part of the weapon in hydrochloric acid and used an electron microscope to take a closer look. The steel contained carbon nanotubes, one of the strongest materials known to humanity, each one slightly larger than half a nanometer. It isn't clear how blacksmiths produced the nanotubes, but the research team believed it was partly due to the quenching, as the legends had stated. The wootz contained small traces of different metals, and alternating hot and cold phases during the manufacture of the steel caused these impurities to segregate and become catalysts for the formation of the carbon nanotubes. The nanotubes then formed cementite nanowires, which formed along the planes of the steel, explaining the wavy bands that were the hallmark of Damascus swords. [6]

While all of the smiths, armorers, and artists who mastered these techniques produced amazing art and weaponry, it's almost impossible that they understood what was going on. Researchers were only able to get a grasp of that understanding as microscopes became increasingly powerful. Right at the turn of the twentieth century, Max Planck and Albert Einstein produced theoretical evidence that a range of tiny particles existed which obeyed their own laws but weren't visible using the apparatus of the time. Improvements in those tools proved the pair correct—and spawned a whole new world of scientific study.[7]

Nanotechnology research was first predicted by the physicist and Nobel Prize–winner Richard P. Feynman in 1959. His paper, "There's Plenty of Room at the Bottom: An invitation to enter a new field of physics," talked about the production and control of tiny machines through quantum mechanics and foresaw that the development of microscopes would enable scientists to arrange atoms any way they wanted them. The paper makes no mention of the word nanotechnology but is still seen as the founding text of the field.[8]

"It would be interesting in surgery if you could swallow the surgeon. You put the mechanical surgeon inside the blood vessel and it goes into the heart and 'looks' around . . . It finds out which valve is the faulty one and takes a little knife and slices it out. Other small machines might be permanently incorporated in the body to assist some inadequately-functioning organ," Feynman wrote. [9]

His paper piqued the interest of the scientific world, and a new field of research was born. Two schools of thought emerged on how to make his ideas reality. The first was to shrink existing machines and instruments. The second, far-more-sensible-sounding approach was to build complex nanostructures atom by atom. The latter was popularized by one of the most important books on the subject by a man considered one of the godfathers of nanotechnology.[10]

In the 1970s, K. Eric Drexler spent most evenings as an MIT undergraduate studying the latest research in genetic engineering. He began to wonder if it would be possible to mimic the role cells play in the body with mechanical replacements. If you could recreate the functions of DNA and proteins with tiny machines, he thought, you could do anything that biology does, and a whole lot more. This theory took inspiration from genetic engineering but was in fact molecular engineering, a technology with the potential to change the world. In 1977 this led him to an incredible idea—a host of minuscule robots that could move around molecules so quickly and precisely they could produce almost any substance in the world with basic ingredients. In Drexler's theory, you would feed these robots a few cheap chemicals and they would produce gasoline, diamonds, or anything you wanted. If you were to put these miniature bots into the bloodstream, they could fight off disease. Put them in the air and they'd clean it of pollution.

Two years later, Drexler read Feynman's paper and realized he wasn't alone in his thinking, but he struggled to get the idea taken seriously at MIT, partly because he was seen as something of an outcast. In the 1980s he was known to organize retreats with his wife where students could discuss topics including cryonics and immortality. Regardless, he was able to publish his first book in 1986, *Engines of Creation*, which popularized the term nanotechnology. The book explained all the potential benefits of this molecular manufacturing he intended to invent, but it also highlighted the dangers. Chief among those was the gray goo scenario: the prospect of self-reproducing assemblers escaping a lab and eating up anything in their path, turning the Earth into a blob of gray goo.[11]

Drexler's writing inspired scientists eager to make the jump into a new field (it also fascinated science fiction writers). Drexler earned his PhD in 1991, receiving the first ever degree in molecular nanotechnology from MIT. The following year he took his theories to Congress, telling the Senate Subcommittee on Science, Technology, and Space this new field could lead to "new technologies for a sustainable world." Al Gore, the subcommittee chair, declared his support and wanted exploratory research funded. Drexler published his masterpiece the same year—a 550-page paper laying out a molecular manufacturing system in detail. "Nanosystems: Molecular Machinery, Manufacturing and Computation" used illustration, charts, and equations to show objects could be built from the molecules up. But the paper did not receive the kind of recognition Drexler hoped for, perhaps partly because it was neither one scientific discipline or another; it was a mix of different fields. [12]

Over the next decade, doubts began to emerge not just over the feasibility of molecular manufacturing, but whether we should do it at all. Prominent scientists suggested nanotechnology could easily be weaponized and used for military purposes, so should be left in the metaphorical box with the lid firmly shut. When the author Michael Crichton read about the gray goo theory, he depicted such a catastrophe in his bestselling novel *Prey*. In the book, a cloud of nanoparticles is released from a lab and quickly reproduces, evolves intelligence, and causes mayhem in the Nevada desert. Crichton prefaced the story with an introduction that claimed although the events in the book were made up, the technology behind it was a very real possibility. The book played into the hands of a growing group of scientists who believed Drexler was peddling nonsense. At the head of that group was Richard Smalley, a chemist from Rice University and a Nobel Prize winner. [13]

In 2004, *Chemical and Engineering News* published a series of letters exchanged between Smalley and Drexler in which the former expressed his doubts that molecular manufacturing was even possible. "Chemistry of the complexity, richness, and precision needed to come anywhere close to making a molecular assembler—let alone a self-replicating assembler—cannot be done simply by mushing two molecular objects together," he wrote. But Smalley wasn't done there.

He also accused Drexler of terrorizing the world with the concept of gray goo. "You and people around you have scared our children," the letter read. "I don't expect you to stop, but I hope others in the chemical community will join with me in turning on the light and showing our children that, while our future in the real world will be challenging and there are real risks, there will be no such monster as the self-replicating mechanical nanobot of your dreams."

Two days later, Drexler's hopes of establishing molecular manufacturing as a recognized field of research were dealt a further blow. That day, President George Bush signed the 21st Century Nanotechnology Research and Development Act, which earmarked $3.7 billion for molecular-scale technologies. In the run-up to the signing of the bill, Drexler had expected the announcement to catapult his research to the next level, putting it at the forefront of the nation's scientific agenda. But no money was allocated to molecular manufacturing as he imagined it, and almost all of it was instead put aside for projects using the technology to attempt to develop new materials. Drexler, the godfather of nanotechnology, had been sidelined from the field he established.[14]

In the aftermath, the young field of nanotechnology was divided. Drexler stood on one side with his molecular assembly theory, something he still hasn't been able to master. On the other was Smalley and the vast majority of scientists, who saw nanotechnology as any work carried out at the nanoscale. Immortalists like Aubrey de Grey see Drexler as not just one of their own, but also believe he'll end up on the right side of history.[15] The science community has another view. Kostas Kostarelos, a professor of nanomedicine at the University of Manchester in the United Kingdom, sees Drexler as a fringe actor in a field he's been a significant part of since its inception.[16]

Kostarelos, born and raised in Athens, Greece, started research at the nanoscale in 1990, studying double-stranded DNA at the University of Leeds before he moved to Imperial College London in the chemical engineering department. He was tasked with working

on delivery systems, tiny man-made methods to carry chemicals, vitamins, and medical treatments. He worked with liposomes to create fatty molecular envelopes—later referred to as lipid nanoparticles.
While colleagues in his department accepted lucrative jobs in the pet-
rochemicals industry in the Middle East, Kostarelos moved to the
United States, where he was paid just $40,000 a year to continue his
study of liposomes at medical school at the University of California,
San Francisco. By 1994, the liposome research area was beginning
to boom. They were used to deliver a vaccine in Switzerland and approved by the FDA in the United States for the treatment of Kaposi's
sarcoma in AIDS patients. The field was called colloidal chemistry,
physical chemistry, formation chemistry, but never nanotechnology,
despite scientists working at nanoscale.

Kostarelos later moved to the East Coast, taking a position at
Memorial Sloan Kettering, the renowned cancer center in New York
City. There, he attempted to create a better form of radiotherapy by
using liposomes to irradiate cancerous tissues from within. He then
switched his attention to gene therapy, another medical field that required innovative ways to deliver drugs to the human body. After
the Gelsinger incident mentioned in the previous chapter, nonviral
vectors were in high demand. Around the turn of the millennium,
Kostarelos moved back to the United Kingdom, at a time when the
definition of nanotechnology was beginning to change. The National
Cancer Institute in the United States made significant investments in
the field, and nanotech began to assume a clear identity, one very different from anything proposed by Drexler. Kostarelos took a position
at University College London and was later named Personal Chair of
Nanomedicine and Head of the Centre in 2007. When the university
asked him what he wanted his chair to be named, his decision drew
taunts from his colleagues in clinical medicine, who reminded him he
was no practitioner of medicine.

I spoke to Kostarelos on a lengthy Zoom call, and he recalled the
difficulties of the early years. "When a new field is morphed, there are

so many influences and actors that it's quite difficult to identify what is the critical parameter that decides things," he told me. "There were a bunch of guys like Drexler who were coming from the semiconducting, hardcore engineering space. These guys were not practicing chemists."

He said the work proposed by Feynman and Drexler used shrunken down machines that came from engineering, while his reality was work in soft biological matter on a similar scale. "At some point in the late '90s and early 2000s, there was a scientific need, the community needed to define 'what the hell do we mean by nano, anyway?' And I think that's where we see the more, kind of boring definitions of the one to one hundred convention. The convention now is that as long as you're between one and one hundred nanometers in scale at least in one dimension of what you're designing, you're doing nano."

Despite progress made at the start of the millennium, the common perception of nanotechnology always involved miniature machines of some kind. "I believe Hollywood has a big play in this, with those movies of miniaturized submarines. I really think that art is affecting conception here," Kostarelos said. That view of nanotechnology was aided by the voices being amplified in the immortalist community.

Ray Kurzweil, the famed inventor, futurist, and expert in AI, is one such voice. He holds a special place in the hopes of immortalists, mostly because of his work predicting a singularity event which will effectively end biological death. In his book *The Singularity Is Near: When Humans Transcend Biology*, he stressed that biology could only take our species so far.

"Biology will never be able to match what we will be capable of engineering once we fully understand biology's principles of operation," he wrote.[17] Concerning nanotechnology, Kurzweil described microscopic machines traveling through human bodies, fixing damaged cells and organs, and wiping out disease. In an interview in 2009, Kurzweil insisted anyone alive by 2040 or 2050 would be close to immortal, mostly due to nanotechnology. He even predicted nanobots would eventually replace biological blood at some point in the future. "It's radical life extension," Kurzweil told ComputerWorld. "The full realization of nanobots will basically eliminate biological disease and aging. I think we'll see widespread use in twenty years of [nanotech] devices that perform certain functions for us. In thirty or forty years, we will overcome disease and aging. The nanobots will scout out organs and cells that need repairs and simply fix them. It will lead to profound extensions of our health and longevity."[18]

Kurzweil and Drexler's visions for nanotechnology gave immortalists exactly the type of hope they crave. But those possibilities remain a long way off, judging by the field today. There are areas of great promise, but putting a timeline on any progress is difficult, partly because the area is so complex. Modern nanotechnology is an interdisciplinary science. Researchers seek to understand and master the tiniest particles and their chemical, physical, and mechanical properties, work that overlaps and blurs the boundaries between physics, chemistry, biology, medicine, electronics, and information technology. Nanomedicine has become a major branch of nanotechnology, and scientists like Kostarelos established that it had the potential to change medicine greatly. They hope nanotechnology can make significant and life-changing progress at every stage of treating disease. Drug delivery, where Kostarelos conducted the bulk of his work, offers the most hope of imminent breakthrough. In fact, the lipid nanoparticles worked on all those years ago recently brought a momentous change to the world, rescuing it from one of its bleakest hours.

. . .

In December 2020, after a year of death, suffering, isolation, and fear, the world finally received some good news: regulators approved two vaccines, one from Pfizer-BioNTech and the other from Moderna, in both the United States and the United Kingdom.[19][20] Finally, some degree of normality appeared to be attainable again. The vaccines were unlike anything used in humans before, and their delivery relied on nanotechnology.

The goal of the vaccines is to deliver mRNA—a genetic messenger instructing cells to develop spike proteins so they can fight the virus before it can do any damage. If the mRNA is the letter containing instructions, then the lipid nanoparticles are the fatty molecular envelopes. These envelopes, which work far more effectively than your average courier, ensure the mRNA evades the biological bouncers guarding what goes in and out of our systems and reaches the targeted cells without losing any of the potency of the message. In the past, lipid nanoparticles have been used to deliver both vaccines and drugs. The chemotherapy Doxil and cholesterol-lowering treatments Repatha and Praluent utilize them to ensure they hit the targeted cells while causing the least amount of damage and side effects. Nanoparticles are also being tested to be used with CRISPR-Cas9 to target organs.[21]

But for those involved in using nanoparticles for drug delivery, the new COVID-19 vaccines were something of a milestone. Dr. Robert Langer, the cofounder of Moderna who boasts an astonishing set of achievements across scientific disciplines, explained to me on a call his hopes, now the vaccine is widely distributed. "I think it's a big moment. Of course, I've been working on this stuff for fifty years, but I think it's a real validation of drug delivery. It's hardly the only one, but it's a very visible one. And it will save millions of lives, and end the pandemic."

Bringing an end to a global pandemic is a good start for any medical technology, yet Langer was also excited for what comes next. He was particularly looking forward to technology that would deliver drugs across the blood-brain barrier, which could help treat Alzheimer's, and targeting of blood vessels to ward off heart disease. Better targeting is a major goal for nanotechnology-enabled drug delivery. "If you have cancer, for example, can you target 100 percent of the drug to a tumor? Probably you can't, but how do you maximize the amount that gets into the tumor? And I would say the same thing for targeting any part of the body for any disease. It's like the idea of Urlich's magic bullet—could you target something it finds where it needs to go, and every bit of it goes there? I think that's the biggest challenge, but that's hardly going to be solved overnight."

Improving the targeting of drugs would make them safer. Cancer patients are often treated with chemotherapy, which makes them ill because the drug goes all over the body. But if you could give someone a drug that specifically targeted the tumor it was going to eradicate, not only would that drug be more effective, but the side effects would be minimal as well.

Drug delivery is not the only use for nanomedicine, of course. The field as a whole is expanding, in part due to a more multidisciplinary approach to education. Like Kostarelos, Langer hopped around disciplines of science. After he got his PhD, he opted to practice his postdoctoral work in a hospital surgery lab, where he was the only engineer.

"I loved it and felt it was very important scientifically, and I felt you could make a real impact, so I've done that all my life," he told me. "I would say in the last ten or fifteen years, that kind of strategy has been adopted more and more. There's a whole area that myself and Phil Sharpe and other people at MIT have called convergence, and I think we see more and more schools adopting that in different institutes." Now he sees more students interested in taking the same route he did, and it's easy to see why, given his long list of accomplishments. Langer's peers gave him the nickname "the Edison of Medicine" after he was awarded an h-index score (which measures the number of papers a person has published and how often they are cited) of 230, the highest ever for an engineer. He has over 1,284 patents issued and pending worldwide, and his lab has produced forty companies, all but one of which are still operating.[22] Moderna is undoubtedly enjoying its high profile and is now worth tens of billions of dollars after its vaccine success. Langer believes the government needs to create the ideal environment for companies like Moderna to thrive in, but his penchant for launching commercial companies from his research doesn't sit well with the entire scientific community, particularly those outside of the United States.

"The important thing about people like Bob, they believe that by spinning out companies and becoming prominent in the biotech field, they are pushing the envelope," argued Kostarelos. "That's a very American approach. It's not how things are done in Europe or the rest of the world. Asia is kind of copying the American paradigm that Bob and others have established. This is where I completely disagree with my American colleagues. I do not think that blind capitalism is a solution to the problem."

Parrish described one of the problems cutting edge medical science faces in the previous chapter—that it takes too long for a discovery to become a drug, and then for the drug to reach patients. The lightning speed at which the COVID vaccines were developed and approved gave some people hope, but Langer feels it won't last long. He recalled to me the negative press attention Moderna got when it was first developing the vaccine, something he said went away when the efficacy data was released. "Now they just say it's all about money and stuff like that, they want it for free, patents should go away. I think people have forgotten about what they thought a year ago, people have short memories. I expect that we're already going back and people are saying medical research costs too much and things like that. I personally don't expect a giant change. I wish I was wrong, and maybe I will be wrong, but I don't think so."

He believes favorable tax systems for biotechnology investors would help advance medical technology further, and he wants to see increased research funding from the National Institute of Health and a beefier budget for the FDA so it can approve more treatments.[23] Kostarelos agrees entirely with the latter two points but laughed when told of the tax breaks for investors. He sees the commercialization of medical technology as one of the great dangers of his field, and something that will only get worse as more progress is made.

Kostarelos is no longer working on drug delivery and has instead turned his attention to an even more complex problem—interfacing with the brain through nanotechnology. He hopes this technology will provide a cure to many neurological problems, including Alzheimer's, Parkinson's, and even blindness. But he's also terrified of making a breakthrough.

"I have this very personal dilemma which I expressed with my very close scientific friends, which is why are we doing this? Why am I developing the next neural interface?" Kostarelos said. "Why do we want to put the research and emphasis in developing the next generation of neural interface technologies? The answer is very simple: because we are trying to make people that suffer now live a better quality of life. That is very straightforward."

But over time, this explanation has made less and less sense to the scientist.

"It's the type of approach I hear when a scientist is interviewed after receiving the Nobel Prize. 'Why did you do this?' 'Well I want to change the world for a better place.' What kind of superficial bullshit is this? Everyone wants to do that."

Kostarelos is worried that someone else is working on the same neural technology but without any kind of transparency or collaboration with the rest of the scientific community. While he wants to use the technology to solve a medical issue and reduce suffering in the world, others may simply want to build a weapon. If nanotechnology were used to create neural interfaces for military purposes, we would enter a new era of warfare featuring super soldiers straight out of Hollywood. A military force might experiment on willing soldiers, but the rest of the world will not have given any kind of consent to develop this world-changing tech.

"What I'm worried about is there will be experimentation done secretly in the context of an elite force that has consented to play a part in this experiment. And then gradually after this failed or not attempt, we will never hear anything, even us scientists," Kostarelos explained. "Suddenly we will see a gradual acceptance and rolling out commercially or capitalistically of those interventions, similar to the plastic surgery body enhancements but in a functional way. And that's where the discussion may start, but that would be too late then. That would be a different type of conversation, by the way. That would be about do we condone or do we have objections on the commercialization of this, not whether we as a society want to go down that route."

"Bob [Langer] and his colleagues have . . . shown that this paradigm of taking technologies and commercializing them and pushing them out into the market very quickly and very profitabl[y] works, at least for the short term. Also, because people are getting more and more accepting of new technologies faster. It's this capitalistic notion of 'let's try it, if it doesn't work we'll drop it and we'll take the new thing coming along.' There's not a lot of conscious thinking of what would be the impact."

My time researching nanotechnology was something of a rollercoaster. I was fascinated by Drexler's vision, then terrified about what it would become. When it appeared to be largely fanciful, the reality seemed much more soothing, especially when used in vaccines and disease-crushing drugs. But even if Drexler's gray goo was nothing more than fantasy, the dangers of developing nanotechnology further are frightening. We cannot continue to have debates over the dangers of technology after the genie has been let out of the bottle. Yet it seemed to me that the immortalists had willingly overlooked the dangers of the path they were advocating. If successful, they could potentially save billions of lives, but at what cost?

13

THE CONSEQUENCE OF
IMMORTALITY

Humanity now has a chance to address some of the devastating effects aging brings to our broken-down bodies, ending the suffering of millions. It remains ambitious to assume this will translate to a longer lifespan or never-ending life, but for immortalists, it's a gigantic step in the right direction. We understand our bodies better than ever, right down to the cellular level. Through gene therapies, stem cell treatments, and other regenerative medicines, we can now attack the overall deterioration that comes from aging, potentially rolling back our bodies' internal clocks. Looking even further into the future, nanotechnology and artificial intelligence promise to rapidly increase the rate of progress.

The influx of Silicon Valley billions has transformed the anti-aging landscape. The days of semi-cults and pseudo-religions now appear numbered as big business takes over. But even with the buckets of cash flowing into age-reversal science, the breakthroughs won't come fast. Federal regulations, clinical trials, and expensive development stages will continue to frustrate the immortalists, who will need to turn to less-reputable solutions to increase their chances of catching the age-reversal wave. In that space, fraudsters and scam artists will profit from the desperation and naiveté of those chasing eternal life. Perhaps, ultimately, the race to live forever is best run by the billionaires and corporations. Given the history of blunders in cryonics and the scandals affecting today's prophets, even if the immortalists were to get their hands on a silver bullet to cure aging, it's likely they'd shoot themselves in the foot with it.

Should the longevity field mature to the point where it brings treatments to the masses, one of two scenarios will play out. Either we'll discover we can make people healthy for longer but our lifespan is quite set, as most gerontologists believe, or de Grey's longevity escape velocity will be proven correct, and we'll vastly extend how long we live. Whatever the outcome, humanity will be changed drastically, and both futures raise significant questions. The most obvious is how we'll cope with people living longer, and potentially forever.

When prominent immortalists go outside the circle of their fanatical followers and explain their plans to others who are less convinced, they are almost always asked about overpopulation.[1] In Russian cosmism, Fedorov proposed colonizing the galaxy and dealing with the problem that way. De Grey has reached the point in presentations where he claims he no longer needs to answer such questions, saying the immortalist movement shouldn't waste time addressing them. But they're not going away.

For many years, experts warned overpopulation could be about to usher in the world's destruction, but while the number of humans on the planet has risen considerably, we appear to be approaching a welcome plateau. It's been estimated that the world's population stood at 190 million two millennia ago around the year "zero." One thousand years later, it was around 250 million.[2] Difficulty in gathering resources and massive infant death rates kept the numbers low. But the Industrial Revolution changed everything. By 1800, the population hit one billion. By 1928 it was two billion, and three billion swiftly followed by 1960. Then, just fifteen years later in 1975, the

figure rose to four billion.[3] The rate of growth seemed completely un-
sustainable, and scientists began forecasting mass starvation, crowded
living conditions, and dystopian laws to control family sizes. In his
1968 book *The Population Bomb*, Stanford biologist Paul Ehrlich predicted that hundreds of millions of people would starve to death in
the 1970s.[4] Of course, none of that happened on a global scale. There
have been plenty of famines across the globe, some cities have been
crowded for decades now, and China and other countries have enforced some draconian rules to combat overpopulation. But it hasn't
been anywhere near as bad as we thought it might be. For some time
now in certain countries—with more regions joining the trend all the
time—birth rates have plummeted. That decline mostly happened in
wealthier countries where women are more educated, and contracep-
tion is readily available. When female populations have more opportunities outside of raising children, the average family size shrinks to
lower than the replacement level (essentially, fewer than two children
per two parents).[5]

In 2019, a Pew Research Center analysis of United Nations data
predicted population growth would stop completely for the first time
in modern history by 2100. At that point, the number of humans on
the planet will reach around 10.9 billion, with annual growth of less
than 0.1 percent. Between 1950 and today, the growth rate has stood
at between 1 and 2 percent per year.[6] This is called the demographic
transition and is hotly debated among experts. When a society becomes richer, and that wealth isn't distributed too unequally, people
don't have to send their children to work to support the family, and
instead put large amounts of money into raising children. That means
there's no longer a financial incentive to have kids. Child mortality
plays an equally important role. When medicine improves and child
death rates drop, initially there is a massive increase in population,
which makes sense—people continue to have a lot of children, but
fewer of them are dying.[7] Some parts of the world went through this
stage in the 1950s and 1960s, and it created the boomer generation.

But that only lasts for one or two generations, and then birth rates begin to decline. This is attributed to increased certainty of the survival
of children, women's rights, the shift where children are no longer an
economic asset, and many other factors. At this point the population
begins to stabilize, and the massive growth is brought under control.
A report by Deutsche Bank predicts the world's population will hit a
peak of 8.7 billion in 2055 and decline to 8 billion by the end of the
century.[8]

So what happens when you throw longevity or immortality into
the mix? De Grey believes lower fertility rates go together with better
health care and longer lifespans, and he expects that trend to continue
even further if aging is reversed. He also pointed to the progression of
technologies in other areas, saying in a 2017 interview:

> Overpopulation is not a matter of how many people there are on the
> planet but rather the difference between the number of people on the
> planet and the number of people that can be on the planet with an
> acceptable level of environmental impact, and that second number is
> of course not a constant; it's something that is determined by other
> technologies.
>
> So as we move forward with renewable energy and other things like
> desalinization to reduce the amount of pollution the average person
> commits, we are increasing the carrying capacity of the planet, and
> the amount of increase that we can expect over the next, say, 20 years
> in that regard far exceeds what we could expect in terms of the tra-
> jectory of rise in population resulting from the elimination of death
> from aging.[9]

On top of that, de Grey believes when these new medical technologies that will usher in escape velocity are presented to the world, they
will come with a choice: if people want immortal life, they will need
to have fewer children. "Ask yourself, which of those two things would
you choose? Would you choose to have your mother get Alzheimer's

disease or to have fewer kids? It's a pretty easy choice, and people just don't do this," he said. To be fair to de Grey, he said this prior to the COVID-19 pandemic and the evidence it brought that, given the choice, a large slice of the population will do what they want rather than what might be better for the collective. Anti-vaxxers, anti-maskers, and the various conspiracy theorists around the world have further eroded our confidence in people's ability to do the right thing. Even faced with as stark a choice as de Grey presents as an example, there's no certainty at all people would willingly accept having fewer kids, even if they knew their relatives could live a little longer.

But his final argument against the overpopulation problem may be his most convincing. He and other immortalists believe we will always have a moral obligation to produce medicines and solutions that extend life. If we have the means to save a life, we almost always have done and will. That makes life extension efforts inevitable. If we're going to do it anyway, why not make it sooner rather than later? "I don't want to be responsible for condemning a vast number of people to death. I don't want to be in that position. I think there's a strong argument that we should get on developing these technologies as quickly as we can," de Grey argued.[10]

The case to speed up age reversal and rejuvenation technologies only gets more convincing when considering the tsunami of issues America's aging population will bring. As the baby boomer generation ages, the appeal of concepts pushed by the likes of the Church of Perpetual Life, People Unlimited, Alcor, and RAADfest will become increasingly tempting. Perhaps they'll navigate those interests safely, sticking to the research, supporting the science, and contributing to the community. But the inevitable draws of scam artist stem cell therapies, dodgy age tests, and bucketloads of supplements will test their ability to sniff out a swindle. And let's be brutally honest, this is not a generation immune to misinformation and selfish behavior.

Critics of the baby boomers say their upbringing made them inherently self-centered, as they spent decades cutting their own taxes and protecting entitlement programs that worked in their favor, all while ignoring major issues like climate change, the student loan crisis, and crumbling American infrastructure.[11] They elected one of their own in 2016 in Donald Trump, despite his appalling track record and twisted character flaws. A large number of them were raised on the lies of Fox News and were happy to reshape their reality as they saw fit, blaming their problems on fabricated boogeymen. Of course, not every baby boomer fits this generalization, but historians will not look back kindly on their actions and inactions in a time of unprecedented wealth. As this generation comes to contemplate their own death, they'll make easy pickings for the conmen and fraudsters ready to offer the next elixir of life. Some of them have clearly already fallen into the trap.

And even if they avoid age-reversal scams, this glut of older people is going to affect the United States in other ways. Data from the latest census showed 16.5 percent, or 54 million, of the current population of 328 million are over the age of sixty-five. That number is expected to rise to 74 million by 2030, and the number of people over the age of eighty-five who will need some kind of care is growing even faster.[12] In July 2021, Commerce Secretary Gina Raimondo said the aging demographics of America will hit the country "like a ton of bricks" if deferral aid isn't increased, and warned the situation was "untenable."[13] It's clear the boomer generation will have a significant impact on the world as it grows old. But even after that generation dies, the world's most populous age group will become older and older as time passes, as fewer people die early and there are not so many new children replacing them. The world's median age, which was twenty-four in 1950 and is around thirty-one now, is expected to increase to forty-two in 2100. And between 2020 and 2100, the number of people ages eighty and older is expected to rise from 146 million to 881 million.[14]

The best way to tackle this impending disaster is to treat aging as a disease which causes all the illness and suffering in the elderly that is so expensive to address. Dr. Ferrucci of the National Institute of Aging explained the benefits of treating aging rather than single diseases better than anyone else I spoke to.

"Many years ago, I [asked someone] what will happen if we can cure cancer? And that guy responded to me, 'Well, we will have a bunch of old people demented, and they won't know what they're doing.' And that's why I think that our approach of addressing aging instead of addressing a single disease is the right one. Because if aging is the underlying mechanism of multiple chronic diseases, then those people that will be aging more will be a little bit cognitively sane, so that bad dream is not going to happen," he said.

But Ferrucci believes the only significant progress science will make is in extended healthspan, not lifespan. He thinks life expectancy will increase slightly as a result of improving our overall health, but we are very close to reaching the limit of human lifespan, so it won't make too much of a difference. "There will be an increase in life expectancy, but it will be small compared to the increase in health expectancy. Which in a way is good, because a larger fraction of our life will be lived in a better health status."

But all the benefits we could enjoy by rolling out anti-aging technologies relies on one of the most corrupt systems in the world—American health care. Being healthy in the United States is a luxury only for those who can afford the eye-watering costs. Judy Campisi, the gerontologist, told me, "If you're poor and old in the US, then you're dead, basically." And the numbers back her up. In the United States, men in the top 1 percent of the income distribution can expect to live fifteen years longer than those in the bottom 1 percent. For women, the difference is ten years. The disparity isn't just seen in those two extreme groups. Men living in the United States who were in the top 5 percent for household income in 2014 had a life expectancy of around 88.5. In contrast, the bottom 5 percent had a life expectancy of 76.5.[15]

David Blumenthal, president of the Commonwealth Fund, a foundation which promotes a better health care system in the United

States, told me the problem of being old and poor gets even worse when you're not white. He believes the onrushing problems an older population brings will hit the whole world hard. "We are dealing with the unintended consequences of our success in extending life expectancy," he said. "The productivity of our employable workforce has to increase dramatically or there is going to be a crisis in financing the means or the welfare of the older population." If we did figure out a way to reverse aging and make those elderly people more productive members of society, it's unlikely that treatment would be rolled out to everyone at the same time, according to Blumenthal. "Unequal distribution of technologies is an age-old issue. And it's been true of just about every new important technology, and still is true for things like vaccination, which we're seeing in real time now . . . I would be surprised if that weren't true of anything that was significantly life extending."

De Grey's answer to this problem has always been the same, that the governments of the world would be crazy not to implement age-reversal technologies on a grand scale because of the savings they would make in the long term.

I put this argument to Blumenthal. He was not impressed. "Our government does not act rationally in that respect, and it's fully capable of making bad long-term decisions in the interest of short-term ideological and political orientations. Just look at the states that have decided not to implement Medicaid, even though it would be worth tens of billions of dollars to them. And they do it because they don't believe in Medicaid, they don't believe in helping people who haven't earned, they don't believe in giving anything away to the poor, and they don't believe in redistributing income," he said.

"They're speaking from the basis of reason and logic. There's no reason and logic operating in the United States at the current time," he added.

If the cure for aging were developed as preventative medicine, it would be even less likely to reach everyone. Blumenthal said preventive treatments are "almost by definition discretionary," and so the financial barriers and access issues are even more severe than therapeutic medicines. "If you look at what happens to prevention spending in the United States, even the most cost-effective types of technologies like vaccines, for example, we have a pretty dismal and variable record of childhood immunization," he told me. "I'm sounding pretty negative, but I think the United States has shown it's very short sighted when it comes to investing in health care for people who can't afford it or people who are unaware or uneducated about the benefits of a treatment, whether it's preventative or therapeutic."

Should de Grey be proved right, and longevity escape velocity occurred, wealth inequality in the United States would need to be fixed quickly. As more people lived longer and hoarded more resources, the opportunities for younger generations would continue to shrink. Today's under-forties already have a hard enough time hoisting themselves onto the property ladder. If the wealthy refused to die and continued to buy up property, only to rent it out at exorbitant prices, some of the basic rights of humanity would feel even more out of reach.

And politics would change as well. Many younger voters have already cursed the number of elderly at the polling booths in the past decade. In the United Kingdom, the Brexit vote was forced through by an older generation who voted for a seismic shift in full knowledge they'd likely die before suffering the aftereffects. It's strange to imagine a political landscape where the boomer generation lives for thirty or even fifty more years. Voting numbers suggest the elderly lean more conversative, possibly because they believe they have more to lose, want to hang on to what they have, or were just brought up racist and didn't see any reason to change. In a world where people lived well into their hundreds, or even forever, the generational shift at the voting booths which brings about much-needed change may never happen.

All these potential challenges come from curing aging, but the Plan B options like cryonics and mind uploading also bring their own problems. Perhaps the worst of these is the danger of creating refugees, ripped out of their own times and forced into the future, with no friends or relatives to talk to and no connection to the futuristic world they find themselves in. While talking to Robert McIntyre about memories, much of what he said was technical and scientific. But toward the end of the conversation he got quite philosophical when pondering the effect of waking up in the future. He told me to imagine two people who had been married for fifty years, and the conversations they have that only really make sense to each other. "It's almost like they're one organism talking to itself rather than two people having a discussion because they're not really sharing that much information. They know where it's going, they do it because it's comfortable and it's fun," he said. "When one of those partners die, and the other one is left alone, I think it's harder for them to access a lot of their memories because the only way you can trigger them is through that other person's interaction."

Aside from being almost poetically tragic, McIntyre raised a legitimate concern for cryonics as well. The same effect could happen with a place or a smell or a taste that would not be available in the future. All those memories linked to the past would be gone forever. McIntyre compared them to encrypted files, with the other person or place acting as the key. "It's important for anyone doing mind uploading to respect the person's human rights and understand that even going through this even in the best of cases is going to be somewhat traumatic, and to do right by them, meaning they're going to need rehabilitation and therapy," he explained.

Whenever a technological breakthrough is made, unforeseen challenges follow. Stopping the push for extended life is a futile gesture, but monitoring, regulating, and ensuring the technology is distributed safely and equally is imperative. Right now, even the hunt for immortality is throwing up issues. Most of them arise from the feverish obsession of those looking to live forever. Eternal life, for obvious reasons, has always been an eye-catching proposal. Some immortalists have used that to

their advantage, flouting the concept of immortality to attract funding
and attention to the less ambitious goals like age reversal and longevity.
In many of the interviews I conducted for this book, I asked scientists
and researchers if they'd accept a chunk of funding from someone asking them to find the key to immortality. Their responses were mixed.
Some said it would be immoral to accept money knowing the end goal
was impossible, but others said they would take the cash and use it to do
some good. Either way, all researchers in the field of aging are subjected
to scrutiny and fandom from an eager crowd of immortalists. To many
scientists working in the field of aging, this is an unwanted distraction which does more harm than good. De Grey claims they need to
say this to distance themselves from opinions grant-giving government
organizations may look down upon, but if that is true, they're doing
an extremely good job putting on that front. Dr. Sean Morrison, for
example, described the immortalist crowd as a nuisance.

"Sometimes you go to these aging meetings and you see this cohort of people there, these guys who are in their middle seventies
but they've got long blonde hair that's clearly been dyed, and they're
clearly doing everything that they can to try to seem young. And
they're listening to the talks so that if somebody identifies a molecular
pathway that regulates aging, they want to start taking a drug that
inhibits that pathway. It's at those aging meetings where you see this
clash between the real legitimate science and the people who are either
victims of the charlatans or the charlatans themselves."

Campisi said she was scrutinized by supporters on both sides of
the argument. Sometimes she got questions from immortalists asking
her why she was being so pessimistic, but others claimed what she
was doing in aging research was immoral. "We can make educated
guesses, and the best educated guess right now is that human lifespan,
maximum human lifespan, will be somewhere around 115, plus or
minus maybe ten years in either direction," she said.

Over the next couple of decades, we'll likely find out just how effective age reversal can be. The early signs are very promising, but we

still don't know if the result will be increased healthspan, lifespan, or neither. Researchers like Campisi believe science should focus completely on the prospect of improved healthspan. She says it's "a concept that the public needs to grab as being more worthy than immortality." Increasing healthspan is a selfless task, with the goal of eliminating the suffering of millions of people as they grow old. Increasing lifespan is generally a more selfish endeavor by people who don't want to die.

When I first encountered the immortalists in Florida, I was highly skeptical about their ambitions. But I quickly saw how enticing their worldview was. The prospect of immortality speaks to something deep within the human instinct to survive, and for the first time in the history of the species, science has offered a glimmer of hope. Characters like de Grey, Parrish, Faloon, and Hoffman all reel in followers with their infectious enthusiasm. We want to believe them because they are saying we won't die, and somehow that seems like our biggest problem.

But suffering is so much worse than dying. And there are many issues staring us right in the face that need to be addressed first. If we don't hold back climate change, our planet will become uninhabitable, and nobody will be living very long at all. If we continue down the path of untempered inequality, we may as well be dead anyway. The real price of immortality may be the distraction from more pressing issues that could immediately raise the life expectancy of the general population. Properly acknowledging and fighting the systemic racism of the United States would give a massive group of people a better chance of living longer and healthier lives. Improving the social safety net so children don't grow up in poverty would do the same. There are so many ways America, and the world, is crying out for help it can seem overwhelming. Perhaps the immortalists think they need more time to deal with all of them, but none of these issues can wait. Ploughing money into long-shot technologies like cryonics or unproven fads like supplements does nothing to ease the global suffering of today.

The tale of Orpheus, which started this book, suggests it does not make sense to dwell on that which is lost, but rather encourages us to mourn, to remember, and to learn from the people in our past. It teaches us to ultimately let them go and move forward. The same can be said of the world today as it grapples with a future after COVID. Our way of living was ripped out from under us and destroyed by a virus. It has taken millions of lives worldwide, crippled economies, and brought everyday life to a standstill. But now is not the time to travel back in an attempt to retrieve what was lost. Now we must build again with the lessons of the old world as a new foundation. Some of the people in this book would do well to heed the lessons of Orpheus in the most literal sense. Others have the chance to play a major part in creating the new world which we may or may not achieve. None of them should be held back by the past.

As I traveled through the immortality industry, I saw scams, frauds, and outrageous misinformation. But I also saw hope. The aging research on which immortalism has piggybacked is an undoubtedly worthy cause for both optimism and encouragement. If the immortal-ists put all their energy into promoting and aiding the development of these treatments, they would be doing the whole world a favor, not just themselves. But the work can't stop at development. There needs to be a system in place, with some kind of equity for all, where these medicines can be distributed universally, not just to those with enough money. Increasing the healthspan is a noble goal for the whole of humanity, but it must be for all, and we shouldn't need the carrot of eternal life to get behind it. If we do these things, and perhaps one day we do actually unlock the secret of living forever, then we'll have built a world worthy of a longer stay.

EPILOGUE

AN APPOINTMENT IN MOSCOW

In November 2021, while Europe braced itself for another COVID-hit winter, I traveled to Moscow, Russia. The city had recently endured a week-long lockdown, intended to lower the number of infected. Masks were enforced on public transit, there were regular signs and posters reminding citizens to get vaccinated, and testing centers were dotted all over the city. And for good reason: deaths had recently topped 1,000 per day, amid disappointing vaccine uptake and the now common conspiracy theories circulating the rest of the world.

I was in Russia to report on the country's warring cryonics factions, but I was also keen to find out more about the prophet so revered back at the Church of Perpetual Life in Florida, where my reporting for this book had begun. On a bitterly cold and snowy evening, I hurried into a Metro station in the middle of the city, just a few minute's walk from the Kremlin. I was greeted by a police officer with a metal detector wand, waiting to check my backpack for weapons, and to also ensure I was wearing a mask. I felt, suddenly, like I had fallen into a dystopian science fiction novel.

Over the past two years, like everyone else, I'd been bombarded by reminders of the fragility of both humanity and our planet. That

evening, the news was dominated by another failed climate conference, anti-vaccine and anti-lockdown protests across Europe, and there
was another, potentially more transmissible, variant of COVID-19
just around the corner. Given the cruelty and suffering we impose on
our fellow humans, animals, and the earth, it's hard to make the case
that we deserve to live longer.

Perhaps it was the cold, the pandemic, or just the location, but the
brutality of nature's indifference to human survival weighed on my
mind as I made my way an hour from the city center to the Konkovo
district, in search of some hope for a better future, no matter how far-
fetched it may be.

When I got off the metro, I walked through a small mall and into
a residential area, hoping my now internet-less Google Maps was taking me in roughly the right direction. After about 15 minutes of speed
walking through the darkened streets, I arrived at a high-rise residential building with a neon sign outside. Here, on the ground floor, was
the N. Fedorov Museum-Library, which was founded in 1993. It was
far removed from the grandiose buildings lining the streets of the city
center, many of them paying tribute to some of the country's greatest
philosophers.

As I walked through the glass doors into the mercifully warm
building lobby, I was greeted with a wide smile by Anna Gorskaja,
who works at the library and had kindly invited me to visit. She welcomed me in, offered me a hot drink and asked me to sit down. Sadly,
Gorskaja told me, the Fedorov exhibits were in temporary storage,
while the Fedorovians found a more suitable display.

There was a painting of Fedorov himself in the corner of the room,
created just a few years after he died. The artist, a friend of the philosopher, couldn't remember what his hands looked like, so he depicted
them hidden away in the sleeves of his coat, Gorskaja told me.

After a short wait, she introduced me to Anastasia Gacheva, the
head of the library and to whom Fedorov and his works have always
been a family endeavor. Her mother, Svetlana Semenova, was credited

with reintroducing his work to the world, and wrote several books about Russian cosmism, the branch of philosophy which grew from Fedorov's thinking. Gacheva's mother first started studying the philosopher in 1972, during the Brezhnev era, when her daughter was just five years old. "From my childhood I have organically absorbed Fedorov's ideas, which is why I feel happy, because they give me optimism of being, which is very important for a child, for a teenager who is always searching, always doubting, always asking why they exist," she said.

Gacheva, Gorskaja and all of Fedorov's followers are immortalists. But there are distinct differences between their interpretation of immortalism and that practiced across the United States, particularly since Silicon Valley started showering its billions upon the industry. As unthinkable as Fedorov's philosophy might be, there's a message at its core that invokes a great sense of hope and empathy, something hinted at in the beliefs of the American immortalists, but seems to be seeping away at an alarming rate as big busines takes control. The Church of Perpetual Life elevated Fedorov to a prophet, many of its followers believed him to be a great man, but did they really understand him?

Fedorov saw immortality as the "common task" that would unite humanity. He didn't believe in eternal life for the few, and he didn't think money had a role to play in its development. His ambitions were much broader and heavily impacted by his Christian faith. As we learned earlier in the book, he said the goal of the planet should be also to resurrect everyone that ever lived and "regulate" nature. That claim seems utterly ridiculous on a practical level, but by making this his ultimate goal, he ensured that everything done in the pursuit of that mission served to unify the whole of humanity. He wanted to bring the world together to create technologies that would make humanity the master of nature and become a God-like figure itself. "Fedorov was in general a very harsh critic of capitalism, because it was, first of all, exhausting to nature, to the earth, and to people. But most importantly, he argued why universality is necessary - for him, man is a being who is necessary to nature, who is necessary to the world. He had a formula that nature in the individual becomes aware of itself and rules itself. That is, man is a part of nature," Gacheva explained.

Gacheva described Fedorov's mission in a way most articles rarely articulate. His quest to end death wasn't just about saving humanity; he wanted to take command of nature, to end death for all species and living things, and to end the food chain so all animals could live like plants, taking the energy from the universal source of the sun. "One cannot attain immortality if everything in nature is mortal," Gacheva said. "In Russian cosmism there was this intuition that nature itself, that living beings want to overcome this law of devouring, fighting. In the Christian picture of the world, the future kingdom will have no death and no enmity. Conventionally speaking, there the wolf and the hare will be friends - one will not eat the other. As the prophet Isaiah says - a doe lies next to a wolf, predators graze peacefully there, they do not eat their own kind. This is the brotherhood of creatures, the brotherhood of all created things."

Many transhumanists talk of Fedorov as the one of the founding fathers of the movement, but Gacheva believes they still have a lot to learn from him. "It's good that they consider him one of them, because if they do, it's a chance for transhumanism to expand its spiritual and creative base a little bit. Transhumanism as it has developed is in many ways the child of this digital, commercial and industrial civilization."

Gacheva's mother Semenova was skeptical of cryonics. She believed in the resurrection of every person in history, even if it was from a single piece of DNA, as Fedorov taught. Cryonics is more of a "secular project," Gacheva said. If the practice were to be proven possible, it would only serve to resurrect those who had been frozen, which would go against Fedorov's teaching of universal immortality. But the concept still has some merit to Gacheva. "To compare: once mankind invented a stone axe, it was the first stick. The killing stick. Then there was a stone axe for work. If a stone axe branched out [to all the] technology we have, cryonics is the stone axe in this future story of resurrection and victory over death. It's the first tool we're trying out. There's probably not much we can do [with it]. There will be some new ones."

Inevitably, our conversation turned to the pandemic. Gacheva believes Fedorov would not have been impressed by the global approach to the spread of COVID-19. She said the restrictions were defensive tactics, while Fedorov preached offensive measures to take control of nature, not just halting death, but natural disasters like earthquakes, hurricanes, and pandemics too. "This pandemic, it shows us that we are not up to the challenges that nature gives us. We should be united by this threat, but it is driving us apart. At first, humanity was a little united in the face of a common threat, and then came the rivalry of pharmaceutical companies for vaccines, for something else. People have realized that it is very convenient to manipulate humanity, to divide it, split it up, fractionalize it and so on," Gacheva said.

When I left the museum, I found myself deeply impressed by the optimism and positivity of the Fedorov way of thinking. I wasn't ready to sign up as a follower, but I felt a little better about the pursuit of immortality regardless. Given the choice between Fedorov's spiritual, all-encompassing version of eternity and a two-tiered world where technology's elite lived on forever, I'd take the old dead Russian philosopher's viewpoint every time.

And despite being thousands of miles away, the Fedorov library and museum reminded me of my trip to the Church of Perpetual Life in Florida, and not just because of the Russian prophet revered in each institution. Both buildings were located in unassuming residential neighborhoods, ill-fitted to the bold and brash causes chased by each institution. Inside, they were a haven for ideas most would find too ambitious or extreme to even ponder, and their followers were, among other things, fueled by a great sense of hope.

But were their efforts misplaced? Back in the biting cold, I put on my mask and scurried into the warmth of the Moscow metro, and pondered my odyssey through the world of immortalism. I'd met all types of believers across many groups. Their quest for immortality would continue, no matter the price. But for me, it was time to move forward— and avoid looking back to see if death was peering over my shoulder.

ACKNOWLEDGEMENTS

Writing a book during a pandemic, it turns out, is really diffi-cult. I mostly got through thanks to the help of others.

Mark Choi, Chrissy Lu, and Amanda Suarez came with me to Florida and kick started the entire adventure.

Ryan Harrington helped me shape the idea into a book. A number of people read pages in various stages of completion, including Alex Morrell, Esme Benjamin, and Amber Snider, who all gave me excellent feedback and criticism. I also need to acknowledge Ryan Kristobak, because I forgot to thank him in my previous book, and Sean Williams, who's always an excellent collaborator.

My family helped me continue working even while I made the painful mid-pandemic move from the United States to the United Kingdom, and were, as ever, immeasurably supportive. They include Janice Ward, Roland Ward, Peter Brown, Alice Ward, Meirion Hughes, and Wendy Hughes.

All the people interviewed for the book were extremely generous with their time and patience, guiding me through this gigantic topic.

The grant I received from the Society of Authors and the K Blundell Trust allowed me to focus in a weird and anxious time.

Carl Bromley, my editor, managed to make sense of everything I wrote and turned it into something readable.

And my wife Seren Hughes, who was always there, and continually inspires and supports me.

ENDNOTES

Notes to the Introduction

1   Becker, Ernest. *The Denial of Death*, chapter 1, p. 2.
2   Interview with George Church, 25 June 2021.
3   "Trends in Number of COVID-19 Cases and Deaths in the US Reported to CDC, by State/Territory." *CDC: COVID Data Tracker*, https://covid.cdc.gov/covid-data-tracker/#trends_totaldeaths|tot_deaths|select.

Notes to Chapter 1

1   "History of Hollywood." *Hollywood, FL*, https://www.hollywoodfl.org/187/History-of-Hollywood.
2   "Odds of Dying." *NSC Injury Facts*, https://injuryfacts.nsc.org/all-injuries/preventable-death-overview/odds-of-dying/.
3   "About the Church of Perpetual Life." *The Church of Perpetual Life*, https://www.churchofperpetuallife.org/about.
4   Cantu, Amanda. "Gilgamesh: The Search for Immortality." *StMU Research Scholars*, https://stmuscholars.org/gilgamesh-the-search-for-immortality/.
5   "How China's First Emperor Searched for Elixir of Life." *BBC News*, 25 Dec. 2017, https://www.bbc.co.uk/news/world-asia-china-42477083.
6   "Longer Daily Fasting Times Improve Health and Longevity in Mice." *National Institute of Aging*, 6 Sept. 2018, https://www.nia.nih.gov/news/longer-daily-fasting-times-improve-health-and-longevity-mice.
7   Pelley, Scott. "A Harvard Geneticist's Goal: Protect Humans from Viruses, Genetic Diseases, and Aging." *CBS News*, 8 Dec. 2019, https://www.cbsnews.com/news/harvard-geneticist-george-church-goal-to-protect-humans-from-viruses-genetic-diseases-and-aging-60-minutes-2019-12-08/.
8   Paddock, Catharine. "Rapamycin Has Anti-Aging Effect on Human Skin." *Medical News Today*, 27 Nov. 2019, https://www.medicalnewstoday.com/articles/327150.

Notes to Chapter 2

1   "The Prospect of Immortality: Murray Ballard." *Impressions Gallery*, 2011, https://www.impressions-gallery.com/wp-content/uploads/2020/04/murray-ballard-info-sheet.pdf.
2   Pilon, Mary. "The Father of Cryonics Never Really Died." *Vice*, 22 Feb. 2017, https://www.vice.com/en/article/pgxa9v/robert-ettinger-cryonics.

3   "Robert Ettinger Biography." *Cryonics Institute*, https://www.cryonics.org/
     about-us/robert-ettiner-biography/.

4   "Robert Ettinger: Scientist Known as the Father of the Cryonics Movement."
     Independent, 23 Oct. 2011, https://www.independent.co.uk/news/obituaries/
     robert-ettinger-scientist-known-father-cryonics-movement-2338622.html.

5   Perry, Mike. "For the Record." *Cryonics*, vol. 13, no. 145, 1992, p. 5. https://
     www.alcor.org/docs/cryonics-magazine-1992-08.txt.

6   Pascal, David. "A Brain Is a Terrible Thing to Waste." *The Crynonics Society*,
     http://www.cryonicssociety.org/articles_mensajournal.html.

7   Ettinger, Robert. *The Prospect of Immortality*, chapter 1, p. 96.

8   Ettinger, Robert. *The Prospect of Immortality*, p. 15.

9   Regis, Ed. *Great Mambo Chicken and the Tranhsuman Condition: Science
     Slightly Over the Edge*, p. 88.

10   Perry, Mike. "For the Record."

11   Perry, Mike. "The First Suspension." *Alcor*, https://www.alcor.org/library/
     bedford-suspension/.

12   Perry, R. Michael. "Suspension Failures: Lessons from the Early Years." *Alcor*,
     Oct. 2014, https://www.alcor.org/library/suspension-failures-lessons-from-
     the-early-years/.

13   Perry, Mike. "The First Suspension."

14   *Freeze, Wait, Reanimate*, May 1965, p. 10.

15   Perry, Mike. "The First Suspension."

16   Sweeney, Emily. "The Great Brink's Robbery, and the 70-year-old Question:
     What Happened to the Money?" *The Boston Globe*, 16 Jan. 2020, https://
     www.bostonglobe.com/2020/01/16/metro/great-brinks-robbery-70-year-old-
     question-what-happened-money/.

17   Nelson, Robert. *Freezing People Is (Not) Easy*, p. 20.

18   Nelson, Robert. *Freezing People Is (Not) Easy*, p. 32.

19   Nelson, Robert. *Freezing People Is (Not) Easy*, p. 38.

20   Nelson, Robert. *Freezing People Is (Not) Easy*, p. 42.

21   Nelson, Robert, *Freezing People Is (Not) Easy*, p. 47.

22   Perry, Mike. "The First Suspension."

23   Perry, R. Michael. "Ev Cooper and the Conference That Didn't Happen:
     Trials of an Early Freezing." *Cryonics*, vol. 35, no. 1, May-June 2016, p. 14.
     https://www.alcor.org/docs/cryonics-magazine-2016-03.pdf.

24   Perry, R. Michael. "Ev Cooper and the Conference That Didn't Happen:
     Trials of an Early Freezing." *Cryonics*, vol. 35, no. 1, May-June 2016, p. 21.
     https://www.alcor.org/docs/cryonics-magazine-2016-03.pdf.

25   Perry, R. Michael. "Ev Cooper." p. 21.

26   Email from Mike Perry, Alcor caretaker and cryonics historian, 4 Feb. 2021.

27   Price, Michael C. "Ev Cooper." *Cryonet*, 17 Dec. 2003, http://www.cryonet.
     org/cgi-bin/dsp.cgi?msg=23124.

28 Perry, R. Michael. "Suspension Failures: Lessons from the Early Years." *Alcor*, Oct. 2014, https://www.alcor.org/library/suspension-failures-lessons-from-the-early-years/.

29 Nelson, Robert. *Freezing People Is (Not) Easy*, p. 70.

30 Nelson, Robert. *Freezing People Is (Not) Easy*, p. 75.

31 Nelson, Robert. *Freezing People Is (Not) Easy*, p. 79.

32 Nelson, Robert. *Freezing People Is (Not) Easy*, p. 84.

33 Nelson, Robert. *Freezing People Is (Not) Easy*, p. 88.

34 Nelson, Robert. *Freezing People Is (Not) Easy*, p. 89.

35 Nelson, Robert. *Freezing People Is (Not) Easy*, p. 95.

36 Nelson, Robert. *Freezing People Is (Not) Easy*, p. 102.

37 Nelson, Robert. *Freezing People Is (Not) Easy*, p. 107.

38 Interview with Mike Darwin, 18 Feb. 2021.

39 Interview with Mike Darwin, 18 Feb. 2021.

40 Nelson, Robert, *Freezing People Is (Not) Easy*, p. 133.

41 Jones, Derek and Sam Shaw. "Mistakes Were Made." *This American Life*, interview by Ira Glass, National Public Radio, 18 April 2008, https://www.thisamericanlife.org/354/transcript. Transcript.

42 Nelson, Robert. *Freezing People Is (Not) Easy*, p. 139.

43 Nelson, Robert. *Freezing People Is (Not) Easy*, p. 141.

44 Nelson, Robert. *Freezing People Is (Not) Easy*, p. 143.

45 Jones, Derek and Sam Shaw. "Mistakes Were Made."

46 Jones, Derek and Sam Shaw. "Mistakes Were Made."

47 Norden, Eric. "Stanley Kubrick: *Playboy* Interview (1968)." *Scraps from the Loft*, 2 Oct. 2016, https://scrapsfromtheloft.com/movies/playboy-interview-stanley-kubrick/.

Notes to Chapter 3

1 "Cryonics: Failure Analysis: Lecture 1: Preface and Initialization Failure, Part 1." *Chronosphere*, 14 April 2012, slide 4, http://chronopause.com/chronopause.com/index.php/2012/04/14/cryonics-failure-analysis-part-i-preface-and-initialization-failure-part-1/index.html.

2 "Michael G. Darwin, a Biographical Précis." *Chronosphere*, 4 April 2011, http://chronopause.com/chronopause.com/index.php/2011/04/04/michael-g-darwin-a-biographical-precis/index.html.

3 Darwin, Mike. "Dear Dr. Bedford – An Open Letter to the First Frozen Man." *Cryonics*, 1991, https://www.alcor.org/library/dear-dr-bedford-an-open-letter-to-the-first-frozen-man/.

4 Interview with Mike Darwin, 18 Feb. 2021.

5 Interview with Mike Darwin, 19 Feb. 2021.

6 Darwin, Mike. "Dear Dr. Bedford."

7 "Michael G. Darwin."

8 Interview with Mike Darwin, 19 Feb. 2021.

9   Interview with Mike Darwin, 19 Feb. 2021.

10 Interview with Mike Darwin, 19 Feb. 2021.

11 "A Timeline on the Events Surrounding the Cryonic Suspension of Dora Kent." *Cryonics*, vol. 9, no. 90, Jan. 1988, https://www.alcor.org/docs/cryonics-magazine-1988-01.txt.

12 "A Timeline."

13 Perry, Michael. "Our Finest Hours: Notes on the Dora Kent Crisis." *Cryonics*, Sept.-Nov. 1992, https://www.alcor.org/library/dora-kent-case/.

14 Interview with Mike Darwin, 19 Feb. 2021.

15 Perry, Michael. "Our Finest Hours."

16 Perry, Michael. "Our Finest Hours."

17 "A Timeline."

18 Interview with Mike Darwin, 19 Feb. 2021.

19 Perry, Michael. "Our Finest Hours."

20 "A Timeline."

21 "A Timeline."

22 "A Timeline."

23 Perry, Michael. "Our Finest Hours."

24 "A Timeline."

25 "A Timeline."

26 Interview with Mike Darwin, 19 Feb. 2021.

27 Perry, Michael. "Our Finest Hours."

28 "A Timeline."

29 Interview with Mike Darwin, 19 Feb. 2021.

30 "A Timeline."

31 "A Victory on February 1st." *Cryonics*, vol. 9, no. 91, Feb. 1988, https://www.alcor.org/docs/cryonics-magazine-1988-02.txt.

32 "Coroner's Press Conference." *Cryonics*, vol. 9, no. 90, Jan. 1988, p. 22. https://www.alcor.org/docs/cryonics-magazine-1988-01.txt.

33 "A Victory on February 1st," p. 5.

34 "A Victory on February 1st," p. 4.

35 Perry, Mike. "Alcor's Legal Battles." *Alcor*, https://www.alcor.org/library/alcor-legal-battles/.

36 Perry, Mike. "Alcor's Legal Battles."

37 Perry, Mike. "Alcor's Legal Battles."

38 Verducci, Tom. "What Really Happened to Ted Williams." *Vault*, 18 Aug. 2003, https://vault.si.com/vault/2003/08/18/what-really-happened-to-ted-williams-a-year-after-the-jarring-news-that-the-splendid-splinter-was-being-frozen-in-a-cryonics-lab-new-details-including-a-decapitation-suggest-that-one-of-americas-greatest-heroes-may-never-rest-in.

39 Shorey, Ananda. "Company Denies Report on Williams' Body." Associated Press, 13 Aug. 2003, https://apnews.com/article/a74ad4599120785b7429a9c0c8f530ee.

Notes to Chapter 4

1   Interview with Rudi Hoffman, 20 Jan. 2021.

2   Duhring, Nathan. *Immortality: Physically, Scientifically, Now: A Reasonable Guarantee of Bodily Preservation, a General Discussion, & Research Targets*, Nathan Duhring (Ev Cooper), chapter 1.

3   *The Prospect of Immortality*, Robert Ettinger, chapter 2.

4   Hoffman, Rudi. "Why Fund Your Suspension with Life Insurance?" *Rudi Hoffman, Certified Financial Planner*, https://rudihoffman.com/cryonics.html.

5   Hoffman, Rudi. "Cryonics Sign Up Process." *YouTube*, 21 Aug. 2020, https://youtu.be/h4kYfaujKks.

6   Interview with Patrick Harris, 19 Feb. 2021.

7   Alcor Foundation. "Protecting Yourself in Medical Emergencies." *Alcor*, https://www.alcor.org/library/protecting-yourself-in-medical-emergencies/.

8   "Russian Transhumanists and the Mafia Are in a Cryonics War over Frozen Heads." *Biohackinfo News*, 18 Sept. 2020, https://biohackinfo.com/news-kriorus-cryonics-russia-transhumanism-ndrangheta/.

9   "Building Owner Pleads Guilty to Bribery," FBI Press Release, 4 June 2015, https://www.fbi.gov/contact-us/field-offices/miami/news/press-releases/building-owner-pleads-guilty-to-bribery.

10   Email from Rudi Hoffman, 9 Sept. 2021.

11   Darwin, Mike. "Jerry Leaf Enters Cryonic Suspension." *Cryonics*, vol. 12, no. 9, 1991, https://www.alcor.org/library/complete-list-of-alcor-cryopreservations/case-report-a-1058/.

12   Interview with Mike Darwin, 19 Feb. 2021.

13   Stewart, James B., Matthew Goldstein, and Jessica Silver-Greenberg. "Jeffrey Epstein Hoped to Seed Human Race with His DNA." *The New York Times*, 31 July 2019, https://www.nytimes.com/2019/07/31/business/jeffrey-epstein-eugenics.html.

Notes to Chapter 5

1   Becker, Ernest. *The Denial of Death.*

2   The Dalai Lama. "Reincarnation." *Dalai Lama*, 24 Sept. 2011, https://www.dalailama.com/messages/retirement-and-reincarnation/reincarnation.

3   Chan, Dawn. "The Immortality Upgrade." *The New Yorker*, 20 April 2016, https://www.newyorker.com/tech/annals-of-technology/mormon-transhumanism-and-the-immortality-upgrade.

4   Editors of *e-flux*. "Editorial – Russian Cosmis." *e-flux*, vol. 88, Feb. 2018, https://www.e-flux.com/journal/88/176021/editorial-russian-cosmism/.

5   Editors of *e-flux*. "Editorial."

6   Editors of *e-flux*. "Editorial."

7   "Konstantin E. Tsiolkovsky." NASA, 22 Sept. 2010, https://www.nasa.gov/audience/foreducators/rocketry/home/konstantin-tsiolkovsky.html.

8   "I.O.T.C.→ Timeline." *Institute of the Cosmos*, https://www.cosmos.art/
     timeline.
9   "I.O.T.C.→ Timeline."
10   Nugent, Addison. "The Russian Philosopher Who Sought Immortality in
     the Cosmos." *Atlas Obscura*, 29 May 2018, https://www.atlasobscura.com/
     articles/what-is-russian-cosmism-nikolai-federov
11   "I.O.T.C.→ Timeline."
12   Van Velzer, Ryan. "Immortality Eludes People Unlimited Founder."
     AZ Central, 16 Nov. 2014, https://eu.azcentral.com/story/news/local/
     scottsdale/2014/11/16/people-unlimited-scottsdale-charles-paul-brown-
     immortality/19152253/.
13   Van Velzer, Ryan. "Immortality Eludes People Unlimited Founder."
     AZ Central, 16 Nov. 2014, https://eu.azcentral.com/story/news/local/
     scottsdale/2014/11/16/people-unlimited-scottsdale-charles-paul-brown-
     immortality/19152253/.
14   Van Velzer, Ryan. "Immortality Eludes."

Notes to Chapter 6

1   Interview with Aubrey de Grey, 7 June 2021.
2   Pontin, Jason. "Is Defeating Aging Only a Dream?" *Technology Review*,
     11 July 2006, https://web.archive.org/web/20130216022816/http://www.
     technologyreview.com/sens/.
3   Pontin, Jason. "Is Defeating Aging Only a Dream?"
4   Friend, Tad. "Silicon Valley's Quest to Live Forever." *The New Yorker*, 27
     March 2017, https://www.newyorker.com/magazine/2017/04/03/silicon-
     valleys-quest-to-live-forever.
5   Trotter, J.K. "Someone Is Trying to Discredit the Story of Peter Thiel's
     Interest in Young Blood." *Gizmodo*, 16 June 2017, https://gizmodo.com/
     someone-is-trying-to-discredit-the-story-of-peter-thiel-1796135794.
6   Drange, Matt. "Peter Thiel's War on Gawker: A Timeline." *Forbes*, 21 June
     2016, https://www.forbes.com/sites/mattdrange/2016/06/21/peter-thiels-war-
     on-gawker-a-timeline/.
7   Conger, Kate. "Peter Thiel Plans Speech on Trump Support." *TechCrunch*, 20
     Oct. 2016, https://techcrunch.com/2016/10/20/peter-thiel-plans-speech-on-
     trump-support/.
8   Hamzelou, Jessica. "Blood from Human Teens Rejuvenates Body and Brains
     of Old Mice." *NewScientist*, 15 Nov. 2016, https://www.newscientist.com/
     article/2112829-blood-from-human-teens-rejuvenates-body-and-brains-of-
     old-mice/.
9   Gottlieb, Scott. "Statement from FDA Commissioner Scott Gottlieb, M.D.,
     and Director of FDA's Center for Biologics Evaluation and Research Peter
     Marks, M.D., Ph.D., cautioning consumers against receiving young donor
     plasma infusions that are promoted as unproven treatment for varying

conditions." *FDA*, 19 Feb. 2019, https://www.fda.gov/news-events/press-announcements/statement-fda-commissioner-scott-gottlieb-md-and-director-fdas-center-biologics-evaluation-and-0.

10   Brodwin, Erin. "The Founder of a Startup that Charged $8,000 to Fill Your Veins with Young Blood Says He's Shuttered the Company and Started a New One." *Business Insider*, 14 Aug. 2019, https://www.businessinsider.com/young-blood-transfusions-ambrosia-shut-down-2019-6?r=US&IR=T

11   Mullin, Emily. "Exlusive: Ambrosia, the Young Blood Transfusion Startup, Is Quietly Back in Business." *OneZero*, 8 Nov. 2019, https://onezero.medium.com/exclusive-ambrosia-the-young-blood-transfusion-startup-is-quietly-back-in-business-ee2b7494b417.

12   Friend, Tad. "Silicon Valley's Quest."

13   Philipkoski, Kristen. "Ray Kurzweil's Plan: Never Die." *Wired*, 18 Nov. 2002, https://www.wired.com/2002/11/ray-kurzweils-plan-never-die/.

14   Friend, Tad. "Silicon Valley's Quest."

15   Naughton, John. "Why Silicon Valley Wants to Thwart the Grim Reaper." *The Guardian*, 9 April 2017, https://www.theguardian.com/commentisfree/2017/apr/09/silicon-valley-wants-to-cheat-grim-reaper-google.

16   Friend, Tad. "Silicon Valley's Quest."

17   Regalado, Antonio. "Meet Altos Labs, Silicon Valley's Latest Wild Bet on Living Forever." *Technology Review*, 4 Sept. 2021, https://www.technologyreview.com/2021/09/04/1034364/altos-labs-silicon-valleys-jeff-bezos-milner-bet-living-forever/?utm_source=pocket-newtab-global-en-GB.

18   "The Future of Aging? The New Drugs & Tech Working to Extend Life & Wellness." *CB Insights*, 24 Oct. 2018, https://www.cbinsights.com/research/report/future-aging-technology-startups/.

19   Franck, Thomas. "Human Lifespan Could Soon Pass 100 Years Thanks to Medical Tech, Says BofA." *CNBC*, 8 May 2019, https://www.cnbc.com/2019/05/08/techs-next-big-disruption-could-be-delaying-death.html.

20   O'Farrell, Seth. "Forever Young? Biotech's Next Frontier." *fDi Intelligence*, 12 Feb. 2021, https://www.fdiintelligence.com/article/79406.

21   Mather, Mark, Paula Scommegna, and Lillian Kilduff. "Fact Sheet: Aging in the United States." *PRB*, 15 July 2019, https://www.prb.org/resources/fact-sheet-aging-in-the-united-states/.

22   Mather, Mark, Paula Scommegna, and Lillian Kilduff. "Fact Sheet."

23   Mather, Mark, Paula Scommegna, and Lillian Kilduff. "Fact Sheet."

24   Van Dermyden Makus Law Firm. "Executive Summary of Investigative Findings: SENS Research Foundation, Executive Summary Concerning Conduct by Dr. Aubrey de Grey." *SENS*, 10 Sept, 2021, https://www.sens.org/wp-content/uploads/2021/09/SENS-Executive-Summary-For-Public-Release-FINAL-091021-00323152xC0E95.pdf.

25   Van Dermyden Makus Law Firm. "Executive Summary."

26   Van Dermyden Makus Law Firm. "Executive Summary."

27   Van Dermyden Makus Law Firm. "Executive Summary."

28   Van Dermyden Makus Law Firm. "Executive Summary."

29   Van Dermyden Makus Law Firm. "Executive Summary."

30   Elton, Catherine. "Has Harvard's David Sinclair Found the Fountain of
     Youth?" *Boston Magazine*, 29 Oct. 2019, https://www.bostonmagazine.com/
     health/2019/10/29/david-sinclair/.

31   Elton, Catherine. "Has Harvard's David Sinclair Found the Fountain of
     Youth?"

32   Taylor, Marisa. "A 'Fountain of Youth' Pill? Sure, If You're a Mouse." *KHN*, 11
     Feb. 2019, https://khn.org/news/a-fountain-of-youth-pill-sure-if-youre-a-mouse/.

33   Callaway, Ewen. "GlazoSmithKline Strikes Back Over Anti-Ageing Pills."
     Nature, 2010. https://www.nature.com/articles/news.2010.412.

34   PBR Staff. "GSK Discontinues SRT501 Development Study." *Pharmaceutical
     Business Review*, 2 Dec. 2010, https://www.pharmaceutical-business-review.
     com/news/gsk-discontinues-srt501-development-study-021210/.

35   Edes, Alyssa. "GlaxoSmithKline to Close Sirtris Unit in Cambridge."
     The Boston Globe, 13 March 2013, https://www.bostonglobe.com/
     business/2013/03/12/glaxosmithkline-moving-sirtris-five-years-after-buyout/
     unHXAjB3ZxfSAtMp0LQi5I/story.html.

Notes to Chapter 7

1   López-Otín, Carlos, Maria A. Blasco, Linda Partridge, Manuel Serrano,
     and Guido Kroemer. "The Hallmarks of Aging." *Cell*, vol. 153, no. 5, 2013,
     1194–1217. https://www.cell.com/fulltext/S0092-8674(13)00645-4.

2   "What Is a Genome?" *Your Genome*, https://www.yourgenome.org/facts/
     what-is-a-genome.

3   "What Are the Hallmarks of Aging?" *AFAR*, https://www.afar.org/
     hallmarksofaging.

4   "What Are the Hallmarks of Aging?"

5   You, Jueng Soo, and Peter A. Jones. "Cancer Genetics and Epigenetics: Two
     Sides of the Same Coin?" *Cancer Cell Review*, vol. 22, 2012, 9–20. https://
     www.cell.com/cancer-cell/pdf/S1535-6108(12)00257-7.pdf.

6   "What Are the Hallmarks of Aging?" *AFAR*, https://www.afar.org/
     hallmarksofaging.

7   "What Are the Hallmarks of Aging?"

8   "What Are the Hallmarks of Aging?"

9   "What Are the Hallmarks of Aging?"

10   Fleming, Nic. "Scientists Up Stakes in Bet on Whether Humans Will Live to
     150." *Nature*, 2016, https://www.nature.com/articles/nature.2016.20818.

11   Buck Institute. "Judy Campisi Elected to the National Academy of Sciences
     for Her Pioneering Work on Cellular Senescence." *Buck Institute*, 30 May
     2018. https://www.buckinstitute.org/news/judy-campisi-nas/.

12   Buck Institute. "Judy Campisi Elected."

13   Jiang, Lijing. "Reassessment of Carrel's Immortal Tissue Culture
     Experiments." *The Embryo Project Encyclopedia*, 28 June 2010, https://
     embryo.asu.edu/pages/reassessment-carrels-immortal-tissue-culture-
     experiments.

14   Cepelewicz, Jordana. "Ingenious: Leodard Hayflick." *Nautilus*, 24 Nov.
     2016, https://nautil.us/issue/42/fakes/ingenious-leonard-hayflick.

15   Dolgin, Elie. "Send in the Senolytics." *Nature Biotechnology*, vol. 38, 2020,
     pp. 1371–1377. https://www.nature.com/articles/s41587-020-00750-1.

16   Terry, Mark. "What's the Deal with Longevity Company Unity
     Biotechnology and its $700 Million Valuation?" *BioSpace*, 6 June 2018,
     https://www.biospace.com/article/what-s-the-deal-with-longevity-company-
     unity-biotechnology-and-its-700-million-valuation-/.

17   DeFeudis, Nicole. "A Month After Losing Its Lead Program, Unity
     Biotechnology Cuts 30% of Staff in Restructuring." *Endpoints News*, 15 Sept.
     2020, https://endpts.com/a-month-after-losing-its-lead-program-unity-cuts-
     30-of-staff-in-restructuring/.

18   "SENS Research Foundation Research Advisory Board." *SENS Research
     Foundation*, https://www.sens.org/about-us/leadership/research-advisory-
     board/.

19   "National Center for Health Statistics: Heart Disease." *CDC*, https://www.
     cdc.gov/nchs/fastats/heart-disease.htm.

20   "Cancer: An Update on Cancer Deaths in the United States." *CDC*, https://
     www.cdc.gov/cancer/dcpc/research/update-on-cancer-deaths/index.htm.

21   "Curing Key Diseases Would Add Little to Life Spans, Study Finds." *The
     Washington Post*, 2 Nov. 1990, in *The Los Angeles Times*, https://www.latimes.
     com/archives/la-xpm-1990-11-02-mn-3743-story.html.

22   Bockladnt, Sven, Wen Lin, Mary E. Sehl, Francisco J. Sánchez, Janet S.
     Sinsheimer, Steve Horvath, and Eric Vilain. "Epigenetic Predictor of Age."
     PLoS One, vol. 6, no. 6, 2011, https://www.ncbi.nlm.nih.gov/pmc/articles/
     PMC3120753/.

23   Gibbs, W. Wayt. "Biomarkers and Ageing: The Clock-Watcher." *Nature*, vol.
     508, 2014, pp. 168–170. https://www.nature.com/articles/508168a.

24   Cohen Marill, Michele. "New Tests Use Epigenetics to Guess How Fast
     You're Aging." *Wired*, 19 Dec. 2019, https://www.wired.com/story/new-tests-
     use-epigenetics-to-guess-how-fast-youre-aging/.

25   El Khoury, Louis Y., et al. "Systematic Underestimation of the Epigenetic
     Clock and Age Acceleration in Older Subjects." *Genome Biology*, vol 20,
     2019, https://genomebiology.biomedcentral.com/articles/10.1186/s13059-019-
     1810-4.

26   Schalkwyk, Leonard, and Jonathan Mill. "Ageing: How Our 'Epigenetic
     Clocks' Slow Down as We Get Older." *University of Essex*, 2020, https://
     www.essex.ac.uk/blog/posts/2020/01/16/ageing-how-our-epigenetic-clocks-
     slow-down-as-we-get-older.

27 Armanios, Mary. "Telomeres in the Clinic, Not on TV." *Mayo Clinic Proceedings*, vol. 93, no. 7, 2018, pp. 815–817. https://www.mayoclinicproceedings.org/article/S0025-6196(18)30407-5/fulltext.

Notes to Chapter 8

1 "Catch Up with RAADfest 2020." *RAADfest*, https://www.raadfest.com/2020.

2 Enmozhi, Sukanth Kumar, et al. "Andrographolide as a Potential Inhibitor of SARS-CoV-2 Main Protease: An In Silico Approach." *Journal of Biomolecular Structure and Dynamics*, 2020, pp. 1–7. https://www.ncbi.nlm.nih.gov/pmc/articles/PMC7212536/.

3 Yuvejwattana, Suttinee. "Thailand Clears Use of Herbal Medicine for Covid-19 Treatment." *Bloomberg*, 30 Dec. 2020, https://www.bloomberg.com/news/articles/2020-12-30/thailand-clears-use-of-herbal-medicine-for-covid-19-treatment.

4 Turner, Elle. "Andrographis Is the Superhero Herb That's Scientifically Proven to Boost Immunity." *Glamour*, 13 Feb. 2021, https://www.glamourmagazine.co.uk/article/andrographis-immunity.

5 "CFR Code of Federal Regulations Title 21." *FDA*, 1 April 2021, https://www.accessdata.fda.gov/scripts/cdrh/cfdocs/cfcfr/CFRSearch.cfm?fr=801.415.

6 Curious readers can view the talk online, but they have to pay $150 to access it: "RAADFest 2020." Uploaded by CoalitionRadicalLifeExtension, 19 Oct. 2020, https://vimeo.com/ondemand/raadfest2020/.

7 Cassidy, Anne. "Bulletproof Coffee: Would You Add Butter to Your Brew?" *BBC News*, 24 June 2019, https://www.bbc.co.uk/news/business-48692763.

8 Cassidy, Anne. "Bulletproof Coffee."

9 Cassidy, Anne. "Bulletproof Coffee."

10 Belluz, Julia. "The Bulletproof Diet Is Everything Wrong with Eating in America." *Vox*, 19 Dec. 2014, https://www.vox.com/2014/12/19/7416939/bulletproof-coffee.

11 Hannaford, Alex. "The Bulletproof Diet: Simplistic, Invalid and Unscientific." *The Telegraph*, 27 Nov. 2014 https://www.telegraph.co.uk/books/what-to-read/the-bulletproof-diet-simplistic-invalid-and-unscientific/.

12 Spector, Paul. "A Brief History of Intermittent Fasting." *Elemental*, 13 Jan. 2020, https://elemental.medium.com/natures-anti-aging-resilience-diet-flipping-the-metabolic-switch-6b70c079e6fb.

13 Belman, Orli. "Eat Less, Live Longer? The Science of Fasting and Longevity." *USC Leonard Davis School of Gerontology*, 18 April 2019, https://gero.usc.edu/2019/04/18/eat-less-live-longer-the-science-of-fasting-and-longevity/.

14 Spector, Paul. "A Brief History of Intermittent Fasting."

15 Andrew, Scottie. "Intermittent Fasting: The Benefits and the Limitations." *CNN*, 2 Jan. 2020, https://edition.cnn.com/2019/12/25/health/intermittent-fasting-live-longer-wellness-trnd/index.html.

16   Corrigan, Hope. "The Damaging Double Standard Behind Intermittent Fasting." *Quartz*, 11 Dec. 2019, https://qz.com/1754394/intermittent-fasting-has-become-a-productivity-hack-for-men/.

17   Silva, Christianna. "Food Insecurity in the U.S. by the Numbers." *NPR*, 27 Sept. 2020, https://www.npr.org/2020/09/27/912486921/food-insecurity-in-the-u-s-by-the-numbers?t=1632686264686.

18   VanZile, Jon. "Futurist Ray Kurzweil." *Life Extension Magazine*, Sept. 2005, https://www.lifeextension.com/magazine/2005/9/report_kurzweil.

19   Haspel, Tamar. "Most dietary supplements don't do anything. Why do we spend $35 billion a year on them?" *The Washington Post*, 27 Jan. 2020, https://www.washingtonpost.com/lifestyle/food/most-dietary-supplements-dont-do-anything-why-do-we-spend-35-billion-a-year-on-them/2020/01/24/947d2970-3d62-11ea-baca-eb7ace0a3455_story.html.

20   "Dietary Supplement Use Reaches All Time High." *Council for Responsible Nutrition*, 30 Sept. 2019, https://www.crnusa.org/newsroom/dietary-supplement-use-reaches-all-time-high.

21   Shen, Helen. "Cancer Research Points to Key Unknowns about Popular 'Antiaging' Supplements." *Scientific American*, 30 May 2019, https://www.scientificamerican.com/article/cancer-research-points-to-key-unknowns-about-popular-antiaging-supplements/.

22   Martens, Christopher R. "Chronic nicotinamide riboside supplementation is well-tolerated and elevates NAD $^+$ in healthy middle-aged and older adults." *Nature Communications*, vol. 9, no. 1, 2018, 1286. https://pubmed.ncbi.nlm.nih.gov/29599478/.

23   Dellinger, Ryan W., et al. "Repeat dose NRPT (nicotinamide riboside and pterostilbene) increases NAD$^+$ levels in humans safely and sustainably: a randomized, double-blind, placebo-controlled study." *NPJ Aging and Mechanisms of Disease*, vol. 3, 2017, p. 17. https://www.ncbi.nlm.nih.gov/pmc/articles/PMC5701244/.

24   Emery, Gene. "FDA Ban Nearly Wiped Out Deaths, Poisonings from Ephedra." *Reuters*, 27 May 2015, https://www.reuters.com/article/us-fda-ephedra-idUSKBN0OC2SR20150527.

25   "Beta Carotene (Oral Route): Precautions." *Mayo Clinic*, https://www.mayoclinic.org/drugs-supplements/beta-carotene-oral-route/precautions/drg-20066795.

26   "Prostate Cancer Risk from Vitamin E Supplements." *National Institutes of Health*, 17 Oct. 2011, https://www.nih.gov/news-events/nih-research-matters/prostate-cancer-risk-vitamin-e-supplements.

27   Shen, Helen. "Cancer Research."

28 Nacarelli, Timothy, et al. "NAD⁺ metabolism governs the proinflammatory senescence-associated secretome." *Nature Cell Biology*, vol. 21, no. 3, 2019, 397–407. https://pubmed.ncbi.nlm.nih.gov/30778219/.

29 Haspel, Tamar. "Most dietary supplements don't do anything."

Notes to Chapter 9

1 Sharkis, Saul J. "Canadian Stem Cell Scientists Take the Prize." *Cell*, vol. 122, no. 6, 2005, pp. 817–819. https://www.cell.com/fulltext/S0092-8674(05)00919-0.

2 Evans, M. J., and M. H. Kaufman. "Establishment in Culture of Pluripotential Cells from Mouse Embryos." *Nature*, vol. 292, 1981, 154–156. https://pubmed.ncbi.nlm.nih.gov/7242681/.

3 Thomson, J. A., et al. "Isolation of a Primate Embryonic Stem Cell Line." *Proceedings of the National Academy of Sciences*, vol. 92, no. 17, 1995, pp. 7844–7848. https://pubmed.ncbi.nlm.nih.gov/7544005/.

4 Thomson, J. A., et al. "Embryonic Stem Cell Lines Derived from Human Blastocysts." *Science*, vol. 282, no. 5391, 1998, pp. 1145–1147. https://pubmed.ncbi.nlm.nih.gov/9804556/.

5 "Embryonic Stem Cells Made Without Embryos." *National Public Radio*, 21 Nov. 2007. Transcript. https://www.npr.org/templates/story/story.php?storyId=16493814.

6 Cohen, Philip. "Bush Surprises with Compromise on Stem Cells." *New Scientist*, 10 Aug. 2001, https://www.newscientist.com/article/dn1142-bush-surprises-with-compromise-on-stem-cells/.

7 Murry, Charles E., and Gordon Keller. "Differentiation of Embryonic Stem Cells to Clinically Relevant Populations: Lessons from Embryonic Development." *Cell*, vol. 132, no. 4, 2008, pp. 661–680. https://pubmed.ncbi.nlm.nih.gov/18295582/.

8 Cyranoski, David. "How Human Embryonic Stem Cells Sparked a Revolution." *Nature*, 26 April 2018, https://www.nature.com/articles/d41586-018-03268-4.

9 Takahashi, Kazutoshi and Shinya Yamanaka. "Induction of pluripotent stem cells from mouse embryonic and adult fibroblast cultures by defined factors." *Cell*, vol. 126, no. 4, 2006, 663–676. https://pubmed.ncbi.nlm.nih.gov/16904174/.

10 "Stem Cell Tourism." *Harvard Stem Cell Institute*, https://hsci.harvard.edu/stem-cell-tourism.

11 "Miller sues stem cell therapy provider over deceptive claims." *Iowa Department of Justice Attorney General Tom Miller*, 15 July 2020, https://www.iowaattorneygeneral.gov/newsroom/stem-cell-therapy-elder-deceptive-copd-autor.

12 "Stem cell COPD commercial." Uploaded by AGIowa, 15 July 2020, https://www.youtube.com/watch?v=EzSDg6KzYfQ.

13 "Miller sues stem cell therapy provider."

14 "Miller sues stem cell therapy provider."

15 Clouse, Thomas. "Stem cell therapy clinics are big business in Spokane area, but are desperate patients being sold snake oil?" *The Spokesman-Review*, 15 April 2019, https://www.spokesman.com/stories/2019/apr/14/stem-cell-therapy-clinics-are-big-business-but-are/.

16 Interview with Dr. Sean Morrison, 28 Dec. 2020.

17 "Financing & Discounts." *Stem Cell Power Now*, https://stemcellpowernow.com/financing/.

18 "Veterans, First Responders and Teachers Benefiting from Free Stem Cell Therapy with 'R3 Heroes Program.'" *PR Newswire*, 30 April 2019, https://www.prnewswire.com/news-releases/veterans-first-responders-and-teachers-benefiting-from-free-stem-cell-therapy-with-r3-heroes-program-300840787.html.

19 Wan, William and Laurie McGinley. "'Miraculous' Stem Cell Therapy Has Sickened People in Five States." *The Washington Post*, 27 Feb. 2019, https://www.washingtonpost.com/national/health-science/miraculous-stem-cell-therapy-has-sickened-people-in-five-states/2019/02/26/c04b23a4-3539-11e9-854a-7a14d7fec96a_story.html.

20 Woodworth, Claire F., et al. "Intramedullary cervical spinal mass after stem cell transplantation using an olfactory mucosal cell autograft." *CMAJ*, vol. 191, no. 27, 2019, E761–E764. https://www.cmaj.ca/content/191/27/E761.

21 Freeman, Liz. "Court Upholds License Revocation of Bonita Springs Doctor Zannos Grekos." *Naples Daily News*, 16 Jan. 2015, http://archive.naplesnews.com/news/health/court-upholds-license-revocation-of-bonita-springs-doctor-zannos-grekos-ep-876165328-339821642.html/.

22 "Zannos G. Grekos MD, MAAC." *Regenocyte*, https://www.regenocyte.com/zannos-g-grekos-md-maac/.

23 Dragoo, J. L. "Stem Cell Treatments Flourish With Little Evidence That They Work." *The New York Times*, 13 May 2019, https://www.nytimes.com/2019/05/13/health/stem-cells-fda.html.

24 "Trump Signs Right to Try Act for Terminally Ill Patients." *BBC News*, 30 May 2018, https://www.bbc.co.uk/news/world-us-canada-44305998.

25 "Trump Signs Right to Try Act for Terminally Ill Patients." *BBC News*, 30 May 2018, https://www.bbc.co.uk/news/world-us-canada-44305998.

26 Gottlieb, Scott. "Examining Patient Access to Investigational Drugs." *FDA*, 3 Oct. 2017, https://www.fda.gov/news-events/congressional-testimony/examining-patient-access-investigational-drugs-10032017.

27 "Trump Signs Right to Try Act for Terminally Ill Patients." *BBC*, 30 May 2018, https://www.bbc.co.uk/news/world-us-canada-44305998.

28 Asprey, Dave. "How Adult Stem Cells Can Help Stop Pain and Reverse Aging." *Dave Asprey*, https://daveasprey.com/how-adult-stem-cells-can-help-stop-pain-and-reverse-aging/.

Notes to Chapter 10

1   Cohen, Martin. "Can a Jellyfish Unlock the Secret of Immortality?" *The New York Times*, 28 Nov. 2012, https://www.nytimes.com/2012/12/02/magazine/can-a-jellyfish-unlock-the-secret-of-immortality.html.

2   Piraino, S. "Reversing the Life Cycle: Medusae Transforming into Polyps and Cell Transdifferentiation in Turritopsis nutricula (Cnidaria, Hydrozoa)." *Biological Bulletin*, vol. 190, no. 3, 1996, 302–312. https://pubmed.ncbi.nlm.nih.gov/29227703/.

3   Cohen, Martin. "Can a Jellyfish Unlock the Secret of Immortality?"

4   Langley, Liz. "Meet the Animal That Lives for 11,000 Years." *National Geographic*, 23 July 2016, https://www.nationalgeographic.com/animals/article/animals-oldest-sponges-whales-fish.

5   Hu, Charlotte. "Animals that defy the rules of aging — like naked mole rats — could help scientists unravel the secrets to longevity." *Business Insider*, 15 Aug. 2018, https://www.businessinsider.com/animals-that-defy-aging-rules-offer-longevity-clues-2018-8?r=US&IR=T.

6   Coulter, Martin. "Is world's oldest tortoise gay? Jonathan comes out of his shell as keepers realise partner of 26-years is actually male." *Evening Standard*, 20 Oct. 2017, https://www.standard.co.uk/news/world/is-world-s-oldest-tortoise-gay-jonathan-comes-out-of-his-shell-as-keepers-realise-partner-of-26years-is-actually-male-a3663421.html.

7   Hu, Charlotte. "Animals that defy the rules of aging."

8   Keane, Michael, et al. "Insights into the Evolution of Longevity from the Bowhead Whale Genome." *Cell Reports*, vol. 10, no. 1, 2015, pp. 112–122. https://www.ncbi.nlm.nih.gov/pmc/articles/PMC4536333/.

9   "Secrets of Naked Mole-Rat Cancer Resistance Unearthed." *University of Cambridge*, https://www.cam.ac.uk/research/news/secrets-of-naked-mole-rat-cancer-resistance-unearthed.

10 Hoad, Phil. "'People Are Caught Up in Magical Thinking': Was the Oldest Woman in the World a Fraud?" *The Guardian*, 30 Nov. 2019, https://www.theguardian.com/science/2019/nov/30/oldest-woman-in-the-world-magical-thinking.

11 Hoad, Phil. "'People Are Caught Up in Magical Thinking'."

12 Gallagher, James. "Algae Proteins Partially Restore Man's Sight." *BBC News*, 24 May 2021, https://www.bbc.co.uk/news/health-57226572.

13 Friedmann, T. and R. Roblin. "Gene Therapy for Human Genetic Disease?" *Science*, vol. 175 no. 4025, 1972, pp. 949–955. https://pubmed.ncbi.nlm.nih.gov/5061866/.

14 Mitha, Farhan. "The Return of Gene Therapy." *Labiotech*, 11 April 2020, https://www.labiotech.eu/in-depth/gene-therapy-history/.

15 Mitha, Farhan. "The Return of Gene Therapy."

16   Rinde, Meir. "The Death of Jesse Gelsinger, 20 Years Later." *Science History Institute*, 4 June 2019, https://www.sciencehistory.org/distillations/the-death-of-jesse-gelsinger-20-years-later.

17   Mitha, Farhan. "The Return of Gene Therapy."

18   "FDA Approval Brings First Gene Therapy to the United States." *FDA*, 30 Aug. 2017, https://www.fda.gov/news-events/press-announcements/fda-approval-brings-first-gene-therapy-united-states.

19   Funk, McKenzie. "Liz Parrish Wants to Live Forever." *Outside*, 18 July 2018, https://www.outsideonline.com/health/wellness/liz-parrish-live-forever/#close.

20   "Elizabeth Blackburn: Nobel Prize in Physiology or Medicine 2009." *The Nobel Prize*, https://www.nobelprize.org/womenwhochangedscience/stories/elizabeth-blackburn.

21   Funk, McKenzie. "Liz Parrish."

22   Funk, McKenzie. "Liz Parrish."

23   Funk, McKenzie. "Liz Parrish."

24   Parrish, Liz. "BioViva -- First Gene Therapy To Treat Biological Aging -- Patient Zero - Liz Parrish." *YouTube*, uploaded by BioViva Science, 2 May 2019, https://www.youtube.com/watch?v=f9YSzT_fOHI.

25   Parrish, Liz. "BioViva."

26   "BioViva Treats First Patient with Gene Therapy to Reverse Aging." *PRWeb*, 8 Nov. 2021, https://www.prweb.com/releases/2015/10/prweb12995323.htm.

27   Mohammadi, Dara and Nicola Davis. "Can This Woman Cure Ageing with Gene Therapy." *The Guardian*, 24 July 2016, https://www.theguardian.com/science/2016/jul/24/elizabeth-parrish-gene-therapy-ageing.

28   Funk, McKenzie. "Liz Parrish."

29   Funk, McKenzie. "Liz Parrish."

30   "Advisory Board." *BioViva*, https://bioviva-science.com/pages/advisory-board.

31   "George Church, Ph.D." *Wyss Institute*, https://wyss.harvard.edu/team/core-faculty/george-church/.

32   Regalado, Antonio. "A Stealthy Harvard Startup Wants to Reverse Aging in Dogs." *Technology Review*, 9 May 2018, https://www.technologyreview.com/2018/05/09/142971/a-stealthy-harvard-startup-wants-to-reverse-aging-in-dogs-and-humans-could-be-next/.

33   Interview with Elizabeth Parrish, 27 May 2021.

Notes to Chapter 11

1   Interview with Alexei Turchin, 13 March 2021.

2   "Russian Transhumanists and the Mafia Are in a Cryonics War over Frozen Heads." *Biohackinfo News*, 18 Sept. 2020, https://biohackinfo.com/news-kriorus-cryonics-russia-transhumanism-ndrangheta/.

3   Dimitropoulos, Stav. "A Dyson Sphere Could Bring Humans Back From the Dead, Researchers Say." *Popular Mechanics*, 10 March 2021, https://www.

popularmechanics.com/science/a35788050/dyson-sphere-digital-resurrection-immortality/.

4   Newton, Casey. "Speak, Memory." *The Verge*, https://www.theverge.com/a/luka-artificial-intelligence-memorial-roman-mazurenko-bot#conversation2.

5   Vlahos, James. "A Son's Race to Give His Dying Father Artificial Immortality." *Wired*, 18 July 2017, https://www.wired.com/story/a-sons-race-to-give-his-dying-father-artificial-immortality/.

6   Abramson, Dustin I., et al. *Creating a Conversational Chat Bot of a Specific Person.* 1 Dec. 2020. U.S. Patent 10,853,717. *United States Patent and Trademark Office*, https://pdfpiw.uspto.gov/.piw?PageNum=0&docid=10853717.

7   @_TimOBrien. "I'm looking into this – appln date (Apr. 2017) predates the AI ethics reviews we do today (I sit on the panel), and I'm not aware of any plan to build/ship (and yes, it's disturbing)." *Twitter*, 22 Jan. 2021, 10:55 a.m., https://twitter.com/_TimOBrien/status/1352645952310439936?s=20.

8   Tucker, Neely. "Martine Rothblatt: She Founded SiriusXM, a Religion and a Biotech. For Starters." *The Washington Post*, 12 December 2014, https://www.washingtonpost.com/lifestyle/magazine/martine-rothblatt-she-founded-siriusxm-a-religion-and-a-biotech-for-starters/2014/12/11/5a8a4866-71ab-11e4-ad12-3734c461eab6_story.html.

9   Forbes, Steve. "Making the Impossible Possible: A Conversation with Martine Rothblatt." *Forbes*, 30 Oct. 2020, https://www.forbes.com/sites/steveforbes/2020/10/30/making-the-impossible-possible-a-conversation-with-martine-rothblatt/?sh=229530a6689d.

10 Tucker, Neely. "Martine Rothblatt."

11 "Home." *Terasem Movement Inc,* https://terasemcentral.org/.

12 "Bina: Custom Character Robot." *Hanson Robotics*, https://www.hansonrobotics.com/bina48-9/.

13 Ronan, Alex. "Humanoid Robot Bina48 Wants Cool Friends and Dreams of Pizza." *Garage Magazine*, 4 Sept. 2018, https://garage.vice.com/en_us/article/ne5kym/bina48-profile.

14 Ramani, Madhvi. "Artificial Intelligence." *The Wilson Quarterly*, https://www.wilsonquarterly.com/quarterly/living-with-artificial-intelligence/artificial-intelligence/.

15 Ramani, Madhvi. "Artificial Intelligence."

16 Crawford, Kate. "Artificial Intelligence's White Guy Problem." *The New York Times*, 25 June 2016, https://www.nytimes.com/2016/06/26/opinion/sunday/artificial-intelligences-white-guy-problem.html

17 Angwin, Julia, et al. "Machine Bias." *ProPublica*, 23 May 2016, https://www.propublica.org/article/machine-bias-risk-assessments-in-criminal-sentencing.

18 Harrison, Sara. "Five Years of Tech Diversity Reports—and Little Progress." 1 Oct. 2019, https://www.wired.com/story/five-years-tech-diversity-reports-little-progress/.

19   Interview with Bruce Duncan, 7 April 2021.

20   "The Truths of Terasem." *Terasem Faith*, https://terasemfaith.net/beliefs/.

21   "The Truths of Terasem."

22   DeWeerdt, Sarah. "How to Map the Brain." *Nature*, 24 July 2019, https://www.nature.com/articles/d41586-019-02208-0.

23   DeWeerdt, Sarah. "How to Map the Brain."

24   Interview with Robert McIntyre, 16 April 2021.

25   Interview with Robert McIntyre, 16 April 2021.

26   "Evaluation of Shawn Mikula's Whole Mouse Brain Entry." *The Brain Preservation Foundation*, https://www.brainpreservation.org/mikulaevaluationpage/.

27   "Large Mammal BPF Prize Winning Announcement." *The Brain Preservation Foundation*, https://www.brainpreservation.org/large-mammal-announcement/.

28   Regalado, Antonio. "A Startup Is Pitching a Mind-Uploading Service That Is '100 Percent Fatal.'" *MIT Technology Review*, 13 March 2018, https://www.technologyreview.com/2018/03/13/144721/a-startup-is-pitching-a-mind-uploading-service-that-is-100-percent-fatal/.

29   Begley, Sharon. "After Ghoulish Allegations, a Brain-Preservation Company Seeks Redemption." *Stat News*, 30 Jan. 2019, https://www.statnews.com/2019/01/30/nectome-brain-preservation-redemption/.

30   "San Diego Resources Frozen Zoo." *San Diego Zoo Wildlife Alliance*, https://science.sandiegozoo.org/resources/frozen-zoo%C2%AE.

31   Interview with Robert McIntyre, 16 April 2021.

Notes to Chapter 12

1   *The Lycurgus Cup*. 4th Century Late Roman. *The British Museum*, https://www.britishmuseum.org/collection/object/H_1958-1202-1.

2   Merali, Zeeya. "This 1,600-Year-Old Goblet Shows that the Romans Were Nanotechnology Pioneers." *Smithsonian Magazine*, Sept. 2013, https://www.smithsonianmag.com/history/this-1600-year-old-goblet-shows-that-the-romans-were-nanotechnology-pioneers-787224/.

3   "Air-Purifying Church Windows Early Nanotechnology." *Phys*, 21 Aug. 2008, https://phys.org/news/2008-08-air-purifying-church-windows-early-nanotechnology.html.

4   Yong, Ed. "Carbon Nanotechnology."

5   Sullivan, Walter. "The Mystery of Damascus Steel Appears Solved." *The New York Times*, 29 Sept. 1981, https://www.nytimes.com/1981/09/29/science/the-mystery-of-damascus-steel-appears-solved.html.

6   Yong, Ed. "Carbon Nanotechnology."

7   Krukenmeyer, M. G., et al. "History and Possible Uses of Nanomedicine Based on Nanoparticles and Nanotechnological Progress." *Journal of*

Nanomedicine & Nanotechnology, vol. 6, issue 6, 2015, pp. 1–7. https://www.longdom.org/open-access/history-and-possible-uses-of-nanomedicine-based-on-nanoparticles-and-nanotechnological-progress-2157-7439-1000336.pdf.

8   Feynman, Richard P. "Plenty of Room at the Bottom." American Physical Society, Dec. 1959, Pasadena, CA. https://web.pa.msu.edu/people/yang/RFeynman_plentySpace.pdf.

9   Feynman, Richard P. "Plenty of Room at the Bottom."

10 Krukenmeyer, M. G., et al. "History and Possible Uses of Nanomedicine."

11 Regis, Ed. "The Incredible Shrinking Man." *Wired*, 1 Oct. 2004, https://www.wired.com/2004/10/drexler/.

12 Regis, Ed. "The Incredible Shrinking Man."

13 Regis, Ed. "The Incredible Shrinking Man."

14 Regis, Ed. "The Incredible Shrinking Man."

15 Interview with Aubrey de Grey, 7 June 2021.

16 Interview with Kostas Kostarelos, 13 June 2021.

17 Kurzweil, Ray. *The Singularity Is Near: When Humans Transcend Biology.* 2006, chapter 5, p. 245.

18 "Nanotech Could Make Humans Immortal by 2040, Futurist Says." *Reuters*, 1 Oct. 2009, https://www.reuters.com/article/urnidgns852573c4006938800 02576420037900c-idUS22091879820091001.

19 Ledford, Heidi. "Moderna COVID Vaccine Becomes Second to get US Authorization." *Nature*, 18 Dec. 2020, https://www.nature.com/articles/d41586-020-03593-7.

20 "Pfizer and BioNTech Celebrate Historic First Authorization in the U.S. of Vaccine to Prevent COVID-19." *Pfizer*, 11 Dec. 2020, https://www.pfizer.com/news/press-release/press-release-detail/pfizer-and-biontech-celebrate-historic-first-authorization.

21 Cooney, Elizabeth. "How Nanotechnology Helps mRNA Covid-19 Vaccines Work." *Stat News*, 1 Dec. 2020, https://www.statnews.com/2020/12/01/how-nanotechnology-helps-mrna-covid19-vaccines-work/.

22 Fellman, Megan. "Robert Langer of MIT receives $250,000 Kabiller Prize in Nanoscience and Nanomedicine from Northwestern." *Northwestern Now*, 27 Sept. 2017, https://news.northwestern.edu/stories/2017/september/robert-langer-kabiller-prize-nanoscience-nanomedicine-northwestern/.

23 Interview with Dr. Robert Langer, 4 June 2021.

Notes to Chapter 13

1   Winslow, Aaron. "Russian Cosmism Versus Interstellar Bosses: Reclaiming Full-Throttle Luxury Space Communism." *Los Angeles Review of Books*, 18 Aug. 2018, https://lareviewofbooks.org/article/russian-cosmism-versus-interstellar-bosses-reclaiming-full-throttle-luxury-space-communism/.

2   Piper, Kelsey. "We've worried about overpopulation for centuries. And we've always been wrong." *Vox*, 20 Aug. 2019, https://www.vox.com/future-

perfect/2019/8/20/20802413/overpopulation-demographic-transition-population-explained.

3   Piper, Kelsey. "We've worried about overpopulation for centuries."

4   Piper, Kelsey. "We've worried about overpopulation for centuries."

5   Cilluffo, Anthony and Neil G. Ruiz. "World's Population Is Projected to Nearly Stop Growing by the End of the Century." *Pew Research Center*, 17 June 2019, https://www.pewresearch.org/fact-tank/2019/06/17/worlds-population-is-projected-to-nearly-stop-growing-by-the-end-of-the-century/.

6   Cilluffo, Anthony and Neil G. Ruiz. "World's Population."

7   Piper, Kelsey. "We've worried about overpopulation for centuries."

8   Bricker, Darrell and John Ibbitson. "What Goes Up: Are Predictions of a Population Crisis Wrong?" *The Guardian*, 27 Jan. 2019, https://www.theguardian.com/world/2019/jan/27/what-goes-up-population-crisis-wrong-fertility-rates-decline.

9   Illing, Sean. "Scientists are waging a war against human aging. But what happens next?" *Vox*, 6 May 2017, https://www.vox.com/conversations/2017/5/4/15433348/aubrey-de-grey-life-extension-aging-death-science-medicine.

10 Illing, Sean. "Scientists are waging a war against human aging."

11 White, Ben. "How the Baby Boomers Broke America." *Politico*, 26 Oct. 2019, https://www.politico.com/news/2019/10/26/how-the-baby-boomers-broke-america-058122.

12 Shalal, Andrea. "Aging Population to Hit U.S. Economy like a 'Ton of Bricks'—U.S. Commerce Secretary." *Reuters*, 12 July 2021, https://www.reuters.com/world/us/aging-population-hit-us-economy-like-ton-bricks-us-commerce-secretary-2021-07-12/.

13 Shalal, Andrea. "Aging Population to Hit U.S. Economy."

14 Cilluffo, Anthony and Neil G. Ruiz. "World's Population Is Projected to Nearly Stop Growing by the End of the Century." *Pew Research Center*, 17 June 2019, https://www.pewresearch.org/fact-tank/2019/06/17/worlds-population-is-projected-to-nearly-stop-growing-by-the-end-of-the-century/.

15 Chetty, Raj, Michael Stepner, Sarah Abraham, et al. "The Association Between Income and Life Expectancy in the United States, 2001–2014." *JAMA*, vol. 315, no. 16, 2016, 1750–1766. https://jamanetwork.com/journals/jama/article-abstract/2513561.

INDEX

Able, Renault, 28, 30, 33

Abrams, Linda, 54

adenosine deaminase (ADA), 171–72

AgeMeter, 131

age reversal research, 179–81

aging, hallmarks of, 115–20, 121; altered intercellular communication, 118; cellular senescence, 119, 121–26, 146; deregulated nutrient sensing, 117–18; epigenetic alterations, 116–17, 127; genomic instability and compromised DNA repair, 116–17; loss of proteostasis, 117; mitochondrial dysfunction, 117; stem cell exhaustion, 118; telomere attrition, 118–19, 173

aging, scientific research on, 115–31; Austad, 119–21, 129, 131; biological age, 126–29; Campisi, 121–26; cellular senescence, 119, 121–26; commercial testing products, 127–31; epigenetic clocks, 127–29; immortalists and, 123–24; the nine hallmarks of aging, 115–20, 121; senolytics, 121–26

Aging Analytics Agency, 106

aging of the American population, 107, 223–27

Airbnb, 97

Alcor Life Extension Foundation, 45–59, 68–77, 93, 103, 185, 198, 223; and cryonics life insurance policies, 63, 64; Darwin's criticisms of, 73–77; Harris and, 69–71, 73, 77; Kent suspension scandal, 47–58, 73–74; neurosuspension and brain preservation technology, 46–59, 198; protocols for when a member dies, 71–72, 76–77; Williams suspension and lawsuit, 58

Aldrin, Buzz, 21

Allen Institute for Brain Science (Seattle), 195–96

Alphabet, 103

Altos Labs, 105

Alzheimer's disease, 71–72, 107, 116–17, 213, 216

Amazing Stories (science fiction magazine), 19

Amazon, 97, 190, 193

Ambrosia, 101–2

American Cancer Society, 162

American Federation of Aging Research, 119

Amgen, 113

Anderson College (Indiana), 63

Andrews, Bill, 174, 176–77

andrographis, 137, 148

animal species, longer-living, 165–68, 180

Apple, 193

Archer, Audrey, 134

Armanios, Mary, 130

Armstrong, Neil, 21

artificial intelligence (AI): BINA48, 191–93; chatbots, 187–88; and digital immortality, 186–88, 191–93, 196–97; and Kurzweil's concept of the singularity, 103; McIntyre's mind uploading techniques, 196–97; predictive algorithms, 192–93; racial biases, 191–93

Ashworth, Chris, 54–56

Asimov, Isaac, x, 22

As It Happens (radio program), 51
Asprey, Dave, 136–41; biohacking,
    136–41; Bulletproof 360 products
    and the FDA warnings, 148;
    Bulletproof Coffee, 136, 138–40,
    194–95; critics of *The Bulletproof Diet*
    and views on health, 139–41; false
    claims about COVID-19 cures, 137,
    148; and intermittent fasting, 139,
    141, 143; and stem cell therapy, 151,
    154, 160, 163
Astounding (science fiction magazine),
    20–21, 183
Atala, Anthony, 161
Austad, Steven, 119–21, 129, 131
Autor, Travis, 156–57

baby boomer generation, 107, 221–22,
    223–27
Banerji, Versha, 146
Bank of America, 105–6
Bardin, Joe, 135–36
Becker, Ernest, xii, 80–81
Bedford, James, 29–32, 34–35, 42,
    44–47
Bedford, Norman, 29, 31, 46
Belluz, Julia, 140
beta-carotene, 146
*Beyond Tomorrow: The Next Fifty Years in
    Space* (Cole), 26
Bezos, Jeff, 90, 97, 105
Biela's Comet, 86
BINA48 (Breakthrough Intelligence via
    Neural Architecture), 191–93
biohacking, 136–49, 151, 170; anti-
    aging dietary supplements, 143–49;
    Asprey and, 136–41; intermittent
    fasting, 10–11, 118, 139, 141–43;
    NAD+, 144–46; nootropics, 147.
    See also regenerative medicine
biological age, 126–29
biological immortality: theory of,
    7–8, 108; *Turritopsis dohrnii* (the
    "immortal jellyfish"), 165–66
biomarkers, 129

biotechnology, xi; and de Grey's escape
    velocity theory, xi; nanotechnology,
    190, 194, 202, 203–17, 219; Silicon
    Valley biotech companies and field
    of aging research, 97–98, 100–113,
    125, 219–20
BioViva, 174–76
Blackburn, Elizabeth, 173
Black Mirror (British sci-fi TV show),
    187
Blumenthal, David, 225–27
Bogan, Rick, 50–51
Boston University Medical School, 122
bowhead whales, 167, 180
brain preservation: Alcor and the Kent
    suspension scandal, 47–58, 73–74;
    Alcor and the Williams suspension,
    58; brain mapping, 195–96;
    brain slicing, 195; cryonics and
    neurosuspension, 29–30, 46–59,
    197–99, 200; mind uploading and
    digital immortality, 89, 196–202,
    227–28
Brain Preservation Foundation (BPF)
    and Brain Preservation Prize,
    197–99
Brexit, 227
Brin, Sergey, 103, 104
Brink's Robbery (1950), 26
British Dietetic Association, 139
Broughton, Travis, 157
Brown, Bernadeane, 92–95, 134–35
Brown, Charles Paul, 92–95
Brown, Marie, 36–37
Brunol, Dante, 30
Buccelli, John "Fats," 26
Buck Institute, 126
Buddhism, 82–83
Bulletproof 360 (company), 139, 148
Bulletproof Coffee, 136, 138–40,
    194–95
The Bulletproof Diet (Asprey), 139–41
Bush, George W., 152, 209

Calico, 103–5, 123–24

California Medical Board, 56–57

Calment, Jeanne, 121, 168–70, 180

caloric restriction, 112, 141–43, 173. See also intermittent fasting

Campisi, Judith, 121–26, 225, 229–30

Canadian Medical Association Journal, 158

cancer: chemotherapy treatment, 141, 213, 214; deaths, 7, 126–27

cancer research, 122–23; cancer resistance in naked mole-rats, 168; cellular senescence, 122–23, 124, 146; Longo and fasting-mimicking diets, 141–42; nanotechnology, 210, 213–14; on potential risks of dietary supplements, 146; telomerase production in cancer cells, 174

Cannon, Lincoln, 84–85

Canopus in Argos (Lessing series), 68

Carpenter, Adelaide, 99

Carrel, Alexis, 124

Carrillo, Ray, 47, 50, 54–56

CB Insights, 105

Cell (journal), 115, 123

cellular senescence, 119, 121–26, 146

cellular transdifferentiation, 152–53, 166

Centers for Disease Control and Prevention (CDC), 158

cerebral palsy, 22–23

Chamberlain, Fred, 43, 45

Chamberlain, Linda, 43, 45, 61

chatbots, 187–88

Chatsworth disaster in cryonics, 36–40, 43–44, 57

Chemical and Engineering News, 208

child mortality rates, 221

Children's Medical Center Research Institute at UT Southwestern, 154

Christianity, 6, 63–64, 81–82, 83, 85, 94, 235–36

ChromaDex, 145

Church, George, xii, 15, 131, 176, 178–81

Church of Perpetual Life (Hollywood, Florida), 3–17, 95, 113, 223, 237; critics of, 68–69; Fedorov and, 8, 86, 91, 233, 235; founders, 7, 14, 79; hosting First Annual Cryonics Symposium, 6, 16–17, 61–63, 69, 72–73, 79; prophets, 8, 13–14, 86, 91, 235; as religion, 14, 68–69, 79–80, 83, 91

Church of Scientology, 54

Clarke, Arthur C., 8

"Classification of Approaches to Technological Resurrection" (Turchin), 186

climate change, 224, 230

clinical trials: anti-aging dietary supplements, 144–45; and the FDA, 162, 172, 177; gene therapy, 171–73, 176, 177, 178–79, 181; Right to Try Act and experimental drug therapies, 162

cloning, 89, 153

Coalition for Radical Life Extension, 134

Cohen, Jeremy, 93–95

Cole, Danbridge M., 26

Comella, Kristin, 163

Commonwealth Fund, 225–26

Conrad, Andy, 103

The Consequential Frontier (Ward), x

convergence, 214

Conversations with Bina48 (Dinkins art project), 192

Cooper, Bradley, 137

Cooper, Evan, 19, 21–27, 31–34, 40, 62

Cooper, Mildred, 34

Cordain, Loren, 140

cosmism, Russian, 89–91, 220, 235, 236

COVID-19 pandemic, xi–xiii, 61, 133, 174, 212–15, 223, 231, 233–34; Asprey's false claims about cures, 137, 148; and followers of Fedorov, 237; vaccines, 212–15

Crichton, Michael, 208

CRISPR (gene-editing tool), 15, 178, 213

cryobiology, 28

Cryo-Care Corporation (Phoenix, Arizona), 25, 26–27, 31, 35, 45

cryonics, x, 5, 13, 19–40, 41–59, 61–78, 200; Alcor, 45–59, 68–77, 93, 103, 185, 198, 223; Bedford preservation, 29–32, 34–35, 42, 44–47; brain preservation (neurosuspension), 29–30, 46–59, 197–99, 200; Chatsworth disaster, 36–40, 43–44, 57; Cooper, 19, 21–27, 31–34, 40, 62; critics of, 43–46, 73–78, 106–7, 184–85, 200, 228, 236–37; cryogenic capsules, 25–26, 31, 35–37, 38–39, 47; Cryonics Society of California (CSC), 28–34, 36–38, 43–44; Darwin and formative years, 41–59; Darwin's criticisms, 43–45, 73–77; Ettinger, 19–24, 28, 31–34, 40, 62; Ettinger's *The Prospect of Immortality*, 21–23, 32; First Annual Cryonics Symposium, 6, 16–17, 61–63, 69, 72–73, 79; first attempted cryopreservations, 26–27, 29–40; founders and early movement, 19–40; Harris, 69–71, 73, 77; Hoffman, 61–68, 72–73; Kent suspension scandal and legal battle, 47–58, 73–74; Life Extension Society (LES) and newsletter, 22, 23–28, 31–32, 34; life insurance policies, 61, 62–63, 64–68; Nelson, 19, 27–40, 41–45, 59; as Plan B option for immortalists, 5, 183, 184, 227–28; Russia's KrioRus, 72, 184–85; Sweet preservation, 32–36; Turchin on, 184–85; Williams suspension and lawsuit, 58

Cryonics (magazine), 44–45

Cryonics Institute, 40, 68

cryonics life insurance policies, 61, 62–63, 64–68

Cryonics Society of California (CSC), 28–34, 36–38, 43–44

Cryonics Society of New York (CSNY), 25, 42–43

Cult Education Institute, 93

cults and cult-like groups, 16, 91–94

Curcumin Max, 148

CyBeRev, 190

Dadbot (chatbot), 188

The Daily Telegraph, 140

Dalai Lama, 82

Damascus Steel swords, 204–6

Dana-Farber Cancer Institute, 122

Darwin, Mike, 41–55, 57–58, 69, 73–77; criticism of Alcor, 73–77; criticism of Nelson, 43–45

de Blasio, Nick, 38

de Grey, Aubrey, 13–14, 95, 98–100, 107–11, 133, 226, 229; criticism of Calico, 104–5; and dietary supplements, 143, 149; on Drexler and nanotechnology, 209; early life and career, 98–99; on Jeanne Calment, 169; longevity escape velocity theory, xi, 95, 108–9, 181, 220, 222–23, 227; on McIntyre, 200; other scientists' opinions of, 109–10, 126; on overpopulation question, 220, 222–23; rejuvenation theory, 98, 100, 108–9, 223; SENS concept, 99; SENS Foundation, 99–100, 110–11, 126, 173; Sergey Young on, 106; sexual misconduct charge, 110–11; Silicon Valley and anti-aging industry, 95, 98, 100, 105, 106, 107–11, 113

de la Poterie, Genevieve, 38–40

de la Poterie, Guy, 38, 39

Deming, Laura, 110–11

demographic transition, 221–22

The Denial of Death (Becker), xii, 80–81

Derhy, Dvir, 72–73

DeSilva, Ashanthi, 171–72

Dick, Philip K., 21

dietary supplements, anti-aging, 143–49; and Asprey's Bulletproof 360 products, 148; de Grey and, 143, 149; and the FDA, 144–48; NAD+ marketing and longevity claims, 144–46; nootropics, 147

digital immortality, 89, 183–202, 227–28; BINA48, 191–93; BioFiles, 190–91; brain mapping, 195–96; brain preservation and mind uploading research, 89, 196–202, 227–28; chatbots, 187–88; flaws and problems with digital resurrection, 195–96; McIntyre and, 196–202, 228; mindfiles, 190–91; and the preservation of memories, 201, 228; role of AI, 186–88, 191–93, 196–97; Rothblatt's Terasem Movement projects, 190–95; Turchin and, 183–87, 195

Dinkins, Stephanie, 191–93

Disney, Walt, 77

Do Androids Dream of Electric Sheep? (Dick), 21

Doerr, John, 103

Dostoevsky, Fyodor, 88

Doubleday Publishers, 22

Doxil, 213

Drexler, K. Eric, 207–9, 211, 212, 217

Duncan, Bruce, 190–91, 193–94

Dune (Herbert), 21

Dyson Sphere, 186

Ehrlich, Paul, 221

Einstein, Albert, 206

Elysium, 145

End of Life Option Act (California), 199

Engines of Creation (Drexler), 207

Epel, Elissa, 173

ephedra, 145

The Epic of Gilgamesh, 8–9

epigenetic clocks, 127–29

epigenetics, 116–17, 127–29

epigenome, 116–17, 127

Epstein, Jeffrey, 77

escape velocity for longevity, xi, 11, 95, 108–9, 181, 220, 222–23, 227

Ettinger, Robert, 19–24, 28, 31–34, 40, 62

eugenics, 22–23

European Commission, 172

euthanasia, 23

evangelical Christianity, 85, 94

Evans, Martin, 152

Fahy, Greg, 43–44, 198

Faloon, Bill, 7, 8, 14, 79, 129, 133, 144

fasting. See intermittent fasting

Federal Trade Commission, 155

Fedorov, Nikolai, 86–91, 234–38; early life, 87; Fedorov Museum-Library in Moscow, 89, 233–38; as prophet of the Church of Perpetual Life, 8, 86, 91, 233, 235; and Russian cosmism, 89–91, 220, 235, 236; and transhumanism, 88–89, 236; views of death and universal immortality, 86–91, 235–37

Fedorov Museum-Library (Moscow), 89, 233–38

Ferrucci, Luigi, 147, 224–25

Feynman, Richard P., 206, 207, 211

First Annual Cryonics Symposium, 6, 16–17, 61–63, 69, 72–73, 79

The First Immortal (Halperin), 68

Flame Foundation (The Eternal Flame Foundation), 92. See also People Unlimited

Florida Board of Medicine, 159

Florida Department of Health, 159

Food and Drug Administration (FDA): and Asprey's Bulletproof 360 products, 148; Center for Biologics Evaluation and Research, 102; and dietary supplement regulation, 144–48; and experimental gene therapy, 172, 177; libertarian efforts to undermine or abolish, 161–62;

and nanotechnology research, 215;
and ozone therapy, 138; Right to
Try Act and unapproved drugs,
162–63; and stem cell therapy,
154–55, 158, 161–62, 163; and
young blood transfusions, 102
food insecurity, 143
Fox News, 224
free radicals (Reactive Oxygen Species),
117
Freeze, Wait, Reanimate (LES newsletter),
22, 23–24, 25, 26, 31, 32, 34
*Freezing People Is (Not) Easy: My
Adventures In Cryonics* (Nelson),
26–27
Friedmann, Theodore, 171
Friend, Tad, 100

Gacheva, Anastasia, 89, 234–37
Gardner, Michaelann, 85
Garfield, Tepper, Ashworth, and
Epstein (law firm), 54–56
Gawker, 101
Geisen, Michael, 68–69, 71–72
Gelsinger, Jesse, 172, 210
Gendicine, 172
gene therapy, 170–82; China, 172;
Church, 178–81; critics of
immortalists' involvement, 175–76,
178–79, 181; DeSilva case success,
171–72; European, 172–73;
experimental trials, 171–73,
176, 177, 178–79, 181; and FDA
regulation, 172, 177; Gelsinger
tragedy, 172, 210; immortalists and
anti-aging focus, 173–82; Parrish
and self-experimentation, 173–79,
181; Russia, 172; use of viral
vectors, 171–72, 210
"Gene Therapy for Human Genetic
Disease?" (Friedmann and Roblin),
171
genetic engineering, 207

genome, human, 115–17, 178. *See also*
aging, hallmarks of; epigenome;
gene therapy
Geostar, 189
Geron, 174
gerontology, 91, 108, 174
giant tortoises, 167
Gilgamesh epic, 8–9
Gilley, Leonard, 24
GlaxoSmithKline, 112–13
Glendale News-Press, 33
Glybera, 172–73
The God Makers (documentary film), 85
Google, 103–4, 193
Gore, Al, 208
Gorskaja, Anna, 234–35
Gottlieb, Scott, 102, 162
gray goo scenario, 207, 208–9, 217
Greider, Carol, 173
Grekos, Zannos, 159–60
Guarente, Leonard, 112, 113

Haggans, Carol, 145, 146
Halevi, Judah, xii
Halioua, Celine, 110–11
Halperin, James L., 68
Hanson, David, 191
Harrington, Dennis, 37–38
Harrington, Mildred, 37–40
Harrington, Terry, 37–38
Harris, Patrick, 69–71, 73, 77
Harvard Medical School, 112, 178
Harvard University, 15, 178
Haspel, Tamar, 147–48
Hayflick, Leonard, 124
Hayworth, Kenneth, 197–98
health care system: and aging baby
boomer generation, 107, 224–27;
COVID-19 pandemic and, xii;
Ferrucci on necessity of treating
aging as a disease, 224–25;
inequalities, xii, 16, 225–27;
preventative medicine, 226–27
healthspan, extended, 108, 182, 225,
230

heart disease, 7, 122–23, 126–27
Hedley, Douglas, 80
Henderson, Curtis, 25, 42
Herbert, Frank, 21
Here After, 188
Hinduism, 82
histones, 116
Hoffman, Rudi, 61–68, 72–73, 75, 129,
    137; Christian background, 63–64;
    cryonics life insurance policies, 61,
    62–63, 64–68; and First Annual
    Cryonics Symposium, 61–63,
    72–73; receiving stem cell therapy,
    160; on religious resistance to
    cryonics, 65
Hogan, Hulk, 101
Hollywood, Florida, 7
Hope, Ed, 31, 35, 36
Horvath, Steve, 126
Howard Hughes Medical Institute, 154
Human Genome Project, 178
Hwang Woo Suk, 153
hydrozoans, 165–66

immortalists, 3–17, 63; critics of,
    68–69, 76–78, 229; and digital
    immortality, 183–202; and
    escape velocity, xi, 11, 95, 108–9,
    220, 222–23, 227; Fedorov's
    followers, 90–91, 234–37; and
    gene therapy, 173–82; modern
    interpretation of immortalism, x–
    xi; and nanotechnology, 211–12;
    scientists' views of, 121, 123–24,
    181, 229; theory of biological
    immortality, 7–8, 108; unforeseen
    and problematic consequences
    of immortality, 219–31; views of
    death, 13, 87–89, 94, 184, 194, 236.
    See also cryonics; transhumanism
Immortality, Physically, Scientifically, Now
    (Cooper), 21–22
Immortality Communication Exchange
    (ICE), 22

immune system: Asprey's suggestions
    for biohacking and "super
    immunity," 137–38; and gene
    therapy, 171–72; and longer-living
    animals, 168
Imperial College London, 209–10
inflammation, chronic, 118, 125
Institute for Advanced Biological
    Studies (IABS), 45–46
Intellectual Ventures, 100
Intelsat, 189
intermittent fasting, 10–11, 118, 139,
    141–43; Asprey and, 139, 141, 143;
    Longo and fasting-mimicking
    diets, 141–42; Panda and Time
    Restricted Feeding, 142
International Society for Stem Cell
    Research, 154
Ivy Plasma, 102

The Jameson Satellite (Jones), 19–20
Jehovah's Witnesses, 16, 83
jellyfish, 165–66, 180
The Johnny Carson Show, 32
Johnson, Larry, 58
Johnson, Marcelon, 44
Jones, Neil Ronald, 19
Journal of the American Geriatrics Society,
    123
Juno Inc., 25

Kansas City Life, 65–66
Karmazin, Jesse, 101–2
Kaufman, Matthew, 152
Kent, Dora, 47–58, 73–74
Kent, Saul, 7, 25, 42, 47–50, 54, 56
Khaled, Walid, 168
King, Larry, 92
Kline, Helen, 36, 39
Klockgether, Joseph, 35–36, 40
Knoepfler, Paul S., 160–61
Kostarelos, Kostas, 209–11, 212, 215–17
KrioRus, 72, 184–85
Kubrick, Stanley, 21, 40
Kunzman, Alan, 50–51

Kurzweil, Ray, 103, 135, 143–44, 211–
    12; and nanotechnology, 211–12;
    singularity concept, 103, 109, 144,
    181, 211–12
Kuyda, Eugenia, 187–88

Langer, Robert, 213–15, 217
LaPlante, Matthew, 113–14
Leaf, Jerry, 45–46, 48, 50, 52–54, 74
Ledesma, Pedro, 38, 39
Leon, Donald, 92
Lessing, Doris, 68
Liberace, 50
libertarians, 61, 101, 137, 161–62, 177
life expectancy, average, 4–5, 125–26,
    225–26, 229, 230
Life Extension Foundation, 129,
    144–45
Life Extension Society (LES), 22,
    23–28, 31–32, 34
life insurance policies and cryonics, 61,
    62–63, 64–68
LifeNaut, 190
lifespan, extended human, 108, 125–26,
    225, 229–30
Lifespan: Why We Age—and Why We Don't
    Have To (Sinclair and LaPlante),
    113–14
Limitless (film), 137
lipid nanoparticles, 210, 212–13
lipoprotein lipase deficiency, 172–73
liposomes, 210
Liveyon, 158
longevity escape velocity. See escape
    velocity for longevity
Longevity Fund, 110
Longevity Party, 184
Longevity Vision Fund, 106–7
Long John Nebel show (talk radio
    program), 23
Longo, Valter, 141–42
Loyal (biotech company), 110
Luka (chatbot), 187
Lycurgus Cup, 203
Lyft, 97

Mandell, Steven, 38–40
Maris, Bill, 103
Marks, Peter, 102
Martin, George, 176
Massachusetts Institute of Technology
    (MIT), 112, 178, 196–97, 199,
    207–8, 214
Mawson, Tim, 83
Max Planck Institute, 198
Mazurenko, Roman, 187
McCulloch, Ernest, 152
McIntyre, Robert, 196–202, 228
McLaughlin, Wilma Jean, 25–26
McMaster University (Hamilton,
    Ontario), 93
The Mechanical Monarch (Tubb), 42
Medicaid, 226
Medical News Today, 15
melatonin, 145
Memorial Sloan Kettering, 210
Miceli, Victor, 55–56
Microsoft, 100, 188, 193
Mikula, Shawn, 198
Mill, Jonathan, 128
Miller, Tom, 155
Milner, Yuri, 105
mind uploading, 89, 196–202, 227–28.
    See also digital immortality
mitochondria, 117, 144, 167
The Mitochondrial Free Radical Theory of
    Aging (de Grey), 99
MIT Technology Review, 99, 105, 199
Moderna, 212–13, 214–15
Monorhaphis chuni (sponge species), 166
More, Max, 69
Mormonism, 83–86
Mormon Transhumanist Association,
    84–86
Morrison, Sean, 154–55, 157–58,
    160–63, 229
Moscow State University, 184
mRNA, 213
Musk, Elon, 90
Myhrvold, Nathan, 100

NAD+. *See* nicotinamide adenine dinucleotide (NAD+)

naked mole-rat, 168

nanobots, 212

"Nanosystems: Molecular Machinery, Manufacturing and Computation" (Drexler), 208

nanotechnology, 190, 194, 202, 203–17, 219; ancient and medieval uses of, 203–6; COVID-19 vaccines, 212–15; dangers of, 215–17; Drexler's theory of molecular nanotechnology, 207–9, 211, 212, 217; Feynman's 1959 paper, 206, 207, 211; gray goo scenario, 207, 208–9, 217; immortalists and, 211–12; as interdisciplinary science, 212, 214; Kostareolos's research and views on the field, 209–11, 212, 215–17; Kurzweil on, 211–12; Langer on, 213–15, 217; lipid nanoparticles, 210, 212–13; nanobots, 212; nanomedicine, 212–15; nanoparticles and drug delivery, 213–14; neural interface technologies, 216–17; in sci-fi films and TV, 203

nanotubes, 205–6

Nara Institute of Science and Technology (Japan), 153

NASA, 69, 88, 189

National Cancer Institute, 141–42, 210

National Institute of Aging (NIA), 11, 147, 224–25

National Institutes of Health (NIH), 145, 178, 215

National Institutes of Health Centers of Excellence in Genomic Science (CEGS), 178

National Safety Council, 8

Nature Cell Biology, 146

Navitor, 104

Nectome, 199–201

Nelson, Bob, 19, 27–40, 41–45, 59; and the Bedford preservation, 29–32, 34–35, 42, 44–45; and the Chatsworth disaster, 36–40, 43–44, 57; and the Cryonics Society of California, 28–34, 36–38, 43–44; and the Sweet preservation, 32–36

Neovasculgen, 172

Nest, 103

neural interface technologies, 216–17

neuroscience, 195–202

neurosuspension, 29–30, 46–59, 197–99, 200. *See also* brain preservation; cryonics

The New Yorker, 100, 104

The New York Times, 77, 112, 161, 192

nicotinamide adenine dinucleotide (NAD+), 144–46

nicotinamide mononucleotide (NMN), 144–45

nicotinamide riboside (NR), 144–45

Nisco, Louis, 35, 36–37, 39

nootropics, 147

NPR (National Public Radio), 51

nutritional supplements. See dietary supplements, anti-aging

Oakwood Memorial Park Cemetery (Chatsworth, California), 36–40

obesity rates, 107

O'Brien, Tim, 188

Odoevsky, Prince Vladimir, 86–87

Office of Dietary Supplements (ODS) at the National Institutes of Health, 145

Olshansky, Jay, 120

Omni magazine, 64

oncogenes, 122

Ontario Cancer Institute, 152

orange roughy (deep sea fish), 166

ornithine transcarbamylase deficiency, 172

Orpheus, tale of, ix–x, 231

Osiris Cryonics, 72–73

Outside magazine, 176
overpopulation, 220–23
ozone therapy, 138

Page, Larry, 103, 104, 123
The Paleo Diet (Cordain), 140
PanAmSat, 189
Panda, Satchidananda, 142
Pardee, Arthur, 122
Parrish, Liz, 173–79, 181–82, 215
Pennington Biomedical Research
    Center, 11
"The Penultimate Trump" (Ettinger),
    20
People Unlimited, 91–95, 134, 174, 223
Perry, Mike, 48–54, 57, 59, 61
Personal Genome Project, 178
Pew Research Center, 221
Pfizer, 113
Pfizer-BioNTech COVID-19 vaccine,
    212–13
Phaedo (Plato), 80
Phelps-Sweet, Marie. See Sweet, Marie
    Phelps
The Philosophy of the Common Task
    (Fedorov), 87
Pigott, Aisling, 139–40
placebo effects, 157, 178–79
Planck, Max, 206
Plato, 80
PloS Biology, 123
The Population Bomb (Ehrlich), 221
Porter, Sam, 39–40
PPH Cure Foundation, 189
Praluent, 213
Prehoda, Robert, 26, 28–32
preventative medicine, 226–27
Prey (Crichton), 208
Proceedings of the National Academy
    of Sciences of the United States of
    America, 123
The Prospect of Immortality (Ettinger),
    21–23, 32
proteostasis, 117
pulmonary hypertension, 189

Qin Shi Huang, 9–10
Quahog clams, 166
quantum immortality, 184, 186–87
Quartz, 142–43

RAADfest, 133–38, 143, 149, 160, 223;
    and anti-aging dietary supplements,
    143, 149; Asprey and, 136–38;
    founders Brown and Strole, 134–
    36; Parrish's talk on gene therapy,
    177; stem cell therapy discussion,
    160
racism and racial biases, 191–93, 230
Raimondo, Gina, 224
rapamycin, 15, 118
Reactive Oxygen Species (ROS), 117
regenerative medicine, 5; gene therapy
    for anti-aging, 173–82; stem cell
    therapy, 151–63
Regenerative Medicine and Anti-Aging
    Institutes (Omaha, Nebraska),
    155–57
Regenocyte, 159–60
Reibold, Marianne, 205–6
Reikes, Joyce Manulis, 56
Rejuvenate Bio, 179
Rejuvenation Research, 169
religious views of death and
    immortality, 79–95, 194–95; Becker
    and, 80–81; Buddhism, 82–83;
    Christianity, 81–82, 83; Church of
    Perpetual Life, 14, 68–69, 79–80,
    83, 91; Fedorov and resurrection
    of all the dead, 86–91; Hinduism,
    82; immortalists and, 83, 194–95;
    Jehovah's Witnesses, 83; Mormons
    and religious transhumanism,
    83–86; People Unlimited, 91–95;
    Plato and immortality of the soul,
    80; Russian cosmism, 89–91, 220,
    235, 236; Terasem Movement
    Transreligion (TMT), 194–95
Repatha, 213
Replika (chatbot), 187–88
resveratrol, 112–13, 145
retinitis pigmentosa, 170

rhodopsins, 170
Rice University, 208–9
Right to Try Act (2018), 162–63
Roblin, Richard, 171
Rohrman, Rae, 41
Ross, Rick, 93
Rostand, Jean, 20
Rothblatt, Martine, 189–91, 193–94
Rumyantsev Museum (Moscow), 87, 88
Russia: cryonics provider KrioRus, 72,
    184–85; experimental gene therapy
    trials, 172; Fedorov Museum-
    Library, 89, 233–38; Fedorov's
    cosmism, 89–91, 220, 235, 236
Russian Orthodox Church, 87
Russian Transhumanist Movement, 184

Salk Institute for Biological Studies, 142
San Diego Frozen Zoo, 200, 202
Schalkwyk, Leonard, 128
Schilman, Eva, 35
Science (journal), 171, 174
The Science and Technology of GROWING
    YOUNG (Young), 106
Science magazine, 112
Scientific American, 120, 146
Seamless, 97
sea sponges, 166–67
Semenova, Svetlana, 234–35, 236–37
Senate Subcommittee on Science,
    Technology, and Space, 208
Senescence-Associated Secretory
    Phenotype (SASP), 123
senolytics, 121–26
SENS (strategies for engineered
    negligible senescence), 99–100
SENS Foundation, 100, 110–11, 126,
    173
SENS Research Advisory Board, 126
severe combined immunodeficiency,
    171–72
Sharpe, Phil, 214
Sierra Sciences, 174
Silicon Valley (HBO comedy drama), 101

Silicon Valley biotech startups, 8,
    90, 95, 97–114, 125, 219–20,
    235; Ambrosia and young blood
    transfusions, 101–3; anti-aging and
    longevity industry, 97–98, 100–113,
    125, 219–20; de Grey's SENS
    Foundation, 100, 110–11, 126;
    Google and Calico, 103–5, 123–24;
    Milner's Altos Labs, 105; senolytics
    and Unity Biotechnology, 125;
    Sinclair's anti-aging research and
    claims, 111–14; Young's Longevity
    Vision Fund, 106–7
"Silicon Valley's Quest to Live Forever"
    (Friend), 100
Sinclair, David, 111–14, 131
singularity, concept of, 103, 109, 144,
    181, 211–12
The Singularity Is Near: When Humans
    Transcend Biology (Kurzweil), 211
Sirius, 189
Sirtris Pharmaceuticals, 112–13
sirtuins, 112, 113, 116
Smalley, Richard, 208–9
Smith, Carl, 47
Smith, Joseph, 84
Socrates, 80
Soloviev, Vladimir, 88
Sommer, Christian, 165–66
Soviet Union, 89
Space Race between the US and the
    USSR, 21
Sports Illustrated, 58
Stalin, Joseph, 89
Stanford Medical School, 102
Stanley, Russ, 33, 36, 39
Startling Stories (science fiction
    magazine), 20
Star Trek films, 203
State University of New York at Stony
    Brook, 122
stem cells, 118, 136, 151–63; adult, 151–
    54; cellular transdifferentiation,
    152–53, 166; exhaustion of
    (as hallmark of aging), 118;

hematopoietic, 152; pluripotent (embryonic), 151–54; role of, 118, 151–52; scientific research on, 152–54, 161; somatic-cell nuclear transfer and "therapeutic cloning," 153. *See also* stem cell therapy
stem cell therapy, 151–63; Asprey and, 151, 154, 160, 163; entrepreneurs and fake/fraudulent therapies, 154–60, 163; FDA regulations and enforcement actions, 154–55, 158, 161–62, 163; immortalists and, 160–61, 163; injuries, complications, and deaths resulting from, 158–59; state lawsuits targeting fraudulent advertisers, 155–57
Strole, James, 92–94, 134–36
Suspended Animation (company), 72
Suspended Animation (Prehoda), 26
Sweet, Marie Phelps, 32–36, 39

telomerase, 119, 173–74
Telomere Center in the McKusick-Nathans Institute of Genetic Medicine at Johns Hopkins University School of Medicine, 130
Telomere Diagnostics, 130, 131
telomeres, 69, 118–19, 130–31, 173–77; attrition of (as hallmark of aging), 118–19, 173; Parrish and age-reversal gene therapy, 173–77; and telomerase, 119, 173–74
Terasem Movement Foundation, Inc., 190–95
Terasem Movement Transreligion (TMT), 194–95
TERC (gene), 174
Terminator II (film), 203
theosis, 85
therapeutic cloning, 153
"There's Plenty of Room at the Bottom" (Feynman), 206, 207
Thiel, Peter, 8, 101
This American Life (radio program), 39

Thomson, James, 152–54
Tierney, Tom, 24
Till, James, 152
Tolstoy, Leo, 88, 91
transhumanism: Fedorov and, 88–89, 236; More and, 69; Mormons and religious transhumanism, 83–86; as term, 69; Turchin and digital immortality, 183–87. *See also* immortalists
TransTime, 45
Trinity Ventures, 139
Trump, Donald, 101, 162, 224
Tsiolkovsky, Konstantin, 88
Tubb, E. C., 42
tumor suppression, 122
Turchin, Alexei, 183–87, 195; on brain slicing, 195; on cryonics, 184–85
Turritopsis dohrnii, 165–66
turtles, 167
21st Century Medicine, 198–99
21st Century Nanotechnology Research and Development Act, 209
2001: A Space Odyssey (film), 8, 21, 40

Uber, 97, 103
Ullah, Assad, 205
United Nations population growth data, 221
United States Transhumanist Party, 133–34
United Therapeutics, 189–90
Unity Biotechnology, 125
Unity Church, 64
University College London, 210
University of Alabama's Nathan Shock Center of Excellence in the Basic Biology of Aging, 119
University of California, Davis, 160–61
University of California, Los Angeles (UCLA), 57, 127, 189
University of California, San Francisco, 210
University of Cambridge, 80, 99, 168
University of Dresden, 205

University of Essex, 128
University of Exeter, 128
University of Leeds, 209
University of Manchester, 209
University of Manitoba, 146
University of Oxford, 83, 111
University of Pennsylvania, 172
University of Southern California
    (USC) Longevity Institute, 141
University of Wisconsin-Madison, 11,
    152
US Department of Energy Technology
    Center, 178
US Stem Cell, 163
Utnapishtim, 9

VanDeRee, Neal, 5–17, 79, 83, 118, 139
Van Dermyden Makus Law, 110
Van Norden, Russ, 32
Verily, 103
Vidokle, Anton, 89–90
vitamin E, 146
Vlahos, James, 188
Vlahos, John, 188
Vlasuk, George, 104
von Biela, Wilhelm, 86
Vox, 140

Wake Forest Institute of Regenerative
    Medicine, 161
The Washington Post, 147–48, 158, 189
Westphal, Christoph, 112
Whole Foods, 139
Williams, Claudia, 58
Williams, John Henry, 58
Williams, Ted, 58
Wistar Institute (Philadelphia), 124, 146
World War II, x, 20–21, 90
Wyss Institute for Biologically Inspired
    Engineering, 178

Xu Fu, 10

Yamanaka, Shinya, 153
The Year 4338 (Odoevsky), 86–87

Young, Joseph, 7
Young, Sergey, 106–7
young blood transfusions, 101–3, 118

Zak, Nikolay, 169
Zhang, Rugang, 146